Organizing Nonprint Materials

Additional Volumes in Preparation

Organizing Nonprint Materials
Second Edition

Jay E. Daily
Graduate School of Library and Information Sciences
University of Pittsburgh
Pittsburgh, Pennsylvania

MARCEL DEKKER, INC.   NEW YORK · BASEL

Library of Congress Cataloging-in-Publication Data

Daily, Jay Elwood
  Organizing nonprint materials.

  (Books in library and information science ; vol. 48)
  Bibliography: p.
  Includes index.
  1. Cataloging of non-book materials. 2. Libraries--
Special collections--Non-book materials. I. Title.
II. Series: Books in library and information science ;
v. 48.
Z695.66.D34 1986   025.3'4   86-13390
ISBN 0-8247-7504-X

MARCEL DEKKER, INC.
270 Madison Avenue, New York, New York 10016

Current printing (last digit):
10 9 8 7 6 5 4 3 2 1

PRINTED IN THE UNITED STATES OF AMERICA

Preface to the Second Edition

"The object of this book is to establish a means for organizing collections of nonprint material so that greatest efficiency can match most effective service." The first sentence of the preface to the first edition remains as true today as it was then. Much has changed in the dozen years since the first edition was published. The range of nonprint materials has increased and new technology for the recording of sight and sound has produced new equipment, some of which has become popular. A strong bid for popularity was made with the disk players that reproduce motion pictures but the expected widespread use never materialized. Compact discs now produce sound which is virtually the same as that recorded. Whether these players will replace the sound discs and sound cassettes remains to be seen. No one with acute hearing can doubt their superiority.

"Part One of this book is meant to provide something more than the overview found in many other sources. Some elements of traditional librarianship have been challenged, others have been reiterated. The librarian faced with the need to organize a nonprint collection should see how to proceed from idea to accomplishment without the fear that he is missing or misinterpreting something." What concerns librarians today are microcomputers which add to the material to be accounted for and provide a means, possibly, for keeping track of everything. Suppliers advertise special programs for the production of catalog cards or for the arrangement of files in diskette form, but the librarian has no way of knowing which is best or which will accomplish what must be done with a minimum of wasted effort.

Directing the explanation to an audience diffuse in expec-
tations and diverse in backgrounds, scattered among all the types
of libraries that use nonprint material, is as much a problem as
ever without additional differences in the kind of microcomputers
in use to be kept in mind. Part Two is still a collection of
examples, the best way to meet some of the needs of everyone. The
classified list exemplified in the first edition has been expanded.
The example of a community survey has been replaced with examples
of catalog entries of each kind of material, using Anglo-American
Cataloging Rules, second edition, which incorporate the punctuation
of International Standard Bibliographic Description. The details
of community surveys have not changed, hence the outline has been
included in the second chapter, but cataloging is quite different
now from what it was when the first edition of the book was published.

A second edition has an advantage over the first, because the
author can change what he didn't like, correct the errors that
crept in despite his zeal at rooting them out, and add whatever was
lacking but was later discovered to be necessary. Authors can take
advantage of those reviewers who made suggestions and of any
generous readers who wrote for further information. The best source
of revisions comes from discerning students in regular classes.
Those that used the book until it fell seriously out-of-date made many
suggestions through their questions. The new edition was almost dic-
tated by the growing popularity of microcomputers and their use in
libraries. Equally the large literature on the subject has expanded
at the predicted rate.

No matter how things change, as the French proverb observes,
they stay the same. The basis for this book has not shifted a
millimeter. The problem is still what to get, how to keep track of
it, and when to replace it. The material to be collected has
increased in volume and in variety, and just as fast, the methods
of cataloging have undergone a thorough, and welcome, revision.

But in planning the second edition, the author was as much struck by what remains valid as by what has been outdated. Preserving the best of what was done before and adding what must be included makes the work of a second edition equal to that of the first, if not greater.

The changes effected, aside from references to what a micro-computer can do and what it cannot, are largely of organization and of the inclusion of material omitted in the first edition. Print material has been included, despite the title, because it is not book-like and the handling is very different, notably maps. As a student pointed out, pictures are print material as well. I con-sider this no problem at all, consistency never being a bugbear to me once I became adjusted to the vagaries of the English language. Strictly speaking, this book deals with library material either not considered in the new edition of the Anglo-American Cataloging Rules or covered by instructions suitable only for a large research library with time to spare. I challenge anyone to find a title in that statement.

Along with reviewers, students, and those who wrote letters, the author must thank his colleagues whose requests and comments gave him the inspiration and often the direction to continue. The second edition was in his head long before the publisher noticed the need for it. Ms. Beverly MacLay chased down facts and further updated the bibliography nobly begun by Ms. Marilyn Jones, another graduate assistant.

Jay E. Daily

Preface to the First Edition

The object of this book is to establish a means for organizing collections of nonprint material so that the greatest efficiency can match most effective service. No lesser goal is worthy of consideration. In discussing the problems of organization, the examples of material have been used to explain differences in treatment that can be made responsive to the needs of the community that the library serves. Nonprint material is a vital part of a modern library of whatever type. School libraries have made the greatest use of the material so far, to the point of becoming media-centers, but the avalanche of information is not only in print form and the need for information may often be satisfied only by nonprint material.

Part One of this book is meant to provide something more than the overview found in many other sources. Some elements of traditional librarianship have been challenged, others have been reiterated. The librarian faced with the need to organize a nonprint collection should see how to proceed from idea to accomplishment without the fear that he is missing or misinterpreting something. Although not meant as a textbook, the library school student should have a firm basis for his further work in the area of nonprint material, but equally, administrators in charge of libraries and teachers associated with a library should be able to read this section with the idea of gaining some understanding of both the problems and the possibilities of organizing nonprint collections.

Directing the explanation to so diffuse an audience has necessitated some rather more general statements than would be ideal in a textbook on cataloging nonprint material. Part Two is meant as something beyond a collection of examples. Where specialized tools have been advocated, they have been included in Part Two, notably the classified list of subject headings meant to serve not only for picture collections, but for any collection of nonprint materials. A list of uniform titles and subject headings for collections of music phonorecordings is necessary to follow what is quite a departure from the rules established in Part Three of the Anglo-American Cataloging Rules of 1967.

In addition, an example of a community survey, prepared by Ms. Elizabeth Donnan, a student in the Graduate School of Library and Information Sciences, is included. Outlines of the community survey, the guide to the collection, and the procedural manual have been included as well, along with examples of records discussed in the text. There is little need now to argue the value of nonprint materials, because that is assumed. There is a need to emphasize that organization is essential if use of these materials is to be the privilege of anyone the library serves. Unfortunately, many nonprint specialists have assumed that a large collection is more valuable than organization of a somewhat smaller collection. The opposite is the case. A library contemplating locating all nonprint material in its confines— from wherever it has been kept before, because it is almost a certainty that such material exists—must plan to make the material readily available.

A rather elaborate bibliography is included as a summary of the literature and an apology for this book. It would never have been written if the works in the bibliography covered the same area in the same way, but much of this book is quite new to librarianship generally, and all of it has been tested repeatedly not only in the classroom and in laboratory situations but also in a working nonprint library with which the author has been associated. But first the author thanks Mrs. Marilyn Smith for editorial assistance.

The author is indebted to Ms. Ruth Weisberg, librarian of WQED, whom it has been his privilege to serve as consultant. If he was able to give as much in consultation work as he gained in knowledge, he has somehow earned his keep. The author is deeply indebted to his indefatigable secretaries, Ms. Darlene Fawcett and Ms. Barbara Wonders, for their assistance in the preparation of the manuscript. The author is indebted to those most capable teachers, his students, who have materially aided him, as in the case of Mr. Abazar Sepehri and Ms. Almira Freeman, and constantly guided him toward the refinement of his ideas to the point where theory and practicality are happily conjoined. Very many other people aided the author, directly or indirectly, especially his colleagues, Dr. Martha Manheimer, Ms. Mildred Myers, and Mr. George Sinkankas. The author thanks his wife for giving him the inspiration and the surroundings that make his work productive. Obviously there would be no book at all without her infinite patience and endless encouragement.

Jay E. Daily

Contents

PART TWO

Organizing Nonprint Materials

PART ONE

1 Nonbook, Nonprint Materials

The members of the American Library Association, who wrote the rules, and other librarians have no doubt whatever that libraries contain many more things than books, serials, and music scores. The second edition of the Anglo-American Cataloging Rules includes separate chapters for the cataloging of maps, sound recordings, motion pictures, and even computer programs. Evidently, the fight against museums has been concluded in the minds of librarians, although the war was won several decades ago, because an avalanche of informational material has swamped the tired exhibits that used to occupy the second floors of public libraries. Even the 'just-like-books' theory of cataloging has been replaced with both a general bibliographic description and special rules for the particular material. The book of rules has been rearranged and numbered so that the particular kind of material is more readily found and the rule governing one feature or another is clearly tied to the general bibliographic rule covering all material of whatever kind.

New studies of human cognition and educational theory deriving from them have placed increasing emphasis on nonprint materials as a means of instruction, to the point that worriers have written books insisting that books will no longer be read because everything will either be on a diskette for a microcomputer or on videotape. A paperless society is foreseen with information over the television network coming right to the screen in the home to replace our customary method of writing letters and reading books. Schools, in particular, are benefitting from this nonprint revolu-

tion as television programs and video arcade games take over the
job of teaching children something of the heritage of the world and
the motor skills of dealing with it. More libraries than ever, especially public libraries, are turning to nonprint materials as a
way of building collections that are attractive to members of the
community. Pets and games are lent as well as books.

In such halcyon days of nonprint, nonbook materials, it might
seem that all the problems concerning them have been solved. Would
that it were true. Catalogs that advertise diskettes for microcomputers also advertise ways of storing them, because a fact of human
nature clouds the foresight of the paperless society. While no one
wants to do, or is ever willing to do, any more work than he has
to, everyone has a memory which each of us likes to have confirmed
from time to time. So long as our methods of communicating information take real time, we must find a means of storing what was
shown a few minutes, hours, days ago. If that weren't the case,
video cassette recorders would not be the appliance that many families are buying and using. Significantly, studies have shown that
viewers who record a television program very rarely watch it more
than once. The virtue is in the saving, not in the recording or
reviewing, or what is more common in rearranging the programming.
What has been called "time shifting" accounts for most of the
recording done, the videocassette recorder solving the problem of
what to do when one program is at exactly the same time as another
and neither can be missed.

A definition of nonbook, nonprint material is easier than
before. All the material requiring special methods of acquisition,
cataloging, use, and storage not described by standard rules for
books, serials, and music scores constitutes the working definition
of what this book covers. All the material considered in this book
needs special means of storage and requires special equipment for
use.

I. ACQUISITIONS

The book trade is a well-defined and important part of the eco-
nomic picture of a country. Literacy governs many of the activities of an industrial society, so that a country which has a system
of commercial dealers specializing in books can be identified at
once as made up of literate citizens who enjoy intellectual freedom. Equally important are dealers in the special materials used
in schools: models, charts, mock-ups, realia, globes, and other
items used in the educational process. Consumer stores now offer
for sale, or rent, video cassettes of motion pictures, some made
especially for sale as educational material. These stores and
methods match the availability of sound recordings in various
shapes all of which are listed in the Schwann Catalogue. Now consumer stores advertise programs as well as microcomputers, and a
new industry has sprung up designing these programs and offering
them for sale. Each of these: computer programs, sound recordings,
video cassettes, charts and models, and books derives from separate
industries. A modern industrial country is an information society
with more than fifty percent of the work force devoted to the production, handling, and sale of material meant to educate the popu-
lace in one way or another.

As in the manufacture and sale of books, each industry that
packages information for sale has its own reviewing media, even
computer programs, and aggregate listings much like the standard
tools of the book trade. Information about the various items a-
vailable for sale and the sellers combines with announcements of
advances in technology. Interspersed among these articles are summaries and reviews of all the material available, comparing them
and choosing the superior ones.

Aside from periodicals devoted to computers and the canned programs available for them, another good example is the sound record-

ing industry which, like motion pictures, honors the best known and most successful of performers. Several different periodicals discuss technological advances, and others focus on the performers who gain incredible popularity. Because of laser technology, compact discs do not reproduce sound, they recreate it. As the medium becomes more popular, the cost of the technology will decrease, and the advantages over the grooved sound discs, if sufficient, will finally erase that industry. It has happened repeatedly in the past, as flat discs replaced fragile cylinders, long playing discs replaced the original sound recordings, cartridges replaced reels, and cassettes replaced cartridges. The crucial factors are the flexibility of the medium not only for playing but recording sound, its convenience of use, its faithfulness in reproducing, or recreating, the original performance, and the cost of equipment for utilizing the medium. Cassettes, for instance, were more convenient than cartridges because they were smaller and reproduced sound as well as the cartridge. The equipment used to play the cassette was less expensive, and particularly, it could record as well as play prerecorded tapes. The compact disc, so called, is now being tested in the marketplace, the final arbiter of popularity. There is talk that compact disc players may soon go out of date, because new ones will not only recreate sound but record as well.

Users of equipment are accustomed to advertised variations that are touted in an attempt to gain acceptance. The quadrophonic systems of a few years ago have been abandoned because the public refused to invest the money required for additional speakers driven by the new four-channel amplifiers. Long-playing sound discs attract dust that becomes noise in the performance and are so readily damaged that putting a needle down on a particular band of disc is almost invariably a good way to ruin it. While compact discs are not advertised as unbreakable, they cannot be scratched when played, and if properly handled to avoid dirtying the surface with body oil, will last indefinitely. Small accidents may introduce random noises in the recreated performance, but ordinarily, the fiftieth playing of a compact disc produces sound no different from the first because no needle grinds away the grooves. The beam of light which reads the digital information on the disc has no effect on its surface. The equipment has a further advantage in playing a standard size disc, less than five inches in diameter, and keeping accurate count of the time that elapses. Many players can play any passage when directed to do so. All of them can be started at any band on the disc without damaging it.

Usually the librarian is not the first to decide some new type of equipment is essential. The community out of curiosity usually requests it often enough to make its purchase practical. But once it has been bought, the impulse of most librarians is to make a complete collection if the money is available. Public librarians now deal with a wide assortment of information sources in many different forms, and the librarian whose job is acquiring it soon adjusts to the peculiarities of the market place. Video cassettes, for instance, may be rented or purchased like films. Some dealers specialize in material that goes out of print rather quickly. The librarian must be quick to recognize a bargain and knowledgeable about what is contained in a cassette. A large collection can be built up quickly, some of it home-made, much more easily than a similar collection on films. Copyright regulations govern much broadcast information, but the local media shop may make cassettes which are as enduring and valuable as anything purchased.

II. CATALOGING

With the publication of the second edition of Anglo-American Cataloging Rules, many of the problems of cataloging nonbook material vanished. The inclusion of International Standard Bibliographic Description and the development of general rules covering all kinds of media have made the rules so flexible that they may be applied even to a medium unknown when the rules were

developed. This achieves the final step in the development of
rules of description. They become principles as much as rules.

The problems of cataloging are now different from what they
were in 1972. General acceptance of the principle that the method
of cataloging should follow the use of a collection and its size
has been accompanied by a search for easier methods of creating the
catalog format desired. The card catalog, at one time the only
method of maintaining a record of holdings, has been replaced by
variations of book catalogs which are more effective and now more
easily produced. The most significant of these new methods is
on-line storage in a computer system with many outlets having
access to a central memory bank. However, even the largest memory
has limits, and problems of access time for users of the catalog
have to take into account the difference between sitting at a
computer terminal and standing at a card catalog. Aside from the
fact that use of the two systems is widely different, input must be
governed as well to prevent problems of storage of information.

Video systems using a disc and laser technology make collections of pictures much more accessible whether they are slides or
photographs. The individual picture can be subsumed in a general
category and still be accessible if desired. The purpose of the
classified list of headings is at last apparent, because the discs
where the pictures are stored for recreation can be produced from
files already in the library. Selecting the files is quite simple
if the headings for the pictures are already classified. All
those in a given hierarchy or otherwise closely associated can be
combined on a disc and the individual picture numbered and given a
brief description. The problem of how to do this is resolved by
the technology of storage not the rules of cataloging.

The technology that makes this possible must, at some time in
the future, be used for other parts of the collection that are dif-

ficult to store and to handle, for instance maps, plans, blueprints, and so on. The rules now widely used must be interpreted before it is apparent that they cover collections of all kinds, those that are made in the library as well as those that can be purchased.

Similarly, rules must be interpreted if they are to be useful in keeping track of other media in the collection. They are far from perfect, as the editors advise us, and in any case, they are rules not statute law. They govern what must be included in a standardized system but not what exceptions should be made. Cataloging in any given library is a compromise between standardization and local needs. For instance, a high school library may include a collection of sound recordings in various formats for home use by the students and for classroom use by the teachers. The entire collection is about the size of the periodical subscriptions. Why should that be maintained in the form of a list and the sound recordings subjected to the meticulous rules that distinguish similar sound recordings for research libraries in the creation of cards for a general catalog?

This book is written with the object of showing how to interpret rules to meet local needs utilizing technology available with the object of producing maximum results from minimum effort. To do this, the library must conduct a community survey to understand what is needed by the people the library serves, a necessity for libraries of all types and kinds. The members of the community do not know how the library can supply them with what they need. They only know what they want and when they want it, usually at once.

Microcomputers and electronic typewriters have added new dimensions to cataloging which the rules could never have foreseen. On-line storage, like the prime space in a library, must be reserved for items any of which may be sought at any time. Wherever the individual item is of importance only because it is a part of another

larger source, the location and storage of the item changes the
whole direction of the catalog entry. For instance, the slides
gathered together in a disc for use in a high school. A student
must give a report on architecture in the middle ages. He needs
from the disc containing pictures of France several reproductions
of cathedrals, at Chartres, Rheims, and in Paris. Modern tele-
communication will allow him to go right to these pictures, while
in the classroom, and show them on a screen. Technology is really
wonderful. However, the library must have a disc classified 914.4
"France -- Description and travel" and a list on the disc of each
of the pictures, arranged by location. It is a simple matter to
call up the numbers of each of the pictures to produce the
illustrations that the report needs. Groups of pictures can be
classified using the divisions of France in the Dewey Decimal
System so that individual pictures, for instance Notre Dame in
Paris, will have a number for Paris and a number for the building
itself.

As information sources increase in number and variety, how to
handle them depends more than ever on the use that is going to be
made of them. To know this the librarian must know the community
he serves and the characteristics of the institution in which he
works. Catalog entries derived from the needs of the community who
are to be served not subjected to futile training in how to use the
library.

III. THE USE OF NONPRINT MATERIALS

Problems of use arise with nonprint materials that are never
thought of with books. Each of us is his own reading machine, and
the book is a wonderfully compact way of storing information, combining maximum surface with minimum volume. The moment one uses
another format, other equipment is needed. Even books on micro-
fiche or serials in microform require additional equipment. Pro-

posed storage of materials on compact discs will simply transform a book into a nonprint object that contains the information. A characteristic of what this book covers can be summarized under questions of use. The reader must be provided with the information he needs and the equipment necessary to utilize it in all formats except those that are book like, such as serials and music scores. Maps on paper are immediately accessible, like books, but they cannot be stored or lent in the same fashion.

Nonprint material, then, is often used in connection with equipment which must be cataloged (or inventoried) and may be lent along with the material itself. The sightless user of a library is ordinarily lent the cassette player as well as the cassette. A library that decides to acquire material must consider the equipment necessary to use it and establish whether the clientele own the models that will be used with a particular item. Standardization is notedly lacking in computer programs that are sold in commercial outlets. Buying floppy diskettes is simple so long as nothing is recorded on them. If the diskette contains a canned program, the first question is for what computer. A library which invests in computer games that can only be used on IBM equipment may disappoint the many users who have Radio Shack or Apple computers, which are less expensive and rather more common. With the growing popularity of truly portable computers, the question arises whether the library should lend, or rent out, the equipment as well as the programs that run it. Deciding which format of information is equally deciding what equipment will be purchased.

Some second sight appears to be necessary as well, because it is very difficult to know just what material and the equipment that makes it accessible will continue to be marketed. The disk-players are no longer sold, although the disks are still available, because the market was saturated much more rapidly than supposed. Video cassettes, for instance, come in two regular sizes, and may be

replaced by a third which will be used universally. A library
which must buy cassettes in VHS and Beta may find both of these
superseded by new cassettes which are much less expensive and a
different size as well.

The fact that one information source changes may not affect
those already collected in the library. A good example is video
cassettes which did not replace films as a visual medium but added
another dimension. While films are ideal for exhibit to groups of
people, video cassettes are equally ideal for individual use, or at
most a few dozen individuals at once. This introduces new com-
plexities into the usual job of acquiring and making available for
use the information sources available that the community wants.
The same information may be available on film, in VHS and Beta
format, and may be added to by compact disc, cassette, and
long-playing recording of the sound track alone. The question that
a librarian must resolved expands the notion of information
conveyed by print to problems as vast in variety as they are in
size.

IV. STORAGE AND CLASSIFICATION

Each kind of nonprint material must be stored in the fashion
that will best preserve it. Experiments which had another purpose
have always resulted in damage to the material or its loss. While
it is a novel idea to store recorded versions of a work next to the
print version, whether textual or musical, the end result has been
damage to the fragile phonodisc or loss of the readily stolen cassette. The idea is less novel than it seems. It has surfaced
regularly during most of the author's career, from the time that
the organizing librarians of the new Donnell Branch of New York
Public Library decided to do so in the late fifties. They changed
their minds after less than a year's trial.

As a general rule, what must be classified is the information
contained in a nonprint source, rather than the source itself.
Each of these may be marked and parked where they can readily be
supervised and the clients informed both what the material is and
where the equipment can be found that will make its use possible.
The insistence that the card catalog contain records of all the
information available and the argument which supports this idea are
now being replaced by questions about the purpose of cataloging and
its method, and even more, by misunderstandings of classification
and its object. The numbers found on the back of books simply give
the material an address. The numbers used in a classified guide to
the information contained in those books locate the subject in the
context of all other subjects held. Where the public cannot browse,
the addresses of material can locate it in whatever way is easiest
for the librarian to find. The information contained, though, can
be classified for the purpose of avoiding unworkable methods of
relating one subject to another and providing for the integration
of many separately conceived indexes into one file. Information is
not circumscribed by the container in which it is packaged and
relates to all other information anywhere. What to do when the
package decays and the information is still valuable is another
problem.

Fortunately all nonprint material does best in the very climate
that is best for books. Less fortunately, not all is known to be
as durable even as a book printed on woodpulp paper. Some are
readily damaged, some decay, and the containers of others poison
the contents. A major problem developed several years ago when it
was discovered that the cardboard containers of microfilm contained
enough sulphur dioxide to create weak sulphuric acid which made
spots on the film. Whole collections would have vanished if a rush
to obtain inert plastic containers had not made the business highly
profitable. Since that time, cardboard containers are not used at
all, except in shipping, and the microfilm is ordinarily protected

from contamination by being wrapped in inert plastic bags.

In some atmospheres, books should be treated in the same fashion, and the damage that film may suffer is not very much different from the damage that books have already endured. A big topic in the old research libraries of the world is the decay of most of the books of the late nineteenth and early twentieth century. By the twenty-first century this material will either be preserved or will be copied in some more durable form, just like newspapers which are never kept in the original woodpulp format but are copied at once on microfilm. A library is a vast memory subject to damage by the environment.

V. NONPRINT, NONBOOK, AND PRINT MEDIA

An old rule of semantics states that where a group of nouns cannot be covered by a single term, a list will equal what the term would supply if the language contained it. This book will cover (1) maps, pictures, filmslides, transparencies, realia, mock-ups, models, and specimens; (2) sound recordings in various formats; (3) motion pictures, video cassettes, and computer programs; and (4) kits, portfolios, and other collections and mixtures of materials. Books, serials, and music scores will be omitted along with archives and manuscripts.

Both the list and the combinations may seem strange, but a logic guides the decisions. Organizing a library devoted to, or largely containing, nonprint and nonbook material requires decisions that may never arise when all the bookstock is in print form, handily bound, whether books, serials, or music scores, or all three. The inclusion of microforms does not alter the characteristics of the library so far as the organization is concerned. Such few facts as are necessary for the preservation of microforms can be found in several places. They are not specifically treated here. The first chapter on material, the third in the book, takes up the kind for which the records are very like an inventory with possible variation. This kind of material is accessible by subject headings whether the terms are placenames, as for maps, or for objects as for pictures. Not all pictures are meant. Art prints are more like sound recordings so far as the cataloging is concerned than they are anything like pictures of the world around us.

The second category is treated in the next chapter. All the material included can be identified with a person, even recordings of the sounds made by waves as they reach the shoreline. This material represents either phenomenal problems of cataloging or rather simple handling by measures that are as effective and take much less time and effort.

The third category is made up material the use of which by a client is dependent on its contents, hence each different item requires an annotation or summary. If a person must use the material to know whether he wants to use it, a different approach is needed. The ideal example is a motion picture or a video cassette. To know whether to invest the time necessary to watch it, an individual must know the contents before he ever begins. To know whether to watch Debbie Reynold's Workout or Debbie Does Dallas depends on knowing what can be seen in each. One is meant for exercise, the other is hardcore pornography, and both are available at the local outlet of video cassettes.

The fourth category is a catch-all made up of material that does not fit in the other three, usually combinations of filmslides and text that may include pictures and games. A truism of cataloging states that the focus of identification must be on the information conveyed not on the container. However, the container governs the storage of the information in all similar containers, and focussing just on the information will lead either to complete dis-

organization or to irretrievable damage to, or loss of, the container and the information contained. Consequently, this section
deals with the problems of such material, the way catalogers have
tried to provide help, and the most efficient way of achieving what
the catalog entry cannot.

What made this edition necessary was less the changes in the
rules of cataloging than the methods of making entries available to
the public. The author uses an IBM Personal Computer with a program for word processing to create and produce the camera-ready
copy for this book. Much can be accomplished with an electronic
typewriter, using no computer at all, which only does faster and
more accurately what can be done with a muscle-driven machine,
whether typewriter or ball point pen. Each has distinct advantages
and disadvantages. In order to make the work as generally useful
as possible, the author was careful not to make his suggestions
computer-specific. What is discussed can be done on any machine
with sufficient memory and a print-out device. Some possibilities
of a computer are different enough to deserve special attention.

Part two gives model entries of various kinds of materials,
which can serve as examples for the creation of cards, various
lists, or reproduced in a computer display. Each type of material
is covered with emphasis on those not usually found in compilations
of model cataloging cards. The classified list of subject headings
has been enlarged, but suppliers have been omitted. The information is readily available elsewhere. The bibliography that follows
covers major works of the past ten years.

2 Defining the Library and Its Patrons

To create or continue a library, the person in charge has to know what patrons will use the library and what service they will expect. Too often, this information is taken for granted, and the library loses an opportunity to refine its procedures while it enlarges its clientele. The librarian has to answer several questions about the organization and the collection before beginning to make changes or create policy. This holds true as much for the nonbook material as for the books in the collection.

The first question to be answered is whether the parent organization has a workshop where nonbook materials are created. These materials can be produced more easily than they can be organized into a usable collection. The question is not whether they should be cataloged but what purpose that will serve. Materials that are only used once need never be retained except for archival purposes. If the costs of creating the materials has increased from year to year, or if the materials must be re-used, with or without slight modification, some kind of organization is necessary. The mistake is often made of providing organization only for materials that are purchased. But all are bought one way or another. The time and materials that created a source of information is as much the purchase price for a library as the selling price of a commercial vendor.

Material should not be cataloged if the cost of organization exceeds the cost of replacement. This rule has to be understood with its assumptions to be followed. A person who wants material

does not want delays. If delay is of no importance, the material
can be recreated more readily than it can be found. This assumes
that the material can be recreated precisely as it was with no
changes whatever. However, material should not be produced over
and over again. This simply indicates that a real saving of time
and money wil be made by making it available without delay. Finding it is just a matter of having the location of the item indicated and understood.

The publication of the second edition of Anglo-American Cataloging Rules, with its clear and readily understood sections on
nonprint materials, led many librarians to dismiss the problem of
organization as already solved. The rules, however, do not establish the size of the community the library serves nor its makeup.
A high school library serving about four hundred students in all
grades is very different from a public library with a clientele of
several hundred thousand.

The first question to be asked is whether the whole population
the library serves is homogenous, so that a decision made for one
group is true for all. If the answer is yes, then the methods decided upon do not have to be compromised to fit one segment as well
as another. A high school library has two large homogenous groups,
the students and the teachers, but both may be treated as adults,
unlike the public library where an important group that the library
serves is made up of children whose reading skills have not developed to the point of adults, for instance. In general, libraries
usually treat radically different groups as isolated types that do
not use the same collections which need not be organized in the
same way. The adult collection can rely on a certain degree of
knowledge among the users of the library in its organization while
the children's collection must be organized not only to meet needs
but to teach the principles of obtaining needed information. The
degree of personal service must differ in each case, because the

principle that what the organization does not do, the librarian must, holds true if it is understood that service to the patrons assures the continuity of the library. Where each person represents a different approach which must be met without any attempt to change it, the methods of organization can be minimal, fitted especially to the professionals who will be understood to know the most about organization.

A second question is whether the need for information is constant, about the same day in and day out, or varies in response to time-bound pressures, for instance the preparation of research papers with their inevitable deadlines. The library must prepare during slack periods for work at a different pace when an assignment is nearly due or final examinations are scheduled. The number of patrons served is a function of the amount of service needed. A few patrons who need a great deal of attention will take as much time as hundreds who need little or none. If this need for service comes all at once at predictable times, it can be included in the planning for the year. If it is constant, it is even more readily included in the planning and directly affects the budget for staff members. If each occurence is a new experience both when it occurs and how much is needed, then the planning can only be done on the basis of averages.

Finally, the librarian must decide which materials are most often asked for and make them more readily obtained than those that are rarely sought. Cataloging rules are of a little help in making these decisions. Instead the librarian should understand the different levels of organization that will provide each medium of information with the accessibility needed for efficient service. The kinds of organization listed below, beginning with the simplest at the outset and ending with the most elaborate, are not independent of the medium, as many have supposed, but are characteristic of the way information is packaged.

The simplest method of organization is the vertical file under
brief subject headings, suitable for road maps, pictures, slide
sets, and even computer software on floppy disks or cassettes.
Here, the material is not in constant use, though sought from time
to time, and no surrogate for the item itself is needed. A bibliographic entry is a surrogate of the actual material providing the
minimum of information needed to identify the item among all the
others that are similar.

As the collection grows in size and complexity, the need for
organization increases, so that the surrogates as well as the
material must be saved in a way that makes finding either one a
simple matter. Custodial rules that prevent the individual from
inspecting the material itself require that surrogates to be sorted
through be easily accessible. This brings up a question which is
rarely debated: should all the bibliographic entries for whatever
the kind of material be kept together? The judgment of librarians
over the years has been yes, and to provide for some indication to
the user of what the medium is the General Medium Designation (GMD)
has been included in the new edition of the cataloging rules. GMD
is usually put after the title, just where it is least likely to be
noticed. A student under considerable pressure to obtain all the
information possible in the shortest time possible scarcely wants
to consult a likely title only to discover that it is in a form he
cannot use. GMD is most useful when it is positioned above the
entry itself, in a card catalog on the upper right hand corner of
the card.

Next, should a brief description of the work be included with
the bibliographic identification? The rule is that anything which
must be reviewed in order to answer the question whether it should
be reviewed must include some kind of annotation or summary. The
ideal example is a motion picture. In order to decide whether to
look at the film or not, the client of the library must look at the

film, at least to scan it. Video cassettes may be run at high
speeds and enough information picked up to inform the client whether the cassette is what is wanted. Films may be run through in
the same way, stopping the rewinding process from time to time to
review a scene. In both cases annotations with the bibliographic
identification will save time on the machines and wear on the
material.

The three levels of bibliographic description included in the
new edition of the rules are less a matter of necessary information
for a bibliographic entry than a way to save the time and energy of
the cataloger by limiting the amount of detail in the bibliographic
entry to what the most frequent user of the file has to obtain.
The cataloging for an elementary school library must be simpler
than that for a research library, because the children cannot use
the fine distinctions which the searcher of the catalog in a research library utilizes. A new edition in a children's library
usually means that the previous edition has been discarded, but a
research library may collect and distinguish between all the
editions of a work.

Despite dedicated effort, the rules still advocate what has
been called the ideology of the cataloger, beginning with author-
ship. Except for material without a distinctive title, this is
secondary to the name of the item. Title is the easiest way to
locate information sources except for art prints and recorded
music. The name of the artist who creates a picture or a statue
informs the individual seeking a representation of it more than
whatever title was given, many of them no more informative than the
designation of a piece of music by its form and its position among
all others in that form which the composer created.

The cartographer of a map, except for those which have become
objects of art, is less meaningful to the individual than the area

which the map represents. Map cataloging must rely on a clear description of the area so that the user will not be forced to go
through many maps to find what is desired.

Recordings of jazz music are identified not by the composition
played but by the performer playing it. The composition is of less
significance than the performer and the name of the composer less
than the title of the composition. Ideology seems a poor excuse
for excessive work which has no purpose and may serve to lose the
identification in the alphabetic order of the file. The client of
the library is done a disservice by the cataloger's ideology and
will find no reason to appreciate it.

Finally, the rules insist on a date for every item whether it
can be obtained or not. No one doubts the desirability of a date
but the question is whether the creator of the item thought date
was significant enough to be included. If not, then the cataloger
is advised to supply an excuse for the whole date in such doubtful
notations as 19? or 198?.

This book and any others that deal realistically with the organization of material are based on standard cataloging rules. To
use them, the librarian must decide whether the present state of
the development of rules holds true for the community the librarian
serves. The rules which do not supply needed information or mis-
locate it must be amplified, and those which supply excessive detail and demand that the librarian drop everything to find it must
be abbreviated. Some of the rules must be interpreted liberally,
others strictly, all in a way that will enable the library to best
serve its clientele.

The goal of the librarian is to organize the material in the
library so that members of the community can use it without having
trouble to get to it and to create this organization with a minimum

of wasted effort. In each of the chapters that follow, the type of
material and how it may be organized is described in detail. But a
further decision remains. Once the bibliographic entry is created,
in what form should it be kept?

The computer has greatly eased the difficulty of making lists,
because there is no needed to copy all the material in order to
reflect additions and deletions. The first use of the computer is
to make lists which may readily be edited and printed out anew.
This is the equivalent of a book catalog. A special library can
keep a record of its information sources in media other than that
which makes up most of the library in a looseleaf notebook. In
general, if there are fewer than a couple hundred items with
additions or deletions that occur less frequently than once or
twice a month, a list will supply the information needed and may
readily be made using a word-processing equipment.

Where there are more items and more changes, the choice is
between a card catalog and computer access. In both cases the
bibliographic entry is about the same, but computers can hold very
much more information than card catalogs and are not subject to the
same kinds of deterioration. The choice is often made by the
budget available to the library, but this is less realistic than
making the choice according to the needs of the community. Modern
students love to use computers, and the problem is not so much
getting the student to overcome his fear of them -- he has none
after so much experience -- but in getting enough computers so that
the use of one is not the reward for waiting out a queue. Librarians have generally used personal computers as word processing
equipment despite all the discussion of their flexibility.

Modern typewriters with memories and the ability to repeat what
has been input can accomplish almost as much as the personal computer used as a word processor. Various programs exist for the crea-

tion of files which are as accessible as the creator wants, but most of them are meant for business and require a certain adjustment of thinking to be useful for a librarian. The card catalog shows no sign of general abandonment except in very large libraries where, even so, it still has a use.

Card catalogs provide bibliographic identification over a long period of time with a maximum of random access but they are duplicated with great difficulty and the use of one is confined to its location. The principles of filing demonstrate that other things being equal, the efficiency begins to diminish as soon as the catalog reaches a certain size. Small libraries need never worry, but any library with more than five million cards should consider dividing the catalog by publication date as modified by immediate usefulness and keeping separate catalogs for material not in book and periodical form, for the purposes of this book the print material. About fifty years of heavy use will cause all the cards to deteriorate to the point of uselessness even when care has been taken to make the entries on stock not attacked by the atmosphere. Dirty thumb prints and broken cards have had less effect on the closing of card catalogs than errors in filing and cataloging procedure, but even in these enlightened days, the cataloger should keep in mind the transience of all things human and not pretend that his cataloging will endure forever.

Whether produced by a modern typewriter or a computer, the card file is the equipment needed for a list of bibliographic entries which constantly change provided that access to it does not have to be distributed over a wide area, like that of a college or university. The modern equivalent of a book catalog is the computer. Minicomputers will provide ready accessibility to millions of records and mainframe computers even more in many places all at once. Whether on a card, in a list, or on a computer screen, the entry is recorded in a standard form. All the information provided is either derived from the item itself or provides access to the identification developed. In biological terms, a bibliographic entry is made up of exogenous or endogenous information, that supplied independent of the identifying features of the item or those characteristics which are unique to the item.

This distinction is important, because only professional librarians can supply information that provides access to the bibliographic entry, while anyone can be trained to create the entry itself on the basis of what the item supplies. As files grow in size, the problems of identification increase and counter measures must be adopted. The first of these is authority files which supply a standard way of listing authors and provide all the information necessary to identify one person or corporate body from all the others with similar names. At some point, there must be a difference, whether it is the birthdate of the individual or the location of the corporate body.

The second is a standard list of subject headings. So long as relatively few are employed, as a round figure less than a thousand, no organization of the subject headings is necessary. If, however, the number increases beyond a thousand for material of one discipline or as many thousands as there are disciplines with different information sources, some organization of the subject access will greatly aid the person, usually a novice, who needs this method of access to the file of bibliographic entries. Classifying the subject headings will make it easy to add to them or delete from them without ever losing the interconnectedness which enables to the searcher to go from the irrational associations in his head through all the possibilities recorded. It should come as a surprise to no one that people do not think in alphabetic order or remember words that way. The traditional methods of relating subjects to one another have proven to be worse than useless, they change the very nature of the list and prevent it from maintaining currency with constant semantic change. There is much less reason for classifying material than there is for classifying the subjects which locate it.

What binds files of titles and of subject headings together are cross references from what the client may think of to the way the name or heading is listed. A list of subject headings is really a cumulation of formalized titles to the works. Though the work may have any title the author can think of, the librarian wants to be sure that the informational value is clearly shown in the subject heading. In computerized files of catalog entries, access by title or key words of the title have proven to be the most effective way of organizing a collection by subject, provided all the authors cooperate by giving titles that clearly convey what information the work contains. This is true for most of the scientific authors, and rather the exception than the rule for humanistic studies. In a classified list, the cataloger avoids the indication that the searcher has looked in the wrong place by providing the classification number in the alphabetic list to all headings. See in this case means only look for the classification number and then the word next to it because further on you will come to heading you thought of. In a list of names, the similarities that confound are sorted out into the identifying characteristics which distinguish one person from another. Classified lists do away with the necesty for see-also references which only muddle the searcher without helping at all and fix all the headings in rigid perpetuity. Teasing out all the see-also references as the file changes defeats everyone, even when the change is limited to the card catalog as material is added or withdrawn from the collection.

The procedure of cataloging that brings the best results for the least effort is one which begins with an understanding of the community and goes on to organize the material in a way that will provide easy access with a minimum of trouble. This is achieved by

using the various methods available in ways that will be easiest
understood and employed by the members of the community, trying
never to provide more or less than is needed for the identification
of material, and using equipment which takes into account the size
of the collection and the community which uses it, the changes
which occur constantly in different portions of the collection, and
the time available for both the librarians and the people they
serve. Leaving to the reference librarian what the cataloger
should do only transfers the job, it doesn't eliminate it. Even
worse is the expectation that the patron of the library wants to be
trained in lot of special symbols and abbreviations which may save
time for the cataloger only to waste it for everyone else.

The outline below gives the major questions to be settled when a
collection is to be organized. Sometimes the name of the library
helps, but more often it doesn't.

I. What type of library is this? Academic, public, or special?
    A. Academic libraries may be school, college, or university.
       Are the users of the library of one or two homogeneous
       groups? If so, at what level?
    B. Public libraries are either small, medium, or large, depend-
       on the number of clients served. What is the educational
       level of public served, the annual income of the majority,
       their need for the library? How many different groups are
       there? Age groups, groups with handicaps, groups with spe-
       cial language requirements?
    C. A special library is designed for the members of the parent
       organization and limited to material in one discipline.
       What is this library and whom does it serve?

II. How many people will use the collection? How big will the
    collection become? What are the characteristics of the

patrons and the organization of the parent institution?

A. Number of patrons, classes by age and education, expectation of self-service. Amount of help needed.

B. Organization of parent institution. Chief administrative officer, channels of authority, immediate superior. Who expects reports and who will judge them?

III. What are the resources of the library? What materials are on hand? How have they been organized? What has not been organized? Should any re-organization be done.

A. Does the organization fit the community? Is it too elaborate or too simple? What is the comparative cost of changing the organization and the cost of leaving it as is?

B. What equipment is on hand? Where and how is it stored? What provisions have been made for maintenance, spare parts, and repair?

C. What are the sources for new material and equipment? Are any materials made locally? Are they free? Can they be rented? What commercial suppliers provide fastest and least expensive service?

IV. What is the role of the library in the mission of the parent institution?

A. What are the objectives and goals of the institution? What is its governance? Where does the library fit into this pattern? What constitutes successful performance of the library?

B. What budget is provided for the library to fulfill its mission? What priorities can be given to various tasks the library must or should do?

C. What help is available? What is the role of each person who is employed?

D. What other help is available? Can volunteers be recruited? What rewards can be offered to them for their work?

Many of these questions are self-explanatory, some are answered at the time the librarian gets the job, and others must be sought from whatever sources are available. The librarian who expects to succeed in his work should address all of them and keep his answers firmly in mind. Finally, the librarian should take a good look at her (or his) own qualifications and see how they fit into the general plan for the library. Then the librarian is ready to begin the task of public relations that will characterized the work ever after. This generally begins when the librarian meets with whatever group sets policy for the library, possibly for the first time, more usually for the second time, after this group or its representative has employed the librarian. The theme of this meeting is the mission of the parent institution and the role of the library in realizing it.

The important outcome of such a meeting is a definition of what constitutes success in the job. General budgetary constraints must be faced at this time, even in situations where the usual way of solving problems is to throw money at them. A clear understanding of the library's, hence the librarian's, role will avoid the unhappy experience of working at cross-purposes with what the parent institution wishes to do and succeeding only in alienating everyone. Using all the resources of the library, the community, and the world at large, the librarian can succeed in meeting the informational needs of even the most complex organization.

3 Material Cataloged by Content

If the identifying feature of a work is only its content, there is no need to search for anything else. This chapter reviews the two principle types of materials: Maps, which must be treated differently from everything else and the content of which is the area depicted, and literally everything else: pictures, film slides, transparencies, models, and realia. What identifies each of these pieces of material is at the least a sequential number assigned with regard only to the time when the material was acquired or the title of the work and the producer if an inventory record must be made. Optical disks, onto which collections of pictures are often copied, are simply accumulations of the kind of material that is too numerous to be accounted for individually. Each of these is either made by the library or by a commercial firm. In any case, the library itself must assign any identifying features, although only the types of material are essential. Different types can be intermixed, with no harm done to them or to the means of access, but it is generally less confusing to limit each disk to the particular media which will fill it. Optical disks serve both as information sources and as surrogates for other informational sources.

I. MAPS

Access to maps is primarily by subject, and either the classification or the entries for map must show this if the map is to be used. A small collection is most easily handled if arranged in vertical files with the area designated on the file folders. This

assumes that the collection will never grow larger, that each new
map will replace one already in the collection, and that users will
be directed to the vertical file if they ask for a map, or that the
librarian will obtain it.

The question immediately arises whether the file folders should
be labelled in strict alphabetic order of the place-name depicted
in the map or the maps arranged hierarchically using one classification system or another. The places of the universe are a natural
hierarchy: Universe, Milky Way Galaxy, Solar system, Earth, North
America, United States, Pennyslvania, Western Region, Allegheny
County, Pittsburgh, Shadyside. That is where these words are being
written. Each area is contained within a larger area.

An incidental collection of maps too good to be discarded but
not the material of primary interest in the library can be kept, if
folded, in file folders in the commonplace letter file, or left
flat in drawers meant for maps and arranged by the area covered:
Shadyside, Pittsburgh, United States. The full description is
necessary, although Pennyslvania may be substituted for United
States if the collection is in that country. Access to the cartographic
collection depends as much on the librarian as on the file folders
or map labels until the person who uses maps becomes accustomed to
the way they are arranged. No attempt is made to keep a file of
surrogates for the maps; they are not cataloged, and one may be
lost without any particular damage to those kept. If the library
wants to keep a record of the maps, the number of them in a file
folder can be recorded in pencil below the area heading if more
than one. There would be no file folder if there was not at least
one map.

The library should keep several good atlases which represent no
problem whatever to catalog and classify. There is no need to describe the maps in the collection unless the collection is of parti-

cular significance and value to the community. A collection of
rare maps should be fully cataloged if only to justify the custodial procedures and decrease use to essential handling. A person
who really wants to see a particular map will know what it is.
When the bibliographic entry is found, the location of the item is
known and calls for no pawing through the collection. A person who
wants an historical map will be satisfied if an entry can be found
either under a cartographer or under area with the period covered
easily seen.

Libraries which try to keep a collection current and spend time
and money on it will need to catalog the individual items. AACR
and the Library of Congress have now adopted International Standard
Bibliographic Description for Cartographic Materials. The only
difference between a catalog entry in a card catalogs and on a computer screen is in the spacing of the entry. Size, Notes, and ISSN
are indented rather than preceded by the usual computer signal of
space, dash, space.

Title / Statement of Responsibility. -- Edition
statement. -- Statement of scale ; statement of
projection. -- Place of publication : publisher,
Date of publication. -- Size within ruled lines of
map ; color. -- Series. -- Notes. -- International
Standard Serial Number.

Any item after title can be omitted if not found on the map
itself, but the order cannot be changed. Statement of scale and
size are essential to identification of the map, moreso than the
statement of responsibility which is often lacking or is only the
publisher. The date is usually found in a copyright notice. The
International Serial Number is included if the map has one, but no
research is done to find it if the map lacks it. Maps are often
issued as serials, especially by governmental producers and the
number helps to identify these.

Access to this surrogate for the map itself is by area and then
by subject, such as "Population," and by subject followed by the
word "Maps" after a dash. For instance, "Pittsburgh, Pennsylvania," "Population : Pittsburgh, Pennsylvania -- Maps." The
colon replaces a preposition which is generally avoided in subject
headings. Maps are classified using either the Library of Congress
Classification or the Dewey Decimal Classification. Both are
hierarchical for the areas of the world and problems arise as much
with the classification as with the cataloging.

The entry on a computer screen is a unit entry, just like the
card produced to be duplicated, whatever the method. Tracings wll
show just how the surrogate can be found. Because the surrogate
should be in the language of the map so far as Title, Statement of
Responsibility, and Publisher are concerned, the Place of publication can be given in the accepted English name of the locality,
Rome not Roma, if desired. A note would show what language is used
on the map. As many writers have noted, language is much less
important to the user of a map than it is in other printed works.
Nevertheless, access is meant for the people who use the library,
and their language should be employed for all methods of access to
the surrogate.

Notes should also be made when more than one map appears on a
single sheet, whether on one side or on the other. The problem
arises with insets, often small maps of cities in road maps. While
the separate maps for each state would be given by means of analytics, insets seem much less important. Notes can show what is contained in the inset if it shows in greater detail a locality already represented in the map. If the inset is used to conserve paper, as when the map of a panhandle would extend beyond the mar-
gins, then no note need be made. Even the simplest minded person
using the map will understand what the inset means, and it does not
amplify the information contained in the statement of the area.

The cataloger must decide what to do about separate maps on a single sheet. As a general rule, if the map takes up more than a quarter of the page and is not covered above as contiguous territory or enlarged scale of an area already shown it can be cataloged separately with a note explaining with what map it is printed. Maps with collective titles can show each separate area as points of access although cataloged under the collective title. Usually the title will clear up any doubts before they arise.

Two further curiosities of maps make the cataloging difficult. Scale must always be stated as a ratio of measurement on the map to the measurement of the area depicted, that is, 1:63,360 then 1 inch to the mile, if that is the scale given on the map. This may require that the cataloger do some calculations: 12 x 5280, for instance, because there are twelve inches to a foot and a mile is known to be 5280 feet. The calculation is easier in the metric system where moving a decimal point is the only calculation necessary. One centimeter to a kilometer would be shown as 1:100,000 because there are a hundred centimeters in a meter and kilo means thousand. The statement of projection should be given next if shown on the map. If there are several maps and insets on a sheet, the scale would be shown as "Scales vary," and if the map is not drawn to scale, this is stated: "Not drawn to scale."

The other difficulty is with the date. The earth constantly changes and an undated map is much less useful than one with the date of publication clearly shown. Here the rules for supplying date are necessary. If the year of publication or the copyright date is not shown, but there is evidence that the map was printed after some date established on the map, for instance the statement "Prepared from photographs made in the 1985 aerial survey," the supplied date may be "1985?" However, if the date cannot be established at least within a decade, the chances are that the map is invalid in any case. The supplied date "19?" or "18?" at least

tells the century, whatever good that may be. A librarian who
handles maps would go to some effort to find the date for a map
that has historical interest.

The rules prescribe certain options to be taken, for instance
the statement of coordinates and equinox, but these vital cartographic indices are of little use to anyone other than geographers
and cartographers. The rule for the use of the name of the printer
when no publisher can be found is not optional. It gives the
client an idea where and how the map was made and supplies one of
the essential identifying features of the map.

Classification has always been a problem and no system yet
invented can prevent the puzzlement that arises in map cataloging.
Simply stated, the classification is not designed for the maps on
hand, and the standing rule that an item should be given the number
of the narrowest class that will contain all the information given
cannot be used sensibly. A map of North Carolina, Tennessee,
Kentucky, and West Virginia would have to be given the number for
the United States, which is too large, or each separately cataloged
with the number for the first state listed. In an alphabetic file,
the folder or drawer in the map case marked Kentucky would contain
the map. Some librarians would create dummy inserts for each of
the other four states. Others would forget the other maps and per-
haps file it under North Carolina because that is the state first
listed on the map itself. It is apparent that a number just sub-
stitutes for a state or a region, and Dewey's or the classifiers at
the Library of Congress do not have the same concepts of regions.
"Map of the Tri-State Region" could contain parts of many states:
Connecticut, New York, and Northern New Jersey; or the Chicago area
of Illinois, Northwestern Indiana, and Southwestern Michigan; or
Western Pennsylvania, Eastern Ohio, and Northern West Virginia.
Here the title is nondescript and confusing.

The boundaries of maps like the state lines are fictional and
do not necessarily relate to previous practice. The land is all
contiguous, and a hiker is likely not to know when he has crossed
from one state into another. Motorists are assisted by road signs
welcoming the visitor or bidding him adieu. The purpose of cataloging is to make the material findable and usable. The headings
can reflect the reason for the existence of the maps: a large city
with its environs that extend out of the state. New York City
Region; Chicago Region; Pittsburgh Region, and the map can be given
the number of the city which matches the intent of the map maker.

Whether to brieflist, create catalog entries, or simply file
away can be determined by the way the maps are stored. If the
library has a collection large enough to justify the purchase of a
map case, in whatever form it may be found, then the maps must be
cataloged or at least brieflisted. The brieflist entries do not
differ substantially from the unit entries. The essential differences between one map and another constitute the items to be
contained. Statements of authority can be omitted along with place
of publication and series. Notes are not made at all. These
entries are very easily made with word-processor equipment and can
be printed out quite cheaply as needed. It is known that the
chances of duplicate entries are reduced to the vanishing point by
the limits of items to be brieflisted: a thousand at the most. The
chance of duplication increases as the maps become more numerous
finally reaching a point almost of inevitability, but only a very
large collection of maps or one that has many maps of single
area run much risk of two maps having exactly the same identifying
features although they are different entities. A brieflist does
not have to be reprinted with all the items correctly filed more
than once a year, and it represents a good way of leading the user
to the maps available. A computer listing is essentially the same
thing if the items cannot be accessed individually. Whether on
paper or on a computer, the brieflist entries are given twice, once

under title and once under area. In either case, access to the
correct page is by alphabetic range rather than individual item.
If there is any change at all in the holdings, a monthly update of
the paper version can be made. The computer update is too easy and
should not be postponed more than a few days, depending on the
state of crisis in the library. Computer lists are very easily
edited. A new entry can be inserted with easily as the entry for a
discarded item is eliminated.

Maps that present storage problems, such as three-dimension relief maps which show in reduced size all the topographical features
of the land depicted are more a storage problem than a cataloging
puzzle. Globes need to be inventoried only for insurance purposes, although if cataloged, precisely the same rules apply.

II. PICTURES

Two dimensional representations of three-dimensional objects
have much more in common with maps than with books. Scenes may
show in actual form what the map depicts using the conventions of
cartographers. However, pictures are much more easily made and
much more abundant that maps. Great picture libraries clip color
representations from periodicals and file them in manila folders.
This is the paper form of the most modern storage facility: inclusion in the laser-read optical disk with access by computer. The
paper form has the advantage of being available to borrowers who
could never be trusted with easily damaged electronic equipment. A
picture collection has enormous reference value and is almost a
necessity of modern instruction.

Except for art prints which are covered elsewhere, pictures are
as useful in collections as they may be individually. A picture of
renaissance table with an inlaid-marble top may be sought both for
an example of the kind of artwork done in marble and for the period

the table represents. The first decision in organizing a collection of pictures is how to sort them into manageable groups. For this purpose the survey of the library once again serves to provide answers to the question: How are the pictures to be used? Once the pictures have been sorted into groups, the question of numbering the individual items arises.

As with maps, pictures can be placed in file folders, and the number of pictures included may be given in pencil underneath the subject heading. The same is true of slide sets. Each group of slides has a number of examples. If the slides cannot be removed from the storage container, there is no need to list the number except as an aid to the individual who will put a group of spectators to sleep by showing them. Slide sets are widely used in many different disciplines, from geography to medicine, and each can be labeled with the heading that best describes the intent of the set.

Such elaborate systems are best left to very large collections. However, the collections need not be all of the same material. That is, slide sets, realia, and specimens all are organized the same way and can use the same subject headings, it being assumed that the items do not rely on words to convey their messages. Transparencies and film strips which are as much verbal as pictorial should be kept together under headings that describe both the discipline and the subject.

At least in theory, any material can be organized by the subject. In practice, however, where the name of an individual is connected with the material, it is best to provide access by names that the user of the material will remember. A good example of this is in the combinations of material which are sold to schools. Very often, they contain filmstrips, printed material, and sound recordings, all under a title usually descriptive of the subject content. The question whether to provide access by a personal name or by subject is determined on the basis of the use of the material. Very often history is taught in this way. The name of the individual is much less important than the country and the period covered.

Portfolios, kits, and the like are useful because of the items contained, no one of which is meant to be used without the others. In a sense, these kits are very much like books, but the difference in packaging implies a difference in the storage of the material as well as a difference in the use. The portfolio must be kept together and identified by its title and the company that produces it. Access is either by title or by subject.

Many libraries keep a collection of pamphlets in vertical files and the question arise whether maps and pictures should be kept in the same file. If the subject content is considered the most important feature of the material collected, there is no reason why not. All the material is of use and may be considered an unassembled kit. The key to all this is the subject heading list used for the vertical files. In libraries of an earlier time, the subject headings used for items in the vertical files were very much better and of easier access than those used for books. The reason was that the vertical files were in constant movement. Material was added and discarded, and the subject headings had to be has flexible as the rules for storage. The headings used on catalog cards were as permanent as stone monuments, even though the meaning had changed over the years. The Library of Congress List of Subject Headings and the Sears List have become museums of language rather than access points of a living collection.

III. SUBJECT ACCESS

The problem that arises is how to provide subject headings for material in a variety of media. The words used for pictures must depict actual things in the world of events around us. Words that interpret the picture are unsuitable, because everyone has his own interpretation. A heading that is the name of an emotion such as "happiness" or "joy" can be depicted by almost anything while "Children playing" or "Newlyweds cutting cake" implies the emotion while giving an exact description of what the picture shows.

What is needed is a brief description of the center of interest of a picture. To find the center of interest, mentally draw two diagonal lines that intersect. This locates the center, and the purpose of the picture is usually made plain. Slide sets that are grouped are more readily handled because the name of the group defines the pictures included. Semanticists usually label these names second-class abstractions, to distinguish them from the names of individuals.

Subject headings generally should not be more than second-class abstractions, that is the class of items. Classes of classes of items are not desirable but acceptable. For instance, "Actors," includes all the names of actors. A phrase like "Actors and act-resses" is acceptable because there is no word that quite means the same thing. The names of males and females would be included. If separate groups are made, the headings can be "Actors" and "Act-resses." A curiosity of English semantics would make "female actors" not redundant while "female actresses" would be, an indi-tion that the language has made the masculine form acceptable for both when they are not separate. Individual names of men and women can be listed under the actors, if desired.

Canned programs are available which accomplish on the computer
what was done manually before. Each picture is given a number and
each number is followed by a brief description. This is posted
under several different headings to make searching by a combination
of headings possible. Essentially this is what is done in information retrieval systems. For instance, the heading "Motion pictures" is combined with "Actors" and "Animals" to give the names of
animals who became famous in motion pictures, like Rin Tin Tin or
Benji.

Although the method is unpopular, many of the troubles are
solved by using a classified list, just as was done with the Sears
List through the eighth edition. The classification numbers were
dropped because librarians were using them to classify everything.
The principle, however, is correct. Classifying the headings
enables a person to find the heading he needs in association with
others in the same semantic areas. The list can be expanded to
cover material in all the different media in the collection without
doing any harm whatever to the classified list. For instance, a
list of subject headings for pictures, realia, specimens, and maps,
pamphlets, transparencies, and filmstrips can be combined although
each of these differently packaged information sources is stored in
a way that best will protect it.

Maps will require the name of the area covered, given in direct
form, with the names of larger areas following the location given
in the map. The classification of subject headings is hierarchical
so that areas are grouped from larger areas to specific localities.
Pamphlets and portfolios may require subject headings that are unsuitable for pictures, for instance "Poverty," which is more of an
interpretative statement than the rules for classifying pictures
would permit.

Although it would seem that a very large list of subject headings
ought to contain all the terms and names that would ever be needed,

this is not the case for a collection of information sources in as many different forms as that supposed, typical of collections in some schools and most colleges. The librarian is left with the disagreeable task of supplying terms, usually in the form of an index, to a large number of items. If these are pictures or picture-like material, of which realia and models are a good examples, one sort is needed. If maps, another kind of heading entirely is required, and if pamphlets, portfolios, and kits still another.

Before deciding to create a subject-heading list, the librarian must settle for once and all whether it is needed. Usually if a standard list of any kind would contain more revised than acceptable headings, a new list is required. Then, the first decision must be the control of terminology. Proper names, for instance, must be listed so that the most distinct part comes first, that one which is least likely to be duplicated. A list of individual names would be under the surname because the variety of last names, in English usage, is vastly larger than the number of given names. This means that the name must be re-arranged so that the word with the least number of duplicate entries comes first, followed by given names, as many as are needed to make the occasional duplications completely unique. Dates may be added, if needed, and anything else that will provide accurate indentification. To the names of corporate bodies, the city can be added when ambiguity arises. The names should not be re-arranged even though non-descript words come first, because no rule can be stated which would be applied whenever this occurs. "Association" is as often the first word in the name of a corporate body as it is the last. Even so, there is no need to change all those names where it becomes the filing word, even though there are very many of them because the next words are generally unique for the organization.

The more general grammatical form of common words must be used. In English, this means the plural of count nouns and the singular

of mass nouns. People who are native speakers rarely know the
difference although they avoid such wrong-sounding combinations as
"many rice" or "much beans." Bean is the count noun, rice is the
mass noun. The plural, beans, is thought of as the generalized
form of the word. The plural of mass nouns, on the other hand,
means different kinds. For instance, "rices" means different kinds
of rice. Headings should use the plural of count nouns and the
singular of mass nouns because these are the more general form of
the words. The native speaker can test the different forms with
the words "much" and "many" which are usually correctly used, unlike fewer and less. "Much rice" and "many beans" sounds right to
the native speaker. Correctly used, less rice and fewer beans
sounds equally right, although with some nouns the distinction is
being lost.

Another characteristic of the English language is that a part
of speech is not fixed, but it may change according to its uses.
An example is "rice." We can add a noun and get a meaningful
phrase, such as "rice pudding." This phrase-making in the nominal
structure includes not only nouns, but also adjectives or adjec-
tival words. The freedom with which English speakers can establish
a phrase is such that an adjective if placed after a noun will
cease being an adjective and change itself into a noun. In the
example above, if "fluid" is placed in front of the noun it means
one thing and if after, the meaning changes. "Fluid rice" is
not the same thing as "rice fluid." Word order, in any case, is
the most important syntactical device in English, and it is generally unwise to tamper with it.

English uses prepositions with very vague meanings to provide
for further specificity of nouns. Because the meaning of a preposition is impossible to decide exactly, they are best avoided
altogether. Usually they are not needed in a list limited to the
simplest, most exact terms, unless they are part of an accepted

phrase. Kings of England, for instance, is a good subject heading because the preposition can be omitted only with difficulty and lead to statements that some patron of the library will delight in telling the librarian are untrue. English Kings, for instance, would be false so far as James I is concerned, because he was Scottish, and George I, because he was German.

Subject heading lists in the past have always provided for inverted headings on the model of re-arranged personal names. These become a separate subsection of the language and must be understood on that ground, usually far too difficult a job for elementary school children, and confusing for everyone else. It is best to avoid inverted headings altogether unless they have become standard phrases like "Accounts receivable" and "Courts martial." Even though a heading like "Burned forest" seems unfindable, it quickly becomes a phrase that is acceptable to the user and likely to be thought of long before he comes upon "Forest fire aftermath" or its roundabout equivalent.

IV. BUILDING THE ALPHABETIC SUBJECT LIST

So long as it is understood that what is said about collections of photographs is true for all similar material and that a collection of realia, models, posters, charts, film slides, and transparencies is identical, the subject headings provide what may be missing from any identifying label, a title that describes the contents. The alphabetic subject list is the means whereby anyone who needs a picture can find it, even though there is no identificating legend on it.

The first step is to gather a list of subject headings in any order. After a list of a hundred or more terms is assembled, they are classified, following some standard classification system. The

Decimal Classification given in Part Two makes a good place to
begin. Where the terms are identical, the number is taken. Where
they are nearly identical, the number may be taken if the heading
is a second or third level of abstraction. The cataloger must
decide whether the term used in the book is more exact and descriptive than the term thought of first. When the terms are put in
classified order, any near synonyms may be eliminated. A legend is
placed with the picture showing the subject headings and classification numbers chosen and a fuller identification of what the picture shows. Usually all pictures are put in plastic envelopes and
stored with the identifying legend inserted with the picture.
Boxes of film slides may have to be identified with a sequential
number referring to the descriptions put one after another in a
loose leaf notebook on lists made with a computer or a word
processor.

The computer is a wonderful device for making lists and for
containing in stored form what the list shows. Canned programs
exist for locating addresses in a file and for assembling various
combinations of these addresses. They serve as well as a retrieval
device for pictures. Word-processing equipment or programs serve
the same purpose, because it is easy to print-out lists of pictures
which can be compared for similarity. Although no subject heading
can elicit all the variations that make pictures different even
when they are of the same subject, the combination of headings will
make the largest details findable. Using the methods described
above the center of interest is characterized by a subject heading.
Other special features are noted if their importance is understood
by the amount of space they take up in the picture. By using
headings to act as a logical sum, highly specific pictures can be
located. Similarly by using headings to find where there is an
overlap, a logical product, pictures of a special character can be
found.

Take, for instance, pictures of the funeral of President
Kennedy. Included are scenes of that memorable event which show
the White House, the Capitol Rotunda, Memorial Bridge, and so on,
and in general, Washington, D. C. Even if the individual wants
pictures of processions and parades on Pennsylvania Avenue, these
can be found if pictures are identified as above.

To go through the whole process, the librarian has pictures of
the funeral procession of President Kennedy, of King George VI of
England, and of President Roosevelt. Subject headings are assigned
for the first level of abstraction, the individual and the place.
Then the particular event is covered with a term for the second
level, Funeral processions, a term that is not included in the list
in Part Two, but 393 Cemeteries is in that general area, and the
number 393.1 can be assigned for Funerals, Funeral processions.

A person who wants a picture of a funeral procession of presidential funeral processions in Washington, D. C. will find the
pictures listed under Washington, D. C., under Pennsylvania Avenue,
and under Presidents, as well as under Funeral processions. Note
that adjectives tend to increase the specificity of nouns, but this
does not always work in favor of better organization. Presidential
funeral processions is a more exact heading, but that would leave
out pictures of the procession for King George VI of England.
Heads of state is a broader subject heading than Presidents or
Kings, but it serves no purpose if a comparison is made of the
various levels of abstraction in the subject heading list.

A further difficulty may arise in the mind of the librarian
when assigning the name of the individual, because the picture is
not of the individual but of what happened to him. It is understood that a picture of a famous individual deals not with the
appearance of the person but with the life. The subject headings

assigned in the example above would quite correctly be those of the individuals even though neither the faces or figures are shown.

A further temptation, quite commonly unresisted, is to add to the subject heading to provide an exact identification of the picture. This adds greatly to the burden of the user of the library and makes the list impossible to classify and usually filled with ambiguities. The exact identification is provided by the legend filed with the picture. The subject headings serve a funtion much like a title. Combining these headings will yield increasing specificity while preserving the list and minimizing the number of headings that must be added. The numbers assigned for the individual provide a context and relate the heading to all others in the collection.

There is always a choice in classification of individual personal names, but the best is the field in which the person was famous. Pictures of Albert Einstein would be classified under Physicists, and the pictures of heads of state under the history number for the country they represented or ruled.

IV. MAKING A GUIDE TO A PICTURE COLLECTION

Even though slides and print pictures have been transferred to optical disks, by far the best way to store them, the user will have trouble operating the machinery and finding what he wants. Even more important, the librarian must leave behind directions which explain exactly what was done and why. The answer to both these requirements is a guide to the picture collection. A real advantage is that the cataloging system need not be overloaded with picture subject headings. The guide to the collection -- aside from explaining the hours the collection is open to the community and the rules of its use, the nature of any equipment and its use

if the patron is expected to operate it -- provides all the subject
headings both in a classified and in an alphabetic list.

If the decision is made to transfer the collection to optical
disks, the librarian is usually confronted with an urge to put all
similar pictures together, meaning that those with roughly the same
subject will be found on the same disks. While this is appealing,
it is not necessary, because the machinery provides that the pictures will appear when the proper directions are given, and the
classified list of subject headings makes it inconsequential exactly in what order the pictures are stored on the disk. Most
machines will show all the pictures under any one heading and provide the user with a number that shows how many there are. The
guide to the collection, then, will show exactly how the disks are
numbered in the sequential list to give an idea which must be
consulted for what pictures. These machines, while useful for
deciding which picture to use, do not provide the same flexibility
as the picture itself, whether film slide or poster, chart or plan,
or even blueprints. Like all such machines, the patron has no
chance to study the picture, carry it about the library, and often
must speed up thinking processes because other patrons are waiting
to use the machinery.

The guide will also explain the consistencies of the collection. For instance, a retinology clinic in a hospital had several
thousand photographs of the retina taken from the eyes of their
patients. These were filed in plastic containers under the various
conditions the photographs depicted. After much discussion the
question of transferring the color photographs to optical disks was
answered with a demonstration of the device and the realization
that what a student needed was the variety of appearances that
would all be called the same condition. Any other use could be
decided by the photograph itself. Physicians and medical students
referring to the collection could compare a photograph with many
possibilities and arrive at a diagnosis much sooner. The machine

justified its cost, because it reduced the amount of time that had
to be spent for this purpose and preserved the irreplaceable photographs of the eyes of patients who had died or moved away. The
explanation of the collection, the principles which governed the
inclusion of a photograph, and the history of the picture library
clarified exactly what the individual looking for a picture could
expect to find and told him how to look for it. A guide to any
collection can do no more. The guide itself can be included among
the books cataloged by the library so that the entry will lead a
person with a question to the proper place to begin his search for
an answer.

V. CONCLUSION

This chapter has dealt with material that either lacks self-
identification or may quickly be found with no reference to it. If
the identifying features are unimportant and will never be sought
by a patron of the library, there is no reason to include them.
The content of the work is the only thing of interest to a person
wishing information, and the self-identifying features are noted in
a catalog entry only as a kind of knee-jerk reflex of catalogers
who will look for details that fit the rules rather rules to fit
the needs of the community. Any material, including recordings of
the various distinct sounds of nature which have no author-equiva-
lents beyond narrators or authors of the text narrated, can be
cataloged so that access is only by content.

The discussion of pictures follows a section on the organization of a map collection on which all the rest of the chapter is
based. Maps may be kept folded in file drawers if only current ones
are kept and no time or money is spent on the collection. Maps
which are laid flat in file drawers and are expected to be used
frequently can be classified and the entries for them made findable

under the area the map covers. These areas should be listed with
the most exact place-name given first followed by other larger
areas in which it is located, because the classification does exactly the opposite, preserving the natural hierarchical order of
all geographic areas. The entries may either be brieflisted or may
be given relatively full cataloging, but in any case, access to the
surrogate for the map itself is by the area depicted, not the cartographer who is of little importance to anyone who is not himself
a cartographer or geographer of note.

Pictures can be given a subject heading based on the center of
interest and other significant details. The subject headings will
follow rules that control the terminology and prevent the use of
inverted headings and limit the use of prepositions to those of
fixed phrases like "Freedom of Worship." If many headings, that is
more than a few hundred are to be used, classifying the headings
will both prevent the puzzle of near synonyms (which is used for
what pictures?) and the problem of relating one heading to another.
The classification numbers supply a context with each number and
relate it to all other numbers in the classification system. Part
two shows a subject heading list in both classified and alphabetic
form.

The subject headings are used in combinations called logical
sums or logical products to elicit the specific picture desired,
even though the user does not whether such a picture exists. The
usual type of subject heading is avoided, because these logical
sums and products are more easily managed when a simple term is
used, either a single word or a phrase that has the meaning of a
single word. Logical sums add up details, logical products show
how they overlap.

All of these collections need not bulk up the general catalog
because the subject headings can be kept in a looseleaf notebook,

called here, the guide to the collection. Brieflisted entries can be printed out, if not too numerous, or can be retrieved by a computer with a program made originally for keeping a list of addresses and sold commercially. The adaptation of this program is relatively easy and only takes thorough thinking out to be useful, as Part Two describes.

4 Material Cataloged by Identifying Features

If the patrons of a library can be expected to know either the title or the name of individuals associated with the item in hand, it is cataloged using the title and names as points of access. Unlike material which either lacks these features or is not looked for that way, access by subject is secondary. Any material that is temporary in nature and will not be sought by anything other than subject should be so cataloged. Maps and pictures were the two examples used extensively in the previous chapter before beginning a discussion of subject. In this chapter, sound recordings and motion pictures or videotapes are the examples. The difference between these two kinds of materials is that motion pictures require annotations. With other material, an annotation is either unneeded or ludicrous.

The second edition of Anglo-American Cataloging Rules settled the problems that arose with the first edition by pointing out the differences between audio-visual material and books rather than starting out with the assumption that they are just alike. The physical description of the material differs widely from one sort to another, just like the material itself. But the rules fail to settle the problem of access. The assumption is made that access by author or author equivalent is the standard from which all other access varies. The rules were published at the beginning of the great change from manual methods to computerized catalogs of various kinds. The reasons for using title unit entry were not accepted because this concept was not considered a part of the ideology of the cataloger, even though the average user of a library has no

interest in the cataloger's ideology or his lack of it, supposing
it exists in the first place.

Where the cataloging system uses a unit entry, access by title
is usually the most economical way of preparing an entry. This is
a requirement in a significant percent of entries in a main-entry
system, even more since the rules for entry under corporate body
were made more stringent. The main-entry system is used when all
the bibliographic detail will be included under one entry only, a
necessity when catalogs were set in type by hand and printed page
by page on rag paper. With the advent of card catalogs, the distinction between a main-entry systems and unit systems was lost.
If all the bibliographic information is included regardless of the
point of access, entry under title saves time and effort. No entry
is main because none is secondary. The ideal example of this was
the card catalog made up of preprinted cards, just what the wrong-
headed ideologues of old cataloging refused to admit. Computer
entries are by definition unit entries whether they are sought on
terminals or printed out in lists or on cards. Sound recordings
and art prints may be entered under the composer or the artist for
the same reason that everything else is entered under title. It
saves time.

I. SOUND RECORDINGS

Sound recording has changed constantly since Thomas A. Edison
first recited "Mary had a little lamb" into a horn, and his machine
played it back for him. First, cylinders stored the sounds and a-
coustical methods reproduced them. These were replaced by disks,
which were electrically recorded in the mid-1920's, and then by
wires and ferrite-coated plastic tapes, and now by compact discs
which are read by laser beams. The quality of the sounds have constantly improved to the point where a compact disc player will produce sounds that are virtually the same as those originally made.

There seems to be nowhere for the present method to go except
to make minor improvements in the player itself. The compact discs
do not reproduce sound as the acoustical and electrical recordings
did, and the disc is not destroyed by being played. The laser beam
that reads the disc will wear out before the disc does, because no
needle grinds away at the grooves which produce the sound. In the
opinion of most experts, the compact disc player creates the sound
anew just as piano rolls did. In general, the cost of the machines
is now decreasing rapidly, because further improvements are impossible as large companies compete for a share in the available
market.

Cassette players, however, are more numerous and the tapes more
abundant. These have replaced the reel-to-reel tapes which have
been completely outdated and are no longer sold except to recording
studios. Cassette players are commonplace now and have done much
to broaden our understanding of history because of their importance
in recording the memories of people. Oral history projects, once
the business of such eccentrics as Professor Seagull, are now in
progress in several universities. Cassette players, also, have
become the means whereby an individual can read a book while mowing
a lawn. Blind people have no other means of acquiring the information, and sighted individuals find it convenient to listen while
their bodies are otherwise engaged. Joggers with earphones may be
listening to the recording of an individual reading a book as well
as an orchestra playing music.

In view of this complexity, the first thing the librarian must
do is survey the library to see how sound is recorded and how much
these sound recordings are used. The number and kinds of sound
recordings determine in large part the way the library will be
organized. A library with a few hundred sound recordings all on
phonodiscs needs only brieflisting to make the collection available, while the music library in a college or university may need
full cataloging.

The second edition of AACR II provides for the description of sound recordings to a greater extent than previous standardized rules, but several points remain unsettled:

Main entry. In general, brieflisted entries require only the composer to be findable, if the work is classical music, or by performer if popular music recordings and jazz. Musical comedies and music that is no longer very popular or has yet to be generally accepted widely is known by the title.

Uniform titles. Classical music is often identified by the form of the work, the signature key, and the number in the composer's list of works. The rules have been clarified greatly for classical music but are unclear for other kinds.

Performer. The Library of Congress gives the performers in a descriptive note, preceding the contents. Jazz, however, relies solely on the performer for identification. The compositions played are of secondary importance.

Date. Expected in all cataloging, date is not readily located on a phonodisc or a cassette, and the user of the library must be satisfied with such uninformative citations as 19? or 194? when he really wants to know when the recording was made.

Analytics. Many works may be combined on one disc or one cassette which the patron of a library will want to find either in other combinations or by the title of a single work.

The rules especially fail for the brieflisting of commercially supplied sound recordings. The rules provide for downscaled cataloging of books, level one in the introductory chapter, but this is only applicable if liberally re-interpreted. While the rules for the cataloging of maps have been clarified, those for cataloging sound recordings remain as opaque as ever, even beyond the problem of main entry. Maps are supposed to be entered under the person responsible, just what no library would ever do unless it wants to prevent the use of the maps. Sound recordings of classical music, for example, can be treated this way with great success. However, sound recordings are made which feature the performer, although the rules make scant provision for this fairly commonplace type of collection if they are not treated as an anthology with a collective title. The rules also provide that the General Material Designation be buried in the entry after the title, just where it will most likely be missed.

Anyone who wishes to follow AACR II scrupulously is invited to skip this chapter and go on to the next. What follows is a revision of the rules with the purpose of showing how the most findable entries can be made with least expense of time and effort. Full cataloging is shown and explained first, followed by brieflisting.

The first consideration is to divide the collection into three sorts of sound recordings: recorded speech, classical music, and popular music, which is understood to include all its forms from folksongs to the latest variations of rock. Recorded speech is cataloged exactly like a book if the sound recording is, in fact, the oral edition of a work. Oral history is cataloged under the name of the individual interviewed. Aside from the dates of the interviews, the only other important information is the subject of the reminiscences. This serves as the title of the sound recording and is assigned by individual who conducts the interview.

The format would be: Individual Interviewed, summary title of the interview, date and place of the interview, and number of cassettes. Because all cassettes maintain the same speed through a sound recorder, depending on size, it is not necessary to site the speed in inches per second. However, some machines for recording speech use small cassettes which should be so labelled if these are employed. A better method is to make the cassettes all of a standard size even if this means rerecording the interview on a small compact cassette onto one of standard size. Those who will use the interviews will find it much easier to deal with standard-size cassettes which are sturdier and less subject to accidental unwinding or other accidents.

Recordings of what is, in effect, purely sound effects presents a problem unless narration accompanies the sounds. The narrator, the author of what is narrator, or the producer serve as identifying features of the work, though less so than the title. This is true of all material that will be cataloged only by the content of the work rather than any person connected with its production. If it is desired to make the name of anyone findable, then it can be cataloged like recorded speech.

Popular music is generally recorded on phonodiscs, cassettes, and on compact discs. Large collections on eight-track cartridges were developed only to have the production of playback machinery and of the cartridges themselves cease. The cassette is handier, the equipment for playing it is much less heavy and bulky, and the quality of sound reproduced is the same as that of cartridges. There is no reason other than archival interest to maintain a collection of eight-track cartridges and the playback equipment.

Modern cassette players do not provide the quality of sound of the compact disc, but they have the advantage of coming in very small sizes that make individual listening possible. With amplification, the difference is minimized. Phonodiscs have set the standard for all of these ways of storing sound recordings of pop music. These should be entered under performer with the title following. Other characteristics of the performance can be included, such as time and place if given on the packaging, thence readily available. The names of the back-up performers are generally not necessary, but the company which produced the sound recording is. The date is especially important, because popular music tends to go

out of favor rather quickly, and careers are made and destroyed
inside a year. Usually the copyright date of the album is given,
and lacking anything else, this may be the only source of a date.

Classical music is entered under the composer with the title of
the composition following. A uniform title will precede it if the
title as given on the packaging of the sound recording is not in
the correct order or is not the original title given to the work.
The performer follows and any necessary facts about the date and
place of the performance, followed by the company issuing the sound
recording, and its number. Compact discs should show the time of
the performance after the number of discs. Usually the time is
given very precisely, track by track, but the total time is not.
This is useful to the patron and should be included even if it
means that the cataloger has to do some elementary addition.

Composer
   [Uniform title of composition]
   Title on sound recording. -- Performer(s). -- Company
  issuing the sound recording : number given it. -- Medium of
  sound recording : time. -- (Series) -- Descriptive notes.
  -- Contents notes.

Summarized, the method of listing each item in the collection
is by the individual responsible, the title, and the producer of
the packaging. Many examples are shown in Part Two of this work.
Many problems remain, however, to be discovered when work begins on
a collection.

The first of these is notes. Which should be made and which
should not? One of the reasons for suggesting that performer be
included in the body of the entry is that space for notes should
not be taken up with description of the actual item in hand. The
performer serves a function much like the individual who creates a

later edition of a standard work. This is best put where one would
expect information on the edition of a work.

The first problem is how much of the contents to list for a
collection of music? If the performer is the most important means
of identifying the work, there seems to be either less need or
greater demand for a list of all the compositions performed. The
difference is supplied entirely by the requests of the patrons.
Very often only a single work is enjoyed, and the patron may not
know where it is recorded. This leads to a rule about contents
notes which will always be found workable. Make only those content notes which will become the entries for analytics. If two
works are included in one cassette or on one phonodisc or compact
disc, the contents are shown in a 'with' note. This note is so
named because it begins "With" and is followed by the composer and
title of the other composition. A separate entry is made for each
work with the composer's name and the uniform title. The cataloging remains the same except that the other work is given in the
with note.

A decision must be made for collections of compositions all on
the same cassette or compact disc. Collections with a title are
cataloged under the title and the contents listed if each these
will be separately cataloged as an analytic. Those without a title
may be cataloged under the first composition named with analytics
made for the rest. Or all the works can be listed one after another
in the title area. Only the first work would be findable under its
title, if it has any. If analytics are desired, then contents must
be listed in a note.

However, in brieflisting a work, the librarian is often tempted
to reduce the number of analytics in the belief that this will save
time. It is no saving to make the reference librarian do what the
cataloger has left undone. If requests come for an individual work

which can be found only if listed separately, the extra time needed
for analytics must be taken.

The lists are made up of separate sections for each type of
composition in each medium. For instance, a section on musical
comedies will be divided into those works on phonodisc, those on
cassettes, and those on compact discs, because each of these is
stored differently. The brieflisting cites the composer for works
of classical music, the performer for popular music, and both where
necessary. A good example of a brieflisting is the Schwann Catalogue, and the same space-saving devices may be used. A composer's name or the name of a performer is only listed once with all
the works under that listing cited. It must be clear that the
purpose of the list is less to inventory the collection than to
advertise it for use. An inventory need list works only once,
usually by the number found on the item itself even if the rules
above are followed so that all the works by one composer come
together.

Any material may be organized by identifying features if the
community of the library needs this service, provided that something other than content identifies it. Obviously pictures are not
identified by anything but the content, like realia collected by
the library. However, art prints are important not for the subject
depicted but for the artist who created the depiction. This is
true whether the artist was a painter, photographer, or sculptor.
These are individually cataloged under the name of the artist, like
classical music, because the title given the work may be non-descript, like "Composition number nine." No uniform titles need to
be made for these works, because the subject entry will adequately
cover what might logically be inclduded.

Usually, all art prints are entered under the title of the
artist, when known. Classical works of statuary which are repro-

duced in prints and photographs may be identified by the customary title, for instance "Venus de Milo" which simply identifies where the piece of sculpture was found. Title, when truly an identifying feature of a work, makes a very good entry around which all others may be grouped. Any anonymous work should be entered under the title not under the word anonymous, its abbreviation, or its synonyms.

Examples of other material are games, kits, and portfolios which differ only in the physical description. Although each of these kinds of material was thought up by someone and produced by other people, the names have been lost or blurred in the general history of the work. Even the name of an important person is less meaningful than the title of the work.   What makes these forms of nonbook material confusing is how much physical description is necessary. Customarily a game comes in a box which can be measured and the exact count of the pieces given in a note if that is desirable. All such composite works are entered under the title unless clearly identified with three or fewer individuals.

Counting all the pieces in a game may be a difficult task that is unrewarding because its only purpose is to provide a basis against which the librarian may check to be sure that the borrower has returned everything. If a deposit is required to check out the material, all the pieces must be counted lest a borrower be charged unjustly for what another person has done. Where loans are made for home use this may be necessary if only to prove to the would-be borrower that a game or portfolio has all its parts.

II. ANNOTATIONS OR SUMMARIES

Material that must convey the contents to the user of the library for a decision to be made whether or not the material is what the user wants must contain a summary or an annotation. The two terms are synonymous in library usage and are used especially for motion pictures, video cassettes, or canned computer programs. Many other kinds of material can use annotations, especially pictures, but the annotation is likely to be more an explanation of the subject heading than of the picture.

The annotation of a canned computer program explains exactly what it will do and the amount of random access memory required. The annotation of a video cassette describes the contents as exactly as possible. In no case is the annotation a criticism. The first rule is to leave out all evaluative words and usually the sentence that contains them. The purpose is to allow the patron of the library to decide whether the material is suitable or not.

Annotations are brief statements and some telegraphic prose is acceptable, especially the omission of obvious subjects of sentences, but this cannot be carried very far without baffling the individual who relies on them for an understanding of the contents. All vague, nondescript, terms -- woolly words -- are avoided and those that have a precise meaning chosen instead. The object is to inform rather than mystify.

Annotations are usually from twenty-five to a hundred words in length. If the subject can be perfectly conveyed in fewer than twenty-five words, the sentence is considered ideal, but more often than not, too much has been omitted for the annotation to be accurate. Usually these abbreviated statements are the result of careless or inattentive work. The limit of twenty-five words reflects the amount of space on a card approximately three inches by five. The entries in a computerized system or on a list can be longer but it is always best to aim for the most complete statement that conveys the subject of a work.

The computer used as a word processor aids greatly because of the ease of making revisions. The statement that an annotation cannot be written but it can be rewritten to perfection explains what the difficulty is. In general, annotations cannot be dashed off without careful consideration, because haste or inattention will show at once in the prose. Formal prose is required, because that is the language universally understood by educated people. Slang phrases, although exact, are avoided, but a broader view of colloquialism relieves the severity. The computer will allow the author of the annotation to try many different phrases until the best one is found.

Motion pictures are always cataloged under the title of the work, because they represent what is truly a corporate venture. The director and the actors may be cited in notes but enough space must be left for the annotation. Because of the difficulty of preparing them, usually annotations are copied. Many sources, though, are misleading. The catalogues of video cassettes ordinarily are small enthusiastic reviews which convey little of the subject matter and explain the desire of the company to sell the item.

Finally, the only way to learn to prepare an annotation is to write them and submit them for criticism until enough confidence is gained to make the work as automatic as it ever can be. Doing this will sharpen the ability of the librarian to select and revise the summaries and annotations he finds in source material. Good annotations become fixed with the work and are generally picked up by anyone who has to do this kind of cataloging.

5 Procedural Manual

Many years ago, a student in a seminar decided to send questionnaires to libraries in the state asking each to submit a copy of its procedural manual. She planned then to take what was common to all of them and make a kind of model for any libraries that did not have one to follow. She made an appalling discovery as soon as the answers to her letters came back. Only the rare library makes one and keeps it up to date. She abandoned the project and shifted to a follow-up questionnaire: why didn't the libraries have an up-to-date record of all the rules in force? Her seminar paper reported that the most common reason was that it was too difficult to do and no one had time to devote to a purely housekeeping task. There were clients to serve and material to organize. Although no one suggested a model, several implied that its absence made the work harder.

Nevertheless, a procedural manual must be made if the library is to have any continuity. All the decisions the librarian makes are recorded in the procedural manual along with examples of the bibliographic entries made and statements that may be forgotten although they govern the library. On the basis of this manual, which should not be undertaken as a project but should be included in the daily routines of the library, the guide to the collection can be maintained. Guides were discussed under the section on pictures. A guide is a necessary adjunct to the catalog, regardless of the form in which it is kept. Its primary purpose is to explain to the user how the library puts material away so it can be found again. The following outline shows what the manual must contain, if it is to be useful to any successor to the librarian now at work. Naturally, the larger the library the more elaborate the manual must be.

Outline of Procedural Manual

I. Name of library, position in parent organization, and mission.

II. Kind of material held, kind of bibliographic entries made for the material, means of access to these entries.

III. Rules for use of material, what can be borrowed for home use, what must be used in the library.

IV. Staff and duties of each person.

I. NAME OF LIBRARY

The procedural manual should be kept in a looseleaf notebook and prepared as work proceeds. Because the name of the library and its mission are very slow to change, once this section is written, it does not often need to be rewritten. It is kept because the statements made govern the future of the library and are the controlling principles of all its work. Even so, the purpose of the library may be forgotten. The position of the library in the parent organization is meant especially for special libraries which may have an important place and a special role. Usually this section writes itself. For instance, the statement that the library serves a college and is considered a separate department, however it is phrased, takes care of this section and answers a question the user will have about the library and the position of its director in the college hierarchy.

II. KINDS OF MATERIAL HELD

All the different kinds of material must be listed and the way
each is cataloged must be explained, but more than this, how these
entries will be found by the patron of the library must also be
explained. A decision that has not been made except by accident
must be faced. Will all the bibliographic entries be listed together or will separate catalogs be made? Anything that begins a
new alphabet is a new catalog. Libraries ordinarily keep a file of
all the periodicals, even though a card for each title may be kept
in the dictionary catalog. The decision, then, is whether to keep
one alphabetic file for all the bookstock of a library, meaning
every information source regardless of the way it is packaged, or
to keep separate files for each different medium or keep both.

Most libraries will find it is convenient to keep both a list
or some other equivalent of a book catalog as well as a file of all
these entries in various media. Before the computer was developed
to the point of usefulness for the library, librarians were warned
not to keep making entries for a variety of files the use of which
was only temporary. This is still true, but it is the composition
of the entry that takes the time. Once any material is cataloged
by anybody, it should not have to be done again. Usually where the
work of finding the entry exceeds that of making a new entry, it is
just as easy to make the entry once for the library and afterward
copy it as often as is necessary. However, there are several
things to keep in mind before making a monster file of bibliographic entries of everything. Is the material cataloged only by content? Does the material have no identifying feature which a user
of the library can be expected to know? If so, then a summary does
as much good as a listing of each item.

The ideal example of this is a collection of photographs which
are kept in the original form and on optical disk. The patrons of

the library use the optical disk; the original copies are kept as
back-up for the preparation of these disks. There is no need to
keep an item-by-item list except for each optical disk. The material is sought by content, hence although each item is important,
the patron of the library wants only the photograph which explains
what he is looking for. The greater the number of items, the better
his information will be when he has used it, and the more likely he
will be to have some knowledge of it.

Even if the library does not use the computer as the means for
storing bibliographic entries, keeping entries in machine-readable
form will reduce to one the number of times the entry must be made.
Word processing programs do this quite as well as any other. Files
can be made and maintained with these programs very successfully if
the material to be included is alphabetized in advance of being entered. Most programs include methods of rearranging text where desirable or necessary. The general file, supposing there is enough
memory, can be copied and rearranged into separate files for each
kind of material. The kind of material must be specified. The
general medium designation (GMD) is placed after the title in the
Anglo-American Cataloging Rules, the searcher of a file is aided by
having it first, usually to the right above the first line of the
entry.

A further consideration is whether full cataloging is made or
the item is brieflisted. The procedural manual should contain a
model of the kind of cataloging done for each medium with an explanation of what is always included. This helps both the searcher
and the beginning cataloger. These decisions are not easily made,
and they may change provided very few items have been cataloged.
If any revision of cataloging method is made after much has already
been done, the question should be whether to create a new file of
entries or intermix the old with the new. So long as no searchable
item has been altered, there is nothing wrong with mixing old and

new. The catalogs of large libraries show this to perfection with old style bibliographic entries intermixed among the new.

Brieflisting is suggested when the collection will always be relatively small and the problem of identification of each item is minimal. The entry is a surrogate and should not be mistaken for the material itself. To answer many bibliographic questions, the item itself must be consulted not the surrogate. For instance, a small collection of sound recordings, even if they are in various forms -- phonodiscs, cassettes, and compact discs -- can be listed with only the minimum of information included and divided by the medium if each is stored in a different place. The author of this book would define small as fewer than a thousand items.

Lists are very easily revised and may be copied into different arrangements without great trouble on the computer. The lists can then be kept in a looseleaf notebook, like the old sheaf catalog of many years ago. What made the method inferior was the permanence of the collection and the difficulty of any revisions of the catalog itself. Because the collection is small, revisions can be made as often as necessary without copying and recopying the permanent items in the collection. If a collection is being built, it is best to keep each of the entries in card form, if it is not kept in a computer.

Ultimately, all cataloging will be done on a computer, because the machine is the perfect answer to the two great problems of the format of the catalog: should the entries be made in a list or should each be put in some kind of random access file, in book catalogs and or on cards filed in one alphabet. Although the book catalog can be produced in many copies, it can not be revised without reprinting entries over and over again. The card catalog, although it can be produced in only one copy, provides random access. Entries can be added or subtracted without changing any of

those already made. The computer does both. Terminals may be
located around a college campus so that the faculty has access to
the catalog of the library and can satisfy their curiosity without
ever leaving their chairs. Entries can be added or withdrawn
without changing anything. The computer is at once a book catalog
and the equivalent of a card catalog. As such, its flexibility is
just now being understood.

In the days when literacy was limited rather than being virtually universal, only scholars used libraries, which were made up
entirely of expensive hand printed books. Now, everybody is taught
how to read and is expected to make use of libraries which contain
information in many different forms. The catalogs prepared for
hand printed books are unnecessary today, because much was included
that is no longer significant. Only the information that identifies the item among all others should be included. If the catalog
includes only one medium of information, much of the detail needed
for a larger catalog can be omitted. The question, then, is not
how much detail to include, but what the overall size of the catalog will be. Because it is easier simply to copy information than
to revise it, the entries made for a catalog are copied onto a list
that represents only a part of all the items included in the whole
catalog. Revising each entry because it is in a list rather than
in a catalog is as great a waste of time as making full entries
when only a few items are needed.

For many media, only the title is important. Everything else
identifies the item even when no confounding of one with another is
likely. Brieflisting does not change the principles of cataloging, it only reduces the work. However, a large catalog not only
records what has been obtained for a library, it is hospitable to
future material. That some confusion may arise when more material
is added requires that some information of little or no use to a
searcher be included. The searcher is primarily anxious to find if

a library contains information that he is seeking, either by a part
of an individual item or by the content of information sources in
general. To find material, the searcher must rely on points of access, whether by subject or by creator in one form or another.

Kind of Bibliographic Entry Made

Only two styles of cataloging are recommended: entry under
title for everything except sound recordings and art prints. This
minimizes the amount of unproductive work that must be done to make
a record of the holdings of a library. Access points should be
limited to those that are essential and shown in the entry itself.
The composer or performer of music is the only access point that
will be sought. It is simple convenience to list them at the head
of the entry. However, trying to find access points for other
kinds of material more often gratifies a compulsion than aids the
searcher of the catalog. Similarly, there is little to be listed
after the name of an artist except the title whether or not it is
meaningful. Putting the name of the artist anywhere but at the
head of the entry is a waste of time. Equally, when a number of
different points of access will be sought, it is most convenient to
list each one at the head of the unit entry, when it is sought in a
computerized file, or to duplicate the unit entry for each accces
point.

Once a decision has been reached, the exact model of the cataloging including the preferred style of spacing on a card must be
explained in the procedural manual. Any material that will not be
a part of the general catalog, ever, can have its own catalog in a
guide to the collection. Preparing this guide should be a project
which, when done, requires no further work. The word processing
programs available for a computer will greatly reduce the effort
and make duplication of the work relatively simple.

Means of Access

The public needs to know how material is stored. Much nonbook
nonprint material must be kept away from those who would like to
browse. This is particularly true for cassettes and compact discs
which are readily stolen. Stores where compact discs are sold
package them in large clear plastic containers which are not so
readily concealed as the actual box containing the disc. There is
no point whatever in creating separate classifications for nonprint
material which will be stored away from the public. Whatever the
method of storage is, the address -- which the classification is,
essentially -- should be as simple as possible and should be added
without consulting anything. This can be primary point of access
as well as anything else: composer for classical music, performer
for popular music, title for videocassettes and motion pictures,
and for everything else: games, canned programs, etc.

III. RULES FOR USE

Allied with problems of storage are the rules of the library in
general, the hours it is open, and the requirements for using the
material in the library and for borrowing material. These rules
change much less frequently than it is supposed. The hours are
posted throughout the library, and it might seem useless repetition
to include them in the procedural manual. However, an explanation
of how the hours are decided is not. Equally, the rules for the
registration of borrowers and any exceptions that may be made
should be included as well. Librarians in public schools rarely
consider who their borrowers are and find themselves in a network
of exceptions. Deciding in advance will do much to reduce the
number of contradictory decisions.

For instance, may members of the janitorial staff borrow material? Volunteers? Parents? Members of the school board? These

decisions must be made in any library not open to the general public. The rules for borrowers are especially important if the library is open to the public but only students and faculty can borrow
material. Then the question is whether alumni and staff can as
well.

IV. STAFF AND DUTIES

The work of the library will go much better if each job is
described and if these jobs are then assigned to the staff available. This is a vital part of the budget process, because staff
accounts for most of the money spent, a fact that horrifies some
people who do not know what a library does. In the words of the
old saw, a library is a service not a collection. What the staff
does is to provide the service that the patrons of the library
need. Even if the library has only one person and some volunteers, the work that each should do should be presented in two
ways: the tasks listed individually with cross references to the
rest of the procedural manual and grouped under the names of each
of the staff members.

To hire librarians or staff members the job description is
usually required by the parent authority. If this is done in advance, the need is much more clearly understood and explained. As
strange as it may sound, more staff members do not make more efficient work, and excess money in the budget does not define compe-
tency in the librarian. Only by knowing exactly what the mission
of the library is, what work must be done to carry out this mission, and who will do the work can the librarian competently use
the money made available in the budget. Excess funds only means
that the librarian has run out of ideas.

Small libraries, especially those in schools, may make use of
volunteers, although the several disadvantages of this kind help

should be known in advance of any concerted effort to find them.
Volunteers will generally regard the work they do as the lowest
priority and sacrifice their work time to almost everything else.
As a result, volunteers should not be given tasks to complete which
are necessary if other work is to proceed. A volunteer should fill
in with help in the regular work of the library and do what the
librarian has always meant to accomplish if there was ever enough
time. Volunteers are not chosen; they're accepted. This may mean
difficulties with personalities, so that a librarian must have a
means of "firing" a volunteer, if necessary without endangering
anyone's reputation. Most volunteer programs work best if roughly
the same requirements for the volunteer as for a paid employee are
maintained and the same requirements for success in the job. This
means that the number of volunteers is limited by the mission of
the library as much as the number of employees, the difference
being the amount of money available. An employee is necessary if
the library's work cannot proceed unless someone can be assigned to
do it and held accountable if it is not done. The key to success
in any volunteer program is the enjoyment of the work on the part
of the volunteer and the librarian's flexibility in fixing the
times the volunteer will work in the library.

Granting all these difficulties, volunteers can nevertheless
accomplish a great deal in a library, depending on how clearly the
librarian understands the work that must be done and the abilities
of the volunteers. The ideal is a librarian who is no longer
employed for one reason or another. College graduates who need
something beside their duties at home to keep them interested in
the world around them will be found almost as suitable as librarians in the performance of many library tasks, and in some cases,
even better. The volunteer should be given work at the level of
his ability. Professional librarians who do not have a job should
not be given strictly routine tasks to perform, which they may do
without complaint, because their error rate is much higher than

that of volunteers who have very limited ability. Payment has
nothing to do with ability.

The college graduate can be taught how to catalog pictures, and
both professional and nonprofessional volunteers can review motion
pictures or videocassettes. College graduates can be taught how to
write annotations. Often they are better at the job than a
professional librarian because they may have more experience in
writing and are able to concentrate better on what they see rather
than on some problem in the library waiting to be solved.

If a librarian decides to embark on a volunteer program, the
first job is to prepare a pamphlet describing the duties that will
be assigned and what conditions of employment, other than pay, will
govern them. The more closely the volunteer programs resemble good
personnel management, the more successful they are likely to be. The
administrative authorities should be consulted and should approve
the pamphlet before the search for volunteers begins if it is to be
more than a haphazard arrangement for extra work.

The first level of paid employee is the clerical assistant
whose duties are limited to routine work that requires little or no
judgement. Duties that can be taught generally fit this category,
such as reshelving material, checking it out, or discharging loans.
The great disadvantage of clerical assistance is the high rate of
turnover, almost as high as that of volunteers. The time needed to
train the employees of the library, paid and unpaid, constitutes an
important expense, so that the procedural manual lessens job training and helps assure accuracy. The clerical assistant's duties
should never include making policy decisions, although the clerical
staff must be included when a decision that affects them is being
formulated.

Unless the clerk is working at much below his capacity, he

cannot catalog pictures, review motion pictures and videocassettes, or write annotations, and yet he can do much more than type letters and enter material into the computer. Rules for the descriptive cataloging of almost all material are so precise that in time the clerical assistants can do it all, depending on the amount of training they receive. If the library has the services of a library technical assistant, it is generally best to leave the cataloging to that individual.

Library technical assistants have two years of college, possibly an Associate of Arts degree, and ideally will be able to do the descriptive cataloging of nonbook, nonprint material. Usually, considerable training is necessary, one of the most important reasons for a procedural manual that becomes the textbook in the library's in-house education programs. However, depending on the interests and abilities of the technical assistant, they cannot write annotations and often cannot catalog pictures, even after considerable time has been spent on training them.

Professional assistants are understood to have a college education, the fifth year of which is library science. They can do anything in the library. The question is not their ability but their time. It is simply wasteful to assign routine work, requiring no judgement, to professional librarians. Some is inevitable, but the greater part of their time must be spent in assisting those who rely on the library for information and its resources. They can formulate policy, conduct experiments, and especially supervise the work of clerical assistants. The professional is trained to be a supervisor, whether that has been realized in his education or not. Keeping in mind that the professional librarian is a manager, even in the cataloging room of a large library, the job descriptions of technical assistants, clerical help, and volunteers can make the managerial function clear. Only professional librarians can supervise the work of other professionals. Only the snags of cataloging are left to the professional after the policy has been set, along with the selection of materials, and the establishment of work to be done by others. Professionals should never do easy work.

Some librarians have difficulty writing job descriptions, but if the procedural manual has been carefully prepared, the work derives from the mission of the library, and the tasks are fully detailed and accomplish this mission. Assigning the tasks to the individual prepares the description in large part and provides a clue to the increase of the staff. Increased work to be done, whether it is a new field or new medium to be included, indicates that a new employee must be sought, but this follows everything else: the tasks to be accomplished, who can do these tasks, and the provision for the payment in the budget. A person who meets the stated or implied previous education to do what it has been decided must be done can be found among all the librarians who graduate every year from library schools.

V. THE PROCEDURAL MANUAL

Like many other tasks of the librarian, once the procedural manual has been prepared, its upkeep is easy. Primarily, the procedural manual records decisions. Those that are made after due reflection rarely have to be changed, although they may need to be updated. This part of the book is meant to serve as a background for the preparation of the manual. The results of the community survey are a part of it and form the basis on which all the methods rest. In general, librarians have worked on the principle that if a method causes no trouble it is kept, but apparently successful methods may be very roundabout when diagrammed in a flow chart of operations. When this is discovered, ways of shortening preparation must be sought if the goal of maximum output at minimum cost is ever to be realized.

The flow chart follows the floor pattern of processing if more than two or three people are involved. If material is shunted back and forth without being completed at one sitting, some slippage is occurring without being addressed. A good example of this is the processing of motion picture films or videocassettes. The librarian selects the material, the technical assistant makes out the order, the film or videocassette is received, and then someone must review it and make an annotation. The technical assistant makes a card for the catalog and completes the Motion Picture Sheet for a looseleaf notebook, giving more than the title information, because facts about the distributor and purchase price are included. Should the annotation be included with the title or not? How much should be included on the card?

Because the reviewing of motion pictures is a lengthy process, and the cataloging cannot be finished until the annotation is prepared, some libraries hold up the processing until all that is done for one record is done. However, a microcomputer can keep all the records completed and incompleted until printed out, so that as parts of the process are accomplished, they are written down, with the whole record being completed when possible. This sort of work rather fills in time left available and is not essential wrong or wasteful. One way to shorten the time is to print the annotation that usually accompanies the listing of the motion picture, on film or videocassette, by the commercial supplier. Everything from the point of the order on is revision, so that the end result will be an acceptable annotation and complete identification of the motion picture.

One of the commonest reasons for delay is excessive checking and rechecking of the work done by technical assistants. Each step in the process should be a means whereby the previous steps are reviewed and corrected if incomplete. Sending material back to be revised by a person who has already seen it is wasteful. A good

work flow will assure that the previous step is revised and the
person who made an error is informed and necessary changes are
made. The effort to prevent errors can end by causing more, as the
experience of librarians has proved.

Finally, it is important, and the procedural manual should make
it clear, that cataloging is not a ritual but a necessary service
which makes the holdings of a library available to those who can
use any part of them. There is no right way to catalog anything,
only the way that achieves complete identification within the
library of each individual item and makes its location known to the
person seeking to use it. Beginning with the statement of the
goals of the library, the facts obtained in the community survey,
the kinds of material and the bibliographic listings made, the
rules for the use of the collection, and the duties of each person
in the library, the procedural manual puts in writing what would
otherwise be subject to erring memories. Any person could follow
the procedures listed and maintain the level of service acheived
following the procedural manual as a guide. It therefore serves
its purpose and justifies its preparation and upkeep.

Bibliography

Anglo-American Cataloging Rules / prepared by The American Library Association [et al.]. -- 2nd ed. by Michael Gorman and Paul Winkler. -- Chicago : The association ; Ottawa : Canadian Library Association, 1978. -- xvii, 620 p.

Cook, Sherry [et al.] "Data processing library: a very special library." Journal of Library Automation, 14:52-53 (March, 1981)

Cruse, Larry "Microcartography and cartographic data bases." Library Trends, 29:391-416 (Winter, 1981)

Drolet, Leon L., Jr. "Illinois libraries share audiovisual materials through pioneer multi-media access project." American Libraries, 14:208 (March, 1982)

Egeter van Kuyk, R. H. J. "Historical film documentation at the Netherlands Information Service." Unesco Journal of Information Science, Librarianship, and Archives Administration, 3:227-234 (October, 1981)

Kebabian, Helen "Administration of historical photograph collections." Current Studies in Librarianship, 4:27-35 (Spring, 1980)

Kidd, Betty H. "The Administration of a large map collection." Library Trends, 29:473-481 (Winter, 1981)

Liebman Roy "The Media Index: computer-based access to nonprint materials." Reference Quarterly, 20:291-299 (Spring, 1981)

Martyn, John "UAP [Universal Availability of Publications] and the new information technology." Unesco Journal... 4:38-42 (January, 1981)

Poor, William "STAIRS: a storage and retrieval system applied in online cataloging." Special Libraries, 73:52-62 (January, 1982)

Pugh, Mary Jo "Oral history in the library: levels of commitment." Drexel Library Quarterly, 15:12-28 (October, 1979)

Saldich, Ann "Television news archive: a model for the future." Change, 12:50-52 (September, 1980)

Samuel, Evelyn K. "Microforms and art libraries." Microform Review 10:141-147 (Summer, 1981)

Schroeder, John R. "Perspectives on map cataloging and classification." Library Trends, 29:419-438 (Winter, 1981)

Schurk, William L. "Popular culture and libraries: a practical perspective." Drexel Library Quarterly, 16:43-52 (July, 1980)

Van Rogers, Joann "Mainstreaming media center materials: adopting AACR2." School Library Journal, 27:32-35 (April, 1981)

Walker, David D. "Towards a national software library." Educational Media International, Issue number 3, p. 20-24, 1981.

PART TWO

Examples of Bibliographic Entries

On the following pages, examples of the cataloging of maps, art prints, sound recordings, videocassettes with annotations, and games are shown. These represent the different cataloging that will be encountered when organizing nonprint nonbook material. Following each is an example of brieflisting the material shown in the first part of each section. Next are alphabetic and classified subject heading lists for pictures. A bibliography of recent works on nonprint material precedes this part. An index for the whole book ends it. This second part of the book has been included in the index wherever anything appropriate can be found. For instance, the heading Maps will include the examples shown here.

In this part, the examples are given on the right-hand side of the page, recto, and the explanation of them is given on the facing left-hand page, the verso of this and following pages. After considerable experimentation this seemed the clearest way of presenting the material. The variation from the rules is explained along with the problem the example represents. The entries are shown as they would appear on a computer display screen or cathode-ray tube. This is more compact than the customary system of indentation found in most American cataloging, more like the spacing used in some British libraries. It is a good deal more compact than the method of display used by OCLC, the cataloging network that is used most by American libraries. These examples should clarify the statements made in Part One of this book, but only the actual work of cataloging the material will make everything clear. Motor skills are different from intellectual comprehension.

MAPS: Full Cataloging

Format precedes the first entry shown. The abbreviations and other curiosities of the entry will be explained first, followed by any problems of classification and access to these surrogates.

1. Title unit entry is shown without tracings because the subject would be exactly like the title of this map which begins the entry. This map is an example of the simplest cataloging available. International Standard Bibliographic Description specifies that each area be punctuated in just this way. A program can readily be devised to make each entry searchable on a computer and parts of the entry searchable as well by using the marks of punctuation. The abbreviations used in this entry are "ca." for Latin circa meaning about and [S.l.] for Latin "sine loco" meaning without a place. The scale is not exact because the number following the colon has been rounded out. The map is measured within the ruled lines that almost always surround the map itself. The measurement is always given in centimeters.

This map would be classified 912.73 in the Dewey Decimal system. The number for maps is 912 to which the number for the United States, 73, is tacked on after the decimal point. A library made up solely of maps could very well classify this map 73 and reserve the numbers 100 for areas and regions in general and 200 for material that is not maps: atlases and globes.

FORMAT

Entry
    Title / Cartographer. -- Scale. -- Place : Publisher, Date.
-- Physical description : coloration ; size. -- (Series) --
Notes.
    Tracing.

1.   MAP

    United States / Rand McNally. -- Scale ca. 1:27,600,000.
-- [S.1.] : The Company, 1977. -- 1 map : col. ; 46 x 68 cm.
    73 United States

2. Scale indeterminable as shown in this map indicates that either
a variety of scales was used or it cannot be ascertained what scale
was employed. The phrase in the first map in the area for publisher cannot be utilized here, because "The Society" is not the
same as "The Magazine." The Magazine is as much a division of the
National Geographic Society as the Cartographic Division.

Historical maps, such as this, may be entered under the cartographer or, if revised or redrawn, by the reviser as well as the
area depicted. The bibliographic entry shown opposite can be found
both ways in a computerized system. If an electronic typewriter is
used, storing the title unit entry will leave only the headings to
be put in. It is inconsequential whether this is done first or
after the entry has been printed out. The tracings as shown would
be printed out even though each has been typed at the head of the
entry and then the key pushed to get the typewriter to produce the
stored entry.

This has been classified under maps of the Western Hemisphere,
912.19812. It could also be classified 909.09812, for history of
the area. The number is created by dropping the 1 from -1812, the
subdivision for Western Hemisphere found at the beginning of the
area tables.

A further problem arises with the subject heading. The usual
way of referring to this area of the world is not "America" as in
the Library of Congress Subject Heading list but *Western
Hemisphere as in the Dewey Decimal Classification. The number
shown would be used by a library which uses the Dewey Classifi-
tion only for maps. This can be combined with Library of Congress
classification provided no letter is put in front of the Dewey number. Putting an M in front of the number would create an ambi-
guous number, neither the Library of Congress number for Music or
the Dewey number.

2.   MAP

   Colonization and trade in the New World / produced by
the Cartographic Division, National Geographic Society. --
Scale indeterminable. -- Washington, D. C. : National
Geographic Magazine, 1977. -- 1 map : col. ; 58 x 76 cm.
-- "This map is a composite based on charts designed about
1720 by Cartographer Herman Moll.
   1812 Western Hemisphere. I. Herman Moll   II. National
Geographic Society.

3. The title of this map includes a subtitle. Each is equally searchable in a computerized file. Because there are two maps, one on each side of the page, it might seem that the two scales given would be for each map. However, this is untrue. The different scales both appear on one side of the page, one for the Middle East and in an inset in greater detail than the general map, the map of the Eastern Mediterranean. The scale of the map on the verso of the page is indeterminable. Following this in a statement about the projection. This is always abbreviated proj. and comes after a period and the scale of the map.

This map would be classified 912.56 in the Dewey system. The number for the Middle East in the Area Tables contains a number for the Eastern Mediterranean, -569. Because this part is contained in the hierarchy, it can only be brought out in the subject headings. Cataloging for a map that contains all the areas specified in Dewey, omitting or including nothing else, even though an additional title entry is searchable, does not have to cite each part. Eastern Mediterranean is not given as a subject heading because the method of searching for an item in the tracing is no different from the way the principal title is searched. A further subject heading brings out the historical map on the verso of the one catalog. A separate entry is not needed for this map because the subject heading amply covers the differences that exist between the maps. A different area might make it necessary to catalog each even though they are on the same sheet of paper, because of the complications of trying to combine tracings. These are principles of classification and would not change the way the surrogate is made in a library of maps.

3.   MAP

Middle East : Eastern Mediterranean / produced by the
Cartographic Division, National Geographic Society. -- Scale
1:1,775,000 and 1:6,700,000. Conic proj. -- Washington, D. C.
: National Geographic Magazine, 1978. -- 1 map : col. ; 56 x
78 cm. -- On verso: Early civilization in the Middle East.
Scale indeterminable.
    56 Middle East. 569 Eastern Mediterranean. 35 Ancient
Civilization. I. National Geographic Society.

4. Traveler's maps are as good as any other if drawn to scale. In the decision whether to keep or discard a map, scale is the determinant, especially if combined with a statement about the projection employed. The problem with maps is that a three-dimensional globe has been transferred to two-dimensional sheets. The projection shows how the surface of a globe has been transferred to one flat sheet. The traditional Mercator projection tends to elongate areas near the pole, and other projections have other problems. One of the best, the Conic projection, transfers a map from a sphere to a cone and comes closer to presenting the true proportions of the areas themselves. If the projection is omitted, it does not necessarily eradicate any value the map might have.

An option that the library may wish to adopt is shown here. The scale has been expanded beyond that required and additional statement added to show the English measurement as well as the ratio.

On the verso of this map is a diagrammatic presentation of the counties of England, Scotland, and Wales with a text lengthy and important enough to be signed by the author. Putting the author's name at the head of the entry in a card catalog makes the entry findable but may obscure the author's role in the creation of the map. The tracing includes the name because the notes give it. A good rule to adopt is that a name important enough to be cited in the entry is important enough to be cited in the tracing.

The number for this map is 912.41 in the Dewey Decimal Classification. The number demonstrates the problems with classification of land areas based on politically-determined boundaries. Scotland and Ireland can only be included if a number which apparently leaves out England and Wales is used.

4.   MAP

Traveler's map of the British Isles / produced by the
Cartographic Division, National Geographic Society. -- Scale
1:1,675. 1 inch to 26.4 miles. -- Washington, D. C. : National
Geographic Magazine, 1974. -- 1 map : col. ; 60 x 84 cm. -- On
verso: The British Isles : regal pleasures, rustic charm /
text by Merlo Severy.   Includes diagrams with names of
counties.
    41 British Isles. I. National Geographic Society. II.
Severy, Merlo.

5. The map of Australia has one scale but it is shown in three
different ways. This is optional and its adoption should be given
in the procedural manual. There is no need to cite options not
accepted. In the previous example, the reason was quite plain. An
American traveler will get a better idea of distances from the
English measurement than from the ratio. In this example,
Australia uses the metric system, hence the inclusion of a
statement in that system. Another projection is shown as well. On
the verso there is a relief map in an indeterminable scale as well
as text on the fauna. Relief maps such as this give a good idea of
how the land lies with attempting any degree of accuracy unless the
omission of scale was either accidental or concluded as unnecessary
because it had once been stated.

This map would be classified 912.94 in the Dewey system. The
description of the fauna would be classified 574.994 if desired. A
biological library would prefer the former, because everything in
the library concerns biology. A general library where the map was
kept primarily for its text would prefer the latter.

As in the previous example, an added entry is made for the
author of the text, but not for the relief map. The library may
wish to expand the Dewey Classification to account for the different types of maps, but this would be a local decision, necessary
only in large map libraries (those more than 50,000 maps). In
almost all other maps, the patron of the library can find the one
sought without undue searching.

5.   MAP

   Australia / produced by the Cartographic Division, National
Geographic Society. -- Scale 1:6,399,000. 1 cm. to 63.9 km. 1
in. to 101 miles. Chamberlin trimetric proj. -- Washington, D.
C. : National Geographic Magazine, 1979. -- 1 map : col. ; 51
x 81 cm. -- On verso: Relief map, scale indeterminable.
Australia : land of living fossils / text by John Eliot.
   94 Australia. I. National Geographic Society. II. Eliot,
John.

6. This map is a part of a series and is so listed. Series is not so rare in a collection of maps as these examples may seem to indicate. However, it was important enough to be included in the examples and is justifiably shown here. Otherwise, there is nothing different about the descriptive cataloging.

The principal difference is in the classification. This map clearly shows what the problem is. In the Dewey system, Colorado and New Mexico are considered "Western States" while Utah and Arizona are "Great Basin and Pacific Slope" states. This is good geography, because both lie on the Pacific side of the Continental Divide. The only way out of this problem is to give each state a subject heading, because, contrary to an earlier example, it is not contained within a hierarchy. Great Basin and Pacific Slope regional maps are classified 912.79, and those of Western States are classified 912.78.

7. The Grand Canyon is wholly in Arizona and maps of it are classified 912.79132. There are two maps on one sheet of paper. The one with the smaller ratio depicts land roughly in the center of Grand Canyon National Park. The other map shows just the land in the National Park. It is quite difficult to say just where the Grand Canyon begins and ends. A map of the whole geological feature would have to be classified 912.7913, the larger number indicating a larger area which contains the National Park.

This map shows as well why scale is important and must be included wherever available, in notes as well as in the body of the entry. The Transverse Mercator projection is adequate here because not too great an area is depicted and it is close enough to the equator not to show great exaggeration of scale. The scale is fairly constant.

6.   MAP

The Southwest / produced by the Cartographic Division,
National Geographic Society. -- Scale 1:2,124,000. 1 in.
to 33.5 miles. Albees conical equal-area proj. -- Washington,
D. C. : National Geographic Magazine, 1977. -- 1 map : col. ;
56 x 90 cm. -- (Close-up U.S.A.) -- Map includes Utah,
Colorado, Arizona, and New Mexico.
    792 Utah. 788 Colorado. 791 Arizona. 789 New Mexico. I.
National Geographic Society.

7.   MAP

The heart of the Grand Canyon, Grand Canyon National Park,
Arizona / produced by the Cartographic Division, National
Geographic Society in collaboration with Museum of Science,
Boston, Mass. -- Scale 1:24,000. Transverse Mercator proj.
-- Washington, D. C. : National Geographic Magazine, 1978.
-- 1 map : col. ; 58 x 84 cm. -- On verso: Computer mosaic
and enhancement of the Grand Canyon National Park. Scale
1:289,200.
    79132 Grand Canyon National Park. I. National Geographic
Society.

8. City maps, such as this, are common. Usually the scale is given in a bar graph and must be worked out to a ratio, like this. the abbreviation "ca." means about and is always used when a number has been rounded off. Much nonbook material demands cataloging no more difficult than this, leaving a question whether it should be done at all. There is no problem with the classification either. The Dewey Decimal Classification provides a number in the Area Tables for Chicago: --77311 which means just what this map shows. A library which uses Dewey would classify this map 912.77311.

9. The final map is not drawn to scale, as the bibliographic description shows. Unlike all the other maps shown, this one has an indication of edition. Finally, it was published by a joint author. There are no problems with this map except why it was saved at all.

8.   MAP

    Chicago and vicinity / Rand McNally. -- Scale ca. 1:190,000.
-- [S.l.] : The Company, 1976. -- 1 map : col. ; 46 x 63 cm.
-- On verso: Map of downtown. Scale indeterminable.
    77311 Chicago, Illinois.

9.   MAP

    San Diego visitor's map / by Gaston Lokvig and Carol Mendel.
-- 1979-1980 ed. -- Not drawn to scale. -- San Diego : Carol
Mendel, c1976. -- 1 map : col. ; 47 x 63 cm. -- Includes map
of San Diego County and "detail map of Balboa Park, Old Town,
and Mission Bay Park."
    79498 San Diego County, California. I. Gaston Lokvig

BRIEFLISTING

As shown on this and the facing page, the brieflisted entries greatly simplify finding the maps. The format differs mostly by the omission of notes, physical description, place of publication, and publisher if it is the same as the author. Scale is simplified to either just the ratio or the scale in the common measurement. The title is omitted if it is the area.

Format

Area. Title / individual responsible. -- Scale. -- Publisher, date.

Maps Brieflisted

Arizona. The Southwest / National Geographic Society. -- 1
   in. to 33.5 miles. -- 1977.
Australia. / National Geographic Society. -- 1 in. to 101
   miles. -- 1979.

British Isles. A traveler's map / National Geographic Society.
   -- 1 in. to 26.4 miles. -- 1974.

Chicago. / Rand McNally. -- 1 in. to 3 miles. -- 1976.
Colorado. The Southwest / National Geographic Society. --
   1 in. to 33.5 miles. -- 1977.

Grand Canyon. / National Geographic Society. -- 1:24,000. --
   1978.

Middle East. / National Geographic Society. -- 1:6,700,000. --
   1978.

New Mexico. The Southwest / National Geographic Society. --
   1 in. to 33.5 miles. -- 1977.

San Diego, California. / Gaston Lokvig and Carol Mendel. -- Not
   drawn to scale. -- c1976.

United States. / Rand McNally. -- 1 : 27,600,000. -- 1977.
Utah. The Southwest / National Geographic Society. -- 1 in. to
   33.5 miles. -- 1977.

Western Hemisphere. Colonization and trade in the New World /
   National Geographi Society. -- Scale indeterminable. -- 1977.

ART PRINTS

The following examples are all copies of drawings except for
the two woodcuts from a modern artist. Because the titles are
nondescript, these are entered under the artist. The cataloging is
simple and only rarely are any tracings made, except as shown.

Format

Artist. Title. -- Place : Publisher, date if available. --
Physical description.
Tracing.

1. The artist ordinarily called Raphael is usually labelled
Raffaello Sanzio in Italy. Libraries in the United States do well
to use the name by which an artist is known. The dates, when
readily available are included. This drawning is a study that
Raphael did for a picture in the art gallery of Bologna. As a
rule, the cataloger takes the information from the print itself; in
this case, on the back of the print is a box which is copied here.

DISEGNI DI GRANDI MAESTRI - Fac-simile N. 1078
RAFFAELLO SANZIO (Urbino, 1483-1520)
San Paolo (studio per il quadro della pinac. de Bologna)
VENEZIA - Galleria dell'Accademia
FRATELLI ALINARI S. A. - Istituto di Edizioni Artistiche
via Nazionale 6 - Firenze (Italia)

On the outside of the box is "Printed in Italy. Copyright F.LLI ALI-
NARI FIRENZE." The cataloging as shown on the facing page takes
everything that is of any use in locating this print. The number,
the artist's name, his dates, the title of this drawing, and the
publisher. What has been left out is advertising or unnecessary
information.

1.   ART PRINT

Raphael [Raffello Sanzio] 1483-1520
  San Paolo (studio per il quadro...)
  [Saint Paul : study for the painting in the gallery of
Bologna] -- Firenze : Fratelli Alinari, 19?. -- 1 print :
monochrome ; 38 x 14. -- (Facsimile no. 1078)

2.   ART PRINT

Leonardo da Vinci, 1452-1520
  Santa Famiglia del Museo del Louvre
  [Studies for the Holy Family in the Louvre Museum] --
Firenze : Fratelli Alinari, 19?. -- 1 print : monochrome ;
26 x 18 cm. -- (Facsimile no. 1064)

3.   ART PRINT

Andrea del Sarto [Andrea d'Agnolo] 1486-1531
  Testa di giovane uomo
  [Studies of the head of a young man] -- Firenze : Fratelli
Alinari, 19? -- 1 print : monochrome ; 33 x 26 cm. --
(Facsimile no. 1265)

4.   ART PRINT

Andrea del Sarto [Andrea d'Agnolo] 1486-1531
  Studio di mani
  [Studies of hands] -- Firenze : Fratelli Alinari ; 19? -- 1
print : monochrome ; 17 x 20 cm. -- (Facsimile no. 115)

2. On the previous page three further examples were given all of
which followed exactly what was done in the first example. The
uniform title, put right after the head of the entry, the author,
was in Italian and was quoted from the back of the print. The
translation into English was put in brackets because it was supplied by the cataloger. The name of the publisher was given in
Italian, because the only information available was in that
language. The date is as close as the cataloger can come to
accuracy and is only slightly better than putting in 'no date' or
leaving this area blank.

The painters' names were given as they are generally known
followed by the actual name when available along with the dates.
There are no tracings for any of these art prints, because the only
one that could be made would be for those paintings of which
numbers 1, 2, and 3 are studies. If the library has a copy or an
art print of the Holy Family by Leonardo da Vinci, for example, the
entry for the copy of the drawing would follow right after it
because a uniform title was used.

Example no. 4 is a problem because the information on the back
of this print differs from that given on the back of example no. 3.
The real name of Andrea del Sarto is not given at all there. Both
names are given on the back of example no. 4, with the real name
coming first. However, the artist is known as Andrea del Sarto not
Andrea d'Agnolo. The cataloger is quite correct in choosing the
name given in most encyclopedias and other reference works.

Example number 5 shows another problem with names. Correggio
is the name commonly used in reference sources. It would be misleading to employ the actual name of the artist and even worse to
give it as Allegri, Antonio. Italians very often refer to
individuals with the surname coming before the given name. The
comma wouldn't be necessary even if the entry were right.

5.   ART PRINT

Correggio [Allegri Antonio] 1494-1534
  Testa d'angelo
  [Head of an angel] -- Firenze : Fratelli Alinari, 19? -- 1
print : monochrome ; 36 x 26 cm. -- (Facsimile no. 1254)

6.   ART PRINT

Tintoretto [Jacopo Robusti] 1518-1594
  Testa d'uomo
  [Head of a man] -- Firenze : Fratelli Alinari, 19? -- 1 p
print : monochrome ; 18 x 19 cm. -- (Facsimile no. 219)

7.   ART PRINT

Miller, K   A
  Two men. -- Original linoleum block, copy dated 7/20/78. --
1 print : monochrome ; 34 x 36 cm.

8.   ART PRINT

Miller, K   A
  Old women. -- Original linoleum block, copy dated 7/20/78.
-- 1 print : monochrome ; 34 x 36 cm.

9.   ART PRINT

Homer, Winslow, 1836-1910
  Flower garden and bungalow, Bermuda. -- New York, Metro-
politan Museum of Art, 1984. -- 1 print : col. ; 29 x 38 cm.

6. Tintoretto, as he is widely known, painted in Venice. His real
name was Jacopo Robusti, and this drawing is kept in the cabinet of
drawings in the Uffizi Gallery, all of which can be gathered from
reference sources and the back of this drawing. Many college
libraries frame drawings such as these and lend them to borrowers,
a good way to build up an appreciation of art. The entries shown
here would make a good list for the potential borrowers to choose
the material they want to hang in their dormitory quarters as well
as the basic material for a computerized file of holdings.

7. This and example number 8 are original copies taken from a
linoleum block signed and dated by the artist. Original works of
art, if they are any kind of copy, can be treated exactly like all
other copies shown here. They need no publisher, hence no place,
and the date is exactly as shown. The Anglo-American Rules specify
"Art Original" as a general material designation but not Art Print,
which is preferred here. Art original would be used for a unique
piece of art work, such as a painting or a watercolor.

9. The last example on the previous page was included to show that
whether monochrome or colored is used, there is very little
difference. Colored is taken to mean "in many colors," precisely
the opposite of what monochrome means. This word exactly expresses
what black and white does not. Some examples are various shades of
red (1 through 5) or black (example 6). The linoleum block copies
are black and white. Black and white is useful in other places, but
not in art prints where it is either omitted, as for engravings and
etchings, or changed to monochrome to save space. Putting down the
exact colors for a monochrome print is hard to do and wastes time,
because the user of a library who really cares can consult the
material itself rather than the surrogate.

SOUND RECORDINGS

The Anglo-American Cataloging Rules second edition have been amended here to show performer information in Area 3, reserved in maps for scale, and not used for sound recordings heretofore. What makes a sound recording different from the work as printed is the performer, who may have the final say in what sounds are produced. The current rules and Library of Congress practice put the names of performers in a note, for a reason that is beyond explanation unless it is tradition.

These examples show most of the problems that will be encountered. They are (1) works that have no title beyond the description of the composition; (2) collections with and without a collective title; (3) use of foreign languages; (4) variety of media of recording. Only recorded music is shown, because verbal material without music is cataloged like print and was adequately described in the text; however, one example of an oral history recording is included.

1. The first two examples show this variety of recording technique. The same work has been recorded many times, two of which are shown. The first is on cassette tape, the second on a compact disc. The format is given first. The words on the cassette are:

Virgil Fox /Eugene Ormandy
The Philadelphia Orch.
Saint-Saens: Symphony no. 3 in
C Minor, Op. 78 ("Organ")
I. Adagio; Allegro moderato; Poco adagio
AGK1-3711
(p) 1974 RCA Records . Printed in U.S.A.

2. The compact disc shows a bar code in the upper right hand corner with the numbers 3 259140006329 under it. To the left are the
words COMPACT DISC DIGITAL AUDIO, formed into a logo with the
words "Digital-Aufnahme Digital Recording Enregistrement
numerique Registrazio digitale in a column. In the center is
the logo of DEUTSCHE GRAMMOPHON. There are two problems here:
which language to choose, what to leave out.

Inside ruled lines are these words:

CAMILLE SAINT-SAENS   [1] 1. Adagio - Allegro moderato
(1835-1921)   poco adagio   [22'26]
Symhonie Nr.3 c-moll op. 78   [2] 2. Allegro moderato - presto -
"Orgel-Symphonie"   Allegro moderato   [6'58]
Symphony no. 3 in C minor, op.78 [3] 3. Maestoso - Allegro - Molto
"Organ"   Allegro - Pesante   [8'24]
Symphonie no 3 en ut mineur, op.78
"avec orgue"
Sinfonia n. 3 in do minore, op. 78 (p) 1982 Polydor International
"con organo"   GmbH. Hamburg
                                     Previously released as 2532 045

Pierre Cochereau
an der Orgel der Kathedrale Notre-Dame zu Paris
at the organ of Notre-Dame Cathedrale, Paris
a l'orgue de la Cathedrale de Notre-Dame de Paris
all'organo dell cattedrale Notre-Dame di Parigi
Berliner Philharmoniker
HERBERT VON KARAJAN
Printed in West Germany by / Imprime en Allemagne par Neef,
Wittingen. Made in Germany.

This label is sealed in plastic and cannot be removed. It is
quite as good, if not better, than the words on the disc itself,
and there is no danger in handling it.

FORMAT   Audiorecording
Entry
  [Uniform title]
Title of sound recording. -- Edition of work ; edition of
sound recording. -- Performers. -- Issuing company of sound
recording in hand, date. -- Physical description. : length of
performance in minutes. -- (Series). -- Notes. -- Issuing
company's number.
  Tracing.

  1.   Audiorecording
Saint-Saens, Camille, 1835-1921
  [Symphonies, no. 3, op. 78, C minor "Organ"]
Symphony No. 3 In C Minor, op. 78 ("Organ") . -- Perf. by
Virgil Fox, organist ; Eugene Ormandy cond. Philadelphia
Orch[estra]. -- RCA, p1974. -- 1 cassette ; approx. 38 min. --
AGK1-3711 RCA.
  1. Symphonies. 2. Organ with orchestra. I. Fox, Virgil II.
Ormandy, Eugene cond. Philadelphia Orchestra. III. Philadel-
phia Orchestra cond. by Eugene Ormandy.

  2.   Audiorecording
Saint-Saens, Camille, 1835-1921
  [Symphonies, no. 3, op. 78, C minor "Organ"]
Symphonie Nr. 3 c-moll op. 78 "Orgel-Symphonie." -- [Perf. by]
Pierre Cochereau an der Orgel der Kathedrale Notre-Dame zu
Paris ; Herbert von Karajan [cond.] Berliner Philharmoniker.
-- Deutsche Grammophon, p1982 Polydor International. -- 1
compact disc : 37 min. 48 sec. -- Previously released as 2532
045; stereo 400 063-2.
  1. Symphonies. 2. Organ with orchestra. I. Cochereau, Pierre
II. Notre-Dame Cathedral organ. III. Karajan, Herbert von,
cond. Berlin Philharmonic. IV. Berlin Philharmonic cond. by
Herbert von Karajan.

3. Like the example on the previous page, this is in German, English, French, and Italian. Which language should be chosen is less a problem than it might seem because the important parts of the bibliographic, or possibly audiographic catalog, entry are inserted by the cataloger as shown by the brackets. The statement of the performers governs the language chosen; it is in German, hence the cataloging is in German. However, the form of the composition is the uniform title, and in a library in an English-speaking country, it would be in English. There is another problem with this audiorecording, a variant of sound recording, the term which the AACR II prefers: two works are included in one compact disc. A 'with' note is made showing the other work included in the cataloging of each. This solution makes each of them equally find-able, whether in a computerized file or in a file of catalog cards. The other possibility is to put one title after the other in the proper area. Because the machine does not damage the disc when it begins a band other than the first, by specifying the bands for each work, the titles can be treated separately.

4. This entry shows another possible solution to the problem of two works on one compact disc. As indicated above, each title may be included in the title area after a period. It is wise to provide that this solution is only done when: (1) both works are by the same composer; (2) both works are performed by the same group of people with only the addition of a soloist for one of the works; and (3) the performance of one of the works lasts less than ten minutes. Unless the work meets all of these conditions it should be treated differently. In this example, the second composition, "Finlandia" meets all the requirements.

It should be noted here that since the new copyright law went into effect, the designation (p) has indicated that the sound recording is under copyright. Aside from protecting the holder of the copyright, it serves to provide a date that was lacking before.

3.   Audiorecording
Brahms, Johannes, 1833-1897
[Symphonies, no. 3, op. 90, F major]
Symphonie Nr. 3 F-dur op. 90. -- Perf. by Leonard Bernstein
cond. Wiener Philharmoniker. -- Deutsche Grammophon, p1983
Polydor International. -- 4 bands of 1 compact disc : 41 min.
53 sec. -- With: Variationen uber ein Thema von Joseph Haydn
op. 56 a. -- Live recordings -- Stereo 410-083-2.
  1. Symphonies. II. Vienna Philharmonic cond. by Leonard
Bernstein. III. Bernstein, Leonard, cond. Vienna Philharmonic.

                                          Audiorecording
Brahms, Johannes, 1833-1897
[Variations on a theme by Joseph Haydn, op. 56a]
Variationen uber ein Thema von Joseph Haydn op. 56a. -- Perf.
by Leonard Bernstein cond. Wiener Philharmoniker. -- Deutsche
Grammophon, p1983 Polydor International. -- 1 band of 1
compact disc : 20 min. 26 sec. -- With: Symphonie Nr. 3 F-dur
op. 90. -- Live recordings -- Stereo 410-083-2.
  1. Symphonic variations. II. Vienna Philharmonic cond. by
Leonard Bernstein. III. Bernstein, Leonard, cond. Vienna
Philharmonic.

4.   Audiorecording
Sibelius, Jean, 1865-1957
[Symphonies, no. 2, op. 43, D]
Symphony no. 2 in D. Finlandia. -- Perf. by Yoel Levi cond.
the Cleveland Orchestra. -- Telarc, p1984. -- 1 compact disc :
40 min. 54 sec. : 7 min. 43 sec. -- CD 80095 Telarc.
  1. Symphonies. 2. Tone poems. I. Finlandia. II. Levi, Yoel,
cond. Cleveland Orchestra. III. Cleveland Orchestra cond. by
Yoel Levi.

5. This shows the way a cassette may be treated when each work
is listed on each side of the cassette. Here there is no more
problem of damage than for a compact disc. The two works can be
treated separately, or they can be combined in one entry with
access by either title, as shown opposite.

6. The problem here is different. What is featured is the
conductor, Sir Georg Solti. Not even the orchestras are the same
for each work. This is a collection with a collective title. Only
the paper insert gives all the information needed, including the
names of the composers and the different orchestras that Solti
conducts. The lengthy cataloging required to record all this
variation can be summarized as shown in the section on brieflisting. As shown here, all the variations that appear on the
cassette itself and cannot be lost are shown. To do more is to run
the risk of having the source of information lost. If it is
important to record the names of the orchestras, a separate record
should be kept in a vertical file under Solti's name.

This cataloging assumes that composer – title analytics will be
made. If there is no plan to make analytics, there is no reason to
record all the contents. The interested patron can sign out for
the cassette and play it himself.

5.   Audiorecording
Debussy, Claude Achille, 1862-1918
    La Mer. -- Perf. by Dimitri Mitropoulos cond. Philharmonic
Symphony of N.Y. Iberia. -- perf. by Eugene Ormandy cond. the
Philadelphia Orchestra. -- CSP, A service of CBS Records, 19?
1 cassette : Approx. 90 min. -- Rechannelled for stereo. --
Contents Side one: La Mer: de l'aube a midi sur la mer - Jeux
de vagues - Dialogue du vent et de la mer. Side two: Iberia:
Par les rues et par les chemins - Les parfums de la nuit - Le
matin d'un jour de fete. -- BT 14168.
    1. Tone poems. I. La Mer. II. Iberia. III. Mitropoulos,
Dimitri, cond. Philharmonic Symphony of New York. IV. Philharmonic Orchestra of New York cond. by Dimitri Mitropoulos.
V. Ormandy, Eugene, cond. Philadelphia Orchestra. VI. Philadelphia Orchestra cond. by Eugene Ormandy.

6.   Audiorecording
Solti, Georg, Sir.
    Sir Georg Solti : Bolero : a Solti spectacular. -- Decca
records, p1980 ; London Records c1980. -- 1 cassette : approx.
90 minutes. -- C 233762.
    Contents Side one: Wagner, Die Meistersinger von Nurnberg
Prelude. -Borodin, Prince Igor Polovtsian Dances. -Elgar,
Marches, no. 5, op. 38, C major "Pomp and circumstance"
-Ponchielli, La Gioconda Dance of the hours. -Rossini, Barber
of Seville Overture. Side two: Verdi, La Traviata Prelude Act
I. -Glinka, Russlan and Ludmilla Overture. -Offenbach, The
Tales of Hoffmann Barcarolle. - Debussy, L'Apres midi d'un
faun Prelude. -Moussorgsky, Khovantschina Persian slave dance.
-Ravel, Bolero.
    1. Orchestral music. I. Solti, Georg, Sir.   ANALS.

7. A collection such as this example has a collective title, but that is the only unifying part of compact disc. The label, ordinarily sealed in plastic, is not informative. Below is a copy of everything on it.

PURE

CLASSICS

SABRE DANCE

BOLERO

THE KALENDER PRINCE

RITUAL FIRE DANCE

AN OUTDOOR OVERTURE

BEETHOVEN:

SYMPHONY NO 9 IN D,

(Choral Finale)

WARNING: All Rights Reserved. Unauthorized duplication is a violation of applicable laws. Printed in Japan.

The site of cataloging for compact discs as for phonodiscs and cassettes is the label on the metal disc. It cannot be removed. If the label is sealed in the plastic of the container and could only be removed by destroying it, the information there is acceptable. It is very often more complete. In this case the compact disc has printed on it the following:

PURE CLASSICS

1. Kachaturian: Sabre Dance (2: 20) Enrique Batiz, Conductor Orquestra Sinfonica del Estado de Mexico (From the ballet "Gayne")

2. Ravel: Bolero (Complete) (16: 32 Morton Gould conductor, London Symphony Orchestra

5. Copland: An Outdoor Overture (Complete) (8: 53) Keith Clark conductor, Pacific Symphony Orchestra.

6. Beethoven: Symphony No. 9 in d, op. 125 (excerpts from finale: Allegro Assai Vivace to end) (13: 50) Enrique

7.   Audiorecording
Pure classics. -- Realistic, 198? -- 1 compact disc : approx.
49 min. -- Contents: Band 1, Kachaturian, Gayne selections,
Sabre dance. -Band 2: Ravel, Bolero. -Band 3: Rimsky-Korsakov,
Scheherazade, Second movement, "The Kalender Prince" -Band 4:
Falla, El Amor brujo selections, "Ritual fire dance" -Band 5:
Copland, An Outdoor overture. -Band 6: Beethoven, Symphonies,
no. 9, D, op. 125 "Choral", Finale: Allegro Assai Vivace. --
51-5001. 1. Orchestral music.   Anals.

E.G.   Audiorecording
Kachaturian, Aram, 1903-1978.
     [Gayne. Selections "Sabre Dance"]
Pure classics. -- Realistic, 198? -- Band 1, compact disc : 2
min. 20 sec. -- 51-5001.
                                                Audiorecording
Ravel, Maurice, 1875-1937.
     Bolero
Pure classics. -- Realistic, 198? -- Band 2, compact disc: 16
min. 32 sec. -- 51-5001.
                                                Audiorecording
Rimsky-Korsakov, Nikolai, 1844-1908
     [Scheherazade, second movement]
Pure classics. -- Realistic, 198? -- Band 3, compact disc: 12
min. 6 sec. -- 51-5001.
                                                Audiorecording
Falla, Manuel de, 1876-1946
     [El Amor Brujo. Selections "Ritual fire dance"]
Pure classics. -- Realistic, 198? -- Band 4, compact disc: 3
min. 32 sec. -- 51-5001.
                                                Audiorecording
Copland, Aaron, 1900-1985
     [Outdoor overture]
Pure classics. -- Realistic, 198? -- Band 5, compact disc: 8

8. Other kinds of music are cataloged in the same fashion. With
collections, the question is what is the unifying element? In
example number 6, it was the conductor. If the performer is
featured, the work can be entered under the performer. If there is
no unifying principle, as in example number 7, the collection can
be entered under the name of the collection. This example is a
collection with collective title, in one sense, but in another it
is a series.

The cataloging shows the work as a series in one package. Then
each of the works is cataloged. The feature to be stressed is the
composer and the work by all the ways it is known.

Access to this surrogate is shown as well, at least for one of
the quartets. All the others would be treated in the same fashion.
Because this is a set, in one container, each of the quartets is
findable either under the name of the composer or under the name of
the Russian Ambassador to the Austrian court to whom Beethoven
dedicated the three opus 59 works. Two other sets are available
from the same group, the early quartets and the quartets of the
later period. Quartets numbers 1 through 6 are in one container,
and quartets 12 through 16 in another.

In the description, the equal sign indicates a parallel title,
used when the title is given in several languages. In the example
of Brahms Third Symphony, above, the title in German was in larger
bold face print than the titles in English, French, and Italian.
In this set, the print is the same size and from the same font.
The titles are parallel, which explains why the tracing includes
the title in English.

8.   Audiorecording
Beethoven, Ludwig van, 1770-1827
[Quartets, strings, nos. 7 - 11]
The middle string quartets = Die mittleren Streichquartette =
Les quatuors a cordes, nos. 7 a 11. -- perf. by Alban Berg
Quartet. -- EMI Records, p1979. -- 3 compact discs. --
Contents: Compact disc 1: no. 7, Op. 59 no. 1, F major
"Rasumovsky" - Compact disc 2: no. 8, Op. 59 no 2, E minor
"Rasumovsky" ; no. 11, Op. 95, F minor. - Compact disc 3: no.
9, Op. 59 no. 3 "Rasumovsky" ; no. 10, Op. 74, E flat major
"Harp". -- CDS 7 47131 8, CDCC 47130 USA only.
    1. String quartets. I. Alban Berg Quartet. II. Title: The
middle string quartets. III. Rasumovsky quartets. ANALS

                                               Audiorecording
Beethoven, Ludwig van, 1770-1827
[Quartets, string, no. 7, op. 59 no. 1, F major
"Rasumovsky"]
The middle string quartets = Die mittleren Streichquartette =
Les quatuors a cordes, nos. 7 a 11. -- perf. by Alban Berg
Quartet. -- EMI Records, p1979. -- 1 compact disc. -- [etc.]
                                               Audiorecording
Rasumovsky quartets
Beethoven, Ludwig van, 1770-1827
[Quartets, string, nos. 7 - 9, op. 59]
The middle string quartets = Die mittleren Streichquartette =
Les quatuors a cordes, nos. 7 a 11. -- perf. by Alban Berg
Quartet. -- EMI Records, p1979. -- 3 compact discs. -- [etc.]
                                               Audiorecording
Alban Berg Quartet
Beethoven, Ludwig Van, 1770-1827
[Quartets, string, nos. 7 - 11]
The middle string quartets = Die mittleren Streichquartette =
[etc.]

9. Popular music is treated just like classical music with two
exceptions: Entry is made either under performer or under title of
the album, cassette, or compact disc. Because cassettes and
compact discs are always collections, the unifying feature is
usually the performer. If the performer's name serves as the title
of the collection, it is so given, surname first followed by the
given names. If a group, the name of the group is not repeated if
it serves as the title of the collection; otherwise it is. Nothing
in the example shown indicates the first names of Ferrante &
Teicher who are treated as a group. The cataloger has made no
effort to find the given names of either man. Nor has the
cataloger attempted to find the date of this sound recording.
Neither the printing on the cassette or the paper insert show a
date.

10. These two examples of popular music show how a group of
several people is treated. Contents may be shown or may be
omitted, but usually knowing which songs are sung helps the patron
of the library decide which he wants to listen to. However, no
effort is made to discover the composers of the songs or the
arrangers of the music that is sung. Everything is supplied to the
knowledgeable person with the name of the group.

   In all three of these examples, there are several producers,
manufacturers, and as shown the composers of the songs are given
for one cassette. Just who wrote what song is not shown.

11. A collection of music by one performer is actually no different from the soloists or groups that perform popular music, except
that ordinarily the library will wish to make analytics of the
various compositions which may be available only in this fashion,
especially if they are relatively short. Longer works may have
been recorded many times and be readily available. Shorter works
are not, especially in these days of cassettes and compact discs.

9.   Audiorecording
Ferrante & Teicher
  Golden piano hits. -- Perf. by Ferrante and Teicher, duo
pianists. -- Liberty Records, 19? -- 1 cassette : approx. 60
min. -- Contents: Side 1: Exodus - Tchaikovsky concerto -
Miserlou - Begin the beguine - Nocturne in E flat -- Near you.
Side 2: Till - Canadian sunset -- Autumn leaves -- Bewitched
-- Warsaw concerto -- quiet village. -- C 124174.
  1. Piano music. I. Title.
10.   Audiorecording
  Village People
  Cruisin'. -- Perf. by Village People, male vocal group. --
Casablanca Record and Filmworks, p1978. -- 1 cassette :
approx. 60 min. -- Contents: Side 1: Y.M.C.A. - Medley: The
women / I'm a cruiser. Side 2: Hot cop - My roommate - Ups
and downs. -- C 124276.
  1. Male vocal groups. I. Title.
                                       Audiorecording
Village People
  Macho man. -- perf. by Village People, male vocal group. --
Casablanca Record and Filmworks, p1978. -- 1 cassette :
approx. 60 min. -- Contents: Side 1: Macho man - I am what I
am. Side 2: Key West - Medley: Just a gigolo; I ain't got
nobody - Sodom and Gomorrah. -- 141876.
  1. Male vocal groups. II. Title
11.   Audiorecording
Horowitz, Vladimir
  The Horowitz collection concert favorites. -- perf. by
Vladimir Horowitz, pianist. -- RCA, c1975. -- 1 cassette :
approx. 60 min. -- Contents: Side 1: Czerny, Variations on the
aria "La Ricordanza." - D. Scarlatti, Sonata in E. - Mozart:
Sonata no 12 in F. K 332. - Clementi, Rondo. Side 2: Mendel-
ssohn: Variations serieuses, Op. 54. - Schumann: Variations on
Theme by Clara Wieck. -- ARK 1-2719. -- 1. Piano music. ANALS

12. Typically, sound recordings provide too much information that is not needed and not enough that is. Opera, unlike other forms of music, is as much visual as it is aural. This and example number 13 show two methods of recording opera. In each case, there are problems. Example 12 is fairly typical for cassette recordings which have become increasingly popular because of the fragility of phonodiscs. On each side of each cassette is label showing the title of the opera, the composer with additional information of interest to music historians, the name of the orchestra and its conductor following an indication where the cassette begins, quoting the text. What is not shown is the cast who sings the work: Joan Sutherland, Luciano Pavarotti, Monserrat Caballe, and Peter Pears. Only the last names of these major performers are given on the paper insert, except for Peter Pears who has one of the minor roles. The site of cataloging information is the cassette and its label, hence the cataloging which shows that the names of three major performers have been supplied.

13. The videocassette provides abundant information on the container but virtually nothing on the label. There is less chance that the container will be lost, because like the plastic boxes which hold compact discs, the tape is subject to damage if not protected and the information is printed on a paper which is held in place by transparent plastic fused into the opaque plastic of the container itself. Once that is accepted, the question is not where to find missing information, but what should be left out. Much is valuable and should be included.

This videocassette is an exception to the rule. An annotation is not needed for this any more than it is for the opera in a purely sound recording. Those who don't know the opera will be willing to try it, and those who do know it scarcely need an annotation which will not tell them anything new and may just give them a reason to complain.

12.   Audiorecording
Puccini, Giacomo, 1858-1924
[Turandot]
Turandot ... completed by Alfano; Adami, Simoni. -- Perf. by
London Philharmonic Orchestra cond. by Zubin Mehta [with Joan
Sutherland, Luciano Pavarotti, and Monserrat Cababalle] --
London Records; Decca Record Co. p1973. -- 2 cassettes :
approx. 140 min. -- 60-2124.
    1. Opera. I. Mehta, Zubin, cond. London Philharmonic
Orchestra. II. London Philharmonic Orchestra cond. by Zubin
Mehta. III. Sutherland, Joan. IV. Pavarotti, Luciano. V. Ca-
balle, Monserrat. VI. Title

13.   Videorecording
Verdi, Giuseppe, 1813-1901
[Aida]
Aida. -- Perf. by Maria Chiara, Nicola Martinucci, Fiorenza
Cossotto, Giuseppe Scandola, and Chorus, Orchestra and Corps de
Ballet of the Arena di Verona, cond. by Anton Guadagno. --
Radiotelevisione Italiana ; Polivideo, c1981. -- 1 cassette,
Beta : 150 min. -- TXE 2790.
    1. Opera. I. Guadagno, Anton, cond. II. Arena di Verona Opera
Company. III. Chiara, Maria. IV. Martinucci, Nicola. V.
Cossotto, Fiorenza. VI. Scandola, Giuseppe. VII. Title.

14.   Audiorecording
Verdi, Giuseppe, 1813-1901
[La Traviata]
La Traviata. -- Perf. by Joan Sutherland, Luciano Pavarotti,
Matteo Manuguerra, London Opera Chorus, Richard Bonynge cond.
National Philharmonic Orchesta. -- Decca Record Co., p1983.
-- 3 compact discs : 134 min. + Libretto, by Francesco Maria
Piave: notes by William Weaver; 168 p. -- 410 154-2.
    1. Opera. I. National Philharmonic Orchesta cond. by Richard
Bonynge. II. Bonynge, Richard Cond. National Philharmonic
Orchestra. III. Sutherland, Joan. IV. Pavarotti, Luciano.

14. This method of cataloging can be expanded as desired, and it is quite amenable to computerized usage. For instance, arias from the operas can be shown as [Uniform title. Selections. Arias]. A particular aria from an act would include the act. For instance, [Turandot. Act 3. Selections. "Nessun dorma"]. This would alphabetize after the whole opera, after complete third acts, and with other arias from it. Similarly, arrangements can be shown by the abbreviation "arr." which is spelled out if necessary for clarity. For instance, [Turandot. Selections. Arranged for piano].

Arrangements should not be shown for popular music which is ordinarily performed only in a special arrangement. Some sound recordings will show all the composers, arrangers, producers, and other involved in the performance; others will not. The only consistent way of treating them is to omit everything.

BRIEFLISTING

The cataloging shown above would be suitable for a radio station library of sound recordings, especially where the time has been given in minutes and seconds. A program to make all the features of a sound recording available can be written; several have been done already. What the program must specify are the searchable fields: Title and performers. Other necessary information should appear in a display, very much like all the information shown above. The provision of ANALS, for analytics not shown in the text, or Anals, in the one case which demonstrates how they are made, should make each composition available for search in the contents note area. Most libraries would be contented to list available sound recordings like those shown for example 7.

The examples on the facing page show the brieflisting of information in the entries selected as examples. This would accomplish just what a computerized file of complete cataloging aims for.

FORMAT

Entry.

Composer. -- Uniform title. -- Title of sound recording. --
Performers. -- Record company, date. -- Physical description.
-- Record company number.

Aida   Videocassette
   Verdi, Giuseppe. -- Aida -- Performed by Anton Guadagno ;
Orchestra, Chorus, Corps de Ballet of the Arena di Verona ;
Maria Chiara ; Nicola Martinucci ; Fiorenza Cossotto ;
Giuseppe Scandola. -- Radiotelevisione Italiana ; Polivideo,
c1981. -- 1 Beta cassette. -- TXE 2790.

Alban Berg Quartet
   Beethoven, Ludwig van. -- String quartets, nos. 7 - 11. --
The Middle string quartets. -- Performed by Alban Berg
Quartet. -- EMI Records, p1979. -- 3 compact discs. -- CDS 7
47131 8 : CDCC 47130 USA only.

Arena di Verona   Videocassette
   Verdi, Giuseppe. -- Aida -- Performed by Anton Guadagno ;
Orchestra, Chorus, Corps de Ballet of the Arena di Verona ;
Maria Chiara ; Nicola Martinucci ; Fiorenza Cossotto ;
Giuseppe Scandola. -- Radiotelevisione Italiana ; Polivideo,
c1981. -- 1 Beta cassette. -- TXE 2790.

Beethoven, Ludwig van. -- String quartets, nos. 7 - 11. --
The Middle string quartets. -- Performed by Alban Berg
Quartet. -- EMI Records, p1979. -- 3 compact discs. -- CDS 7
47131 8 : CDCC 47130 USA only.

Beethoven, Ludwig van. -- String quartets, no. 7, op. 59 no. 1
F major. "Rasumovsky" -- The middle quartets. -- Performed
by Alban Berg Quartet. -- EMI Records, p1979. -- 1 compact

disc. -- CDS 7 47131 8 : CDCC 47130 USA only.

Beethoven, Ludwig van. -- String quartets, no. 8, op. 59 no. 2, E minor "Rasumovsky" -- The Middle string quartets. -- Performed by Alban Berg Quartet. -- EMI Records, p1979. -- 1 compact disc. -- CDS 7 47131 8 : CDCC 47130 USA only.

Beethoven, Ludwig van. -- String quartets, no. 9, op. 59 no. 3, F minor "Rasumovsky" -- The Middle string quartets. -- Performed by Alban Berg Quartet. -- EMI Records, p1979. -- 1 compact disc. -- CDS 7 47131 8 : CDCC 47130 USA only.

Beethoven, Ludwig van. -- String quartets, no. 10, op. 74, E flat major "Harp" -- The Middle string quartets. -- Performed by Alban Berg Quartet. -- EMI Records, p1979. -- 1 compact disc. -- CDS 7 47131 8 : CDCC 47130 USA only.

Beethoven, Ludwig van. -- String quartets, no. 11, op. 95, F minor. -- The Middle string quartets. -- Performed by Alban Berg Quartet. -- EMI Records, p1979. -- 1 compact disc. -- CDS 7 47131 8 : CDCC 47130 USA only.

Beethoven, Ludwig van. -- Symphonies, no. 9, op. 125, D. 4th movement. Selections, Finale allegro assai vivace. -- Pure classics. -- Realistic, 198? -- 1 compact disc. -- 51-5001.

Bernstein, Leonard
Brahms, Johannes. -- Symphonies, no. 3, op. 90, F minor. -- Performed by Leonard Bernstein ; Vienna Philharmonic. -- Deutsche Grammophon, p1983. -- 4 bands of compact disc. -- 410-083-2.

Brahms, Johannes. -- Variations on a theme by Joseph Haydn, op. 56a. -- Performed by Leonard Bernstein ; Vienna

Philharmonic. -- Deutsche Grammophon, p1983. -- 1 band of
compact disc. -- 410-083-2.

Bonynge, Richard
Verdi, Giuseppe. -- La Traviata. -- Performed by Richard
Bonynge ; National Philharmonic Orchestra ; Joan Sutherland ;
Luciano Pavarotti ; Matteo Manuguerra ; London Opera Chorus.
-- Decca Record Co. p1983. -- 3 compact discs. -- 410 154-2.

Brahms, Johannes. -- Symphonies, no. 3, op. 90, F minor. --
Performed by Leonard Bernstein ; Vienna Philharmonic. --
Deutsche Grammophon, p1983. -- 4 bands of compact disc. --
410-083-2.

Brahms, Johannes. -- Variations on a theme by Joseph Haydn,
op. 56a. -- Performed by Leonard Bernstein ; Vienna
Philharmonic. -- Deutsche Grammophon, p1983. -- 1 band of
compact disc. -- 410-083-2.

Caballe, Monserrat
Puccini, Giacomo. -- Turandot. -- Performed by Zubin Mehta ;
London Philharmonic Orchestra ; Monserrat Caballe ; Luciano
Pavarotti ; Joan Sutherland. -- Decca Record Co., p1973. -- 2
cassettes. -- (Book-of-the-Month Records) -- 60-2174.

Cleveland Orchestra
Sibelius, Jean. -- Symphonies, no. 2, op. 43, D. Finlandia.
-- Performed by Yoel Levi ; Cleveland Orchestra. -- Telarc,
p1984. -- 1 compact disc. -- CD 80095 Telarc.

Cochereau, Pierre
Saint-Saens, Camille. -- Symphonies, no. 3, op. 78, C minor
"Organ" -- Performed by Pierre Cochereau ; Herbert von Karajan
; Vienna Philharmonic. -- Deutsche Grammophon, p1982. -- 1

compact disc. -- 400 063-2.

Copland, Aaron. -- Outdoor overture. -- Pure classics. --
Realistic,   198? -- 1 band of 1 compact disc. -- 51-5001.

Cruisin'. -- Performed by Village People, male vocal group. --
Casablanca Record and Filmworks, p1978. -- 1 cassette. -- C
124276.

Debussy, Claude Achille. -- Iberia. -- Performed by Eugene
Ormandy ; Philadelphia Orchestra. -- CBS Records, 19? -- 1
side of 1 cassette. -- BT 14168.

Debussy, Claude Achille. -- La Mer. -- Performed by Dimitri
Mitropoulos ; Philharmonic Symphony of New York. -- CBS
Records, 19? -- 1 side of 1 cassette. -- BT 14168.

Falla, Manuel de. -- El Amor brujo. Selections "Ritual fire
dance" -- Pure classics. -- Realistic,   198? -- 1 band of 1
compact disc. -- 51-5001.

Ferrante & Teicher. -- Golden piano hits. -- Performed by
Ferrante and Teicher, piano duo. -- Liberty Records, 19? --
1 cassette. -- C 124174.

Finlandia
Sibelius, Jean. -- Symphonies, no. 2, op. 43, D. Finlan-
dia. - Performed by Yoel Levi ; Cleveland Orchestra. --
Telarc, p1984. -- 1 compact disc. -- CD 80095 Telarc.

Fox, Virgil
Saint-Saens, Camille. -- Symphonies, no. 3, op. 78, C minor
"Organ" -- Performed by Virgil Fox, organist ; Eugene Ormandy
; Philadelphia Orchestra. -- RCA, p1974. -- 1 cassette. --

AGK1-3711 RCA.

Horowitz, Vladimir
The Horowitz collection concert favorites. -- Performed by
Vladimir Horowitz, pianist. -- RCA, p1978. -- 1 cassette. --
ARK 1-2719.

Iberia
Debussy, Claude Achille. -- Iberia. -- Performed by Eugene
Ormandy ; Philadelphia Orchestra. -- CBS Records, 19? -- 1
side of 1 cassette. -- BT 14168.

Karajan, Herbert von
Saint-Saens, Camille. -- Symphonies, no. 3, op. 78, C minor
"Organ" -- Performed by Pierre Cochereau ; Herbert von Karajan
; Vienna Philharmonic. -- Deutsche Grammophon, p1982. -- 1
compact disc. -- 400 063-2.

Kachaturian, Aram. -- Gayne. Selections "Sabre dance" -- Pure
classics. -- Realistic, 198? -- 1 band of 1 compact disc. --
51-5001.

Levi, Yoel
Sibelius, Jean. -- Symphonies, no. 2, op. 43, D.   Finlan-
dia -- Performed by Yoel Levi ; Cleveland Orchestra. --
Telarc, p1984. -- 1 compact disc. -- CD 80095 Telarc.

London Opera Chorus
Verdi, Giuseppe. -- La Traviata. -- Performed by Richard
Bonynge ; National Philharmonic Orchestra ; Joan Sutherland ;
Luciano Pavarotti ; Matteo Manuguerra ; London Opera Chorus.
Decca Record Co. p1983. -- 3 compact discs. -- 410 154-2.

London Philharmonic Orchestra
    Puccini, Giacomo. -- Turandot. -- Performed by Zubin Mehta ;
London Philharmonic Orchestra ; Monserrat Caballe ; Luciano
Pavarotti ; Joan Sutherland. -- Decca Record Co., p1973. -- 2
cassettes. -- (Book-of-the-Month Records) -- 60-2174.

Macho man. -- Performed by Village People, male vocal group.
-- Casablanca Record and Filmworks, p1978. -- 1 cassette. -- C
141876.

Manuguerra, Matteo
    Verdi, Giuseppe. -- La Traviata. -- Performed by Richard
Bonynge ; National Philharmonic Orchestra ; Joan Sutherland ;
Luciano Pavarotti ; Matteo Manuguerra ; London Opera Chorus.
-- Decca Record Co. p1983. -- 3 compact discs. -- 410 154-2.

Mehta, Zubin
    Puccini, Giacomo. -- Turandot. -- Performed by Zubin Mehta ;
London Philharmonic Orchestra ; Monserrat Caballe ; Luciano
Pavarotti ; Joan Sutherland. -- Decca Record Co., p1973. -- 2
cassettes. -- (Book-of-the-Month Records) -- 60-2174.

La Mer
    Debussy, Claude Achille. -- La Mer. -- Performed by Eugene
Ormandy ; Philadelphia Orchestra. -- CBS Records, 19? -- 1
side of 1 cassette. -- BT 14168.

Mitropoulos, Dimitri
    Debussy, Claude. -- La Mer. -- Performed by Dimitri
Mitropoulos ; Philharmonic Symphony of New York. -- CBS
Records, 19? -- 1 cassette. -- BT 14168.

National Philharmonic Orchestra
    Verdi, Giuseppe. -- La Traviata. -- Performed by Richard

Bonynge ; National Philharmonic Orchestra ; Joan Sutherland ;
Luciano Pavarotti ; Matteo Manuguerra ; London Opera Chorus.
-- Decca Record Co. p1983. -- 3 compact discs. -- 410 154-2.

New York, Philharmonic Symphony
   Debussy, Claude. -- La Mer. -- Performed by Dimitri
Mitropoulos ; Philharmonic Symphony of New York. -- CBS
Records, 19? -- 1 cassette. -- BT 14168.

Ormandy, Eugene
   Saint-Saens, Camille. -- Symphonies, no. 3, op. 78, C minor
"Organ" -- Performed by Virgil Fox, organist ; Eugene Ormandy
; Philadelphia Orchestra. -- RCA, p1974. -- 1 cassette. --
AGK1-3711 RCA.

Pavarotti, Luciano
   Puccini, Giacomo. -- Turandot. -- Performed by Zubin Mehta ;
London Philharmonic Orchestra ; Monserrat Caballe ; Luciano
Pavarotti ; Joan Sutherland. -- Decca Record Co., p1973. -- 2
cassettes. -- (Book-of-the-Month Records) -- 60-2174.

   Verdi, Giuseppe. -- La Traviata. -- Performed by Richard
Bonynge ; National Philharmonic Orchestra ; Joan Sutherland ;
Luciano Pavarotti ; Matteo Manuguerra ; London Opera Chorus.
-- Decca Record Co. p1983. -- 3 compact discs. -- 410 154-2.

Philadelphia Orchestra
   Saint-Saens, Camille. -- Symphonies, no. 3, op. 78, C minor
"Organ" -- Performed by Virgil Fox, organist ; Eugene Ormandy
; Philadelphia Orchestra. -- RCA, p1974. -- 1 cassette. --
AGK1-3711 RCA.

   Puccini, Giacomo. -- Turandot. -- Performed by Zubin Mehta ;
London Philharmonic Orchestra ; Monserrat Caballe ; Luciano

Pavarotti ; Joan Sutherland. -- Decca Record Co., p1973. -- 2 cassettes. -- (Book-of-the-Month Records) -- 60-2174.

Pure classics. -- Realistic, 198? -- 1 compact disc. -- 51-5001.

Rasumovsky quartets
Beethoven, Ludwig van. -- String quartets, nos. 7 - 11. -- The Middle string quartets. -- Performed by Alban Berg Quartet. -- EMI Records, p1979. -- 3 compact discs. -- CDS 7 47131 8 : CDCC 47130 USA only.

Ravel, Maurice. -- Bolero. -- Pure classics. -- Realistic, 198? -- 1 band of 1 compact disc. -- 51-5001.

Rimsky-Korsakov, Nikolai. -- Scheherazade, 2nd movement. -- Pure classics. -- Realistic, 198? -- 1 band of 1 compact disc. -- 51-5001.

Saint-Saens, Camille. -- Symphonies, no. 3, op. 78, C minor "Organ" -- Performed by Virgil Fox, organist ; Eugene Ormandy ; Philadelphia Orchestra. -- RCA, p1974. -- 1 cassette. -- AGK1-3711 RCA.

Saint-Saens, Camille. -- Symphonies, no. 3, op. 78, C minor "Organ" -- Performed by Pierre Cochereau ; Herbert von Karajan ; Vienna Philharmonic. -- Deutsche Grammophon, p1982. -- 1 compact disc. -- 400 063-2.

Sibelius, Jean. -- Symphonies, no. 2, op. 43, D. Finlandia. -- Performed   by Yoel Levi ; Cleveland Orchestra. -- Telarc, p1984. -- 1 compact disc. -- CD 80095 Telarc.

Solti, Georg, Sir

Sir Georg Solti : Bolero : A Solti spectacular. -- Decca
Records, p1980. -- 1 cassette. -- C233762.

Sutherland, Joan
  Puccini, Giacomo. -- Turandot. -- Performed by Zubin Mehta ;
London Philharmonic Orchestra ; Monserrat Caballe ; Luciano
Pavarotti ; Joan Sutherland. -- Decca Record Co., p1973. -- 2
cassettes. -- (Book-of-the-Month Records) -- 60-2174.

Verdi, Giuseppe. -- La Traviata. -- Performed by Richard
Bonynge ; National Philharmonic Orchestra ; Joan Sutherland ;
Luciano Pavarotti ; Matteo Manuguerra ; London Opera Chorus.
-- Decca Record Co. p1983. -- 3 compact discs. -- 410 154-2.

La Traviata
  Verdi, Giuseppe. -- La Traviata. -- Performed by Richard
Bonynge ; National Philharmonic Orchestra ; Joan Sutherland ;
Luciano Pavarotti ; Matteo Manuguerra ; London Opera Chorus.
-- Decca Record Co. p1983. -- 3 compact discs. -- 410 154-2.

Turandot
  Puccini, Giacomo. -- Turandot. -- Performed by Zubin Mehta ;
London Philharmonic Orchestra ; Monserrat Caballe ; Luciano
Pavarotti ; Joan Sutherland. -- Decca Record Co., p1973. -- 2
cassettes. -- (Book-of-the-Month Records) -- 60-2174.

Vienna Philharmonic
  Brahms, Johannes. -- Symphonies, no. 3, op. 90, F minor. --
Performed by Leonard Bernstein ; Vienna Philharmonic. --
Deutsche Grammophon, p1983. -- 4 bands of compact disc. --
410-083-2.

Brahms, Johannes. -- Variations on a theme by Joseph Haydn,
op. 56a. -- Performed by Leonard Bernstein ; Vienna

Philharmonic. -- Deutsche Grammophon, p1983. -- 1 band of
compact disc. -- 410-083-2.

Saint-Saens, Camille. -- Symphonies, no. 3, op. 78, C minor
"Organ" -- Performed by Pierre Cochereau ; Herbert von Karajan
; Vienna Philharmonic. -- Deutsche Grammophon, p1982. -- 1
compact disc. -- 400 063-2.

Variations on a theme by Joseph Haydn, op. 56a.
Brahms, Johannes. -- Variations on a theme by Joseph Haydn,
op. 56a. -- Performed by Leonard Bernstein ; Vienna
Philharmonic. -- Deutsche Grammophon, p1983. -- 1 band of
compact disc. -- 410-083-2.

                                                  Videocassette
Verdi, Giuseppe. -- Aida -- Performed by Anton Guadagno ;
   Orchestra, Chorus, Corps de Ballet of the Arena di Verona ;
   Maria Chiara ; Nicola Martinucci ; Fiorenza Cossotto ;
   Giuseppe Scandola. -- Radiotelevisione Italiana ; Polivideo,
   c1981. -- 1 Beta cassette. -- TXE 2790.

Verdi, Giuseppe. -- La Traviata. -- Performed by Richard
   Bonynge ; National Philharmonic Orchestra ; Joan Sutherland
   ; Luciano Pavarotti ; Monserrat Caballe ; London Opera Chorus.
   Decca Record Co. p1983. -- 3 compact discs. -- 410 154-2.

Village People
   Cruisin'. -- Performed by Village People, male vocal group.
   -- Casablanca Record and Filmworks, p1978. -- 1 cassette. -- C
   124276.

Macho man. -- Performed by Village People, male vocal group.
   -- Casablanca Record and Filmworks, p1978. -- 1 cassette. -- C
   141876.

EXAMPLES OF ORAL HISTORY SOUND RECORDING

University of Pittsburgh. Cathedral of Learning.
Jamie Thomas relates how Chancellor Bowman planned for and at last succeeded in building the principal structure of the University. Interviewed by Mitzi Fitzgerald, 21 Jan. 1984.
1 cassette : 84 min. + Transcription.

Thomas, Jamie
University of Pittsburgh. Cathedral of Learning.
Jamie Thomas relates how Chancellor Bowman planned for and at last succeeded in building the principal structure of the University. Interviewed by Mitzi Fitzgerald, 21 Jan. 1984.
1 cassette : 84 min. + Transcription.

SUBJECTS

BALLETS, SELECTIONS

Falla, Manuel de. -- El Amor brujo. Selections "Ritual fire
dance" -- Pure classics. -- Realistic,   198? -- 1 band of 1
compact disc. -- 51-5001.

Kachaturian, Aram. -- Gayne. Selections "Sabre dance" -- Pure
classics. -- Realistic, 198? -- 1 band of 1 compact disc. --
51-5001.

MALE VOCAL GROUPS

Village People
Cruisin'. -- Performed by Village People, male vocal group. --
Casablanca Record and Filmworks, p1978. -- 1 cassette. -- C 124276.

Macho man. -- Performed by Village People, male vocal group. --
Casablanca Record and Filmworks, p1978. -- 1 cassette. -- C 141876.

OPERA

Puccini, Giacomo. -- Turandot. -- Performed by Zubin Mehta ; London
   Philharmonic Orchestra ; Monserrat Caballe ; Luciano Pavarotti ;
Joan Sutherland. -- Decca Record Co., p1973. -- 2 cassettes. --
(Book-of-the-Month Records) -- 60-2174.

                                      Videocassette
Verdi, Giuseppe. -- Aida -- Performed by Anton Guadagno ;
   Orchestra, Chorus, Corps de Ballet of the Arena di Verona ; Maria
Chiara ; Nicola Martinucci ; Fiorenza Cossotto ; Giuseppe Scandola.
-- Radiotelevisione Italiana ; Polivideo, c1981. -- 1 Beta
cassette. -- TXE 2790.

Verdi, Giuseppe. -- La Traviata. -- Performed by Richard
  Bonynge ; National Philharmonic Orchestra ; Joan Sutherland ;
  Luciano Pavarotti ; Monserrat Caballe ; London Opera Chorus. --
  Decca Record Co. p1983. -- 3 compact discs. -- 410 154-2.

ORCHESTRAL MUSIC

Bolero. Ravel, Maurice.
  Pure classics. -- Realistic, 198? -- 1 band of 1 compact disc. --
  51-5001.

Solti, Georg, Sir
  Sir Georg Solti : Bolero : A Solti spectacular. -- Decca Records,
  p1980. -- 1 cassette. -- C233762.

Finlandia
  Sibelius, Jean. -- Symphonies, no. 2, op. 43, D. Finlan- dia. -
  Performed by Yoel Levi ; Cleveland Orchestra. -- Telarc, p1984. --
  1 band of 1 compact disc. -- CD 80095 Telarc.

Variations on a theme by Joseph Haydn, op. 56a.
  Brahms, Johannes. -- Variations on a theme by Joseph Haydn, op.
  56a. -- Performed by Leonard Bernstein ; Vienna Philharmonic. --
  Deutsche Grammophon, p1983. -- 1 band of compact disc. --
  410-083-2.

ORGAN MUSIC
Cochereau, Pierre
  Saint-Saens, Camille. -- Symphonies, no. 3, op. 78, C minor
  "Organ" -- Performed by Pierre Cochereau ; Herbert von Karajan ;
  Vienna Philharmonic. -- Deutsche Grammophon, p1982. -- 1 compact
  disc. -- 400 063-2.

Fox, Virgil
Saint-Saens, Camille. -- Symphonies, no. 3, op. 78, C minor
"Organ" -- Performed by Virgil Fox, organist ; Eugene Ormandy ;
Philadelphia Orchestra. -- RCA, p1974. -- 1 cassette. -- AGK1-3711
RCA.

OVERTURES
Copland, Aaron. -- Outdoor overture. -- Pure classics. --
Realistic,   198? -- 1 band of 1 compact disc. -- 51-5001.

PIANO MUSIC

Ferrante & Teicher. -- Golden piano hits. -- Performed by
Ferrante and Teicher, piano duo. -- Liberty Records, 19? -- 1
cassette. -- C 124174.

Horowitz, Vladimir
The Horowitz collection concert favorites. -- Performed by
Vladimir Horowitz, pianist. -- RCA, p1978. -- 1 cassette. -- ARK
1-2719.
STRING QUARTETS

Beethoven, Ludwig van. -- String quartets, nos. 7 - 11. --   The
Middle string quartets. -- Performed by Alban Berg Quartet. --
EMI Records, p1979. -- 3 compact discs. -- CDS 7 47131 8 : CDCC
47130 USA only.
SYMPHONIES

Brahms, Johannes. -- Symphonies, no. 3, op. 90, F minor. --
Performed by Leonard Bernstein ; Vienna Philharmonic. -- Deutsche
Grammophon, p1983. -- 4 bands of compact disc. -- 410-083-2.

Saint-Saens, Camille. -- Symphonies, no. 3, op. 78, C minor

"Organ" -- Performed by Virgil Fox, organist ; Eugene Ormandy ;
Philadelphia Orchestra. -- RCA, p1974. -- 1 cassette. -- AGK1-3711
RCA.

Saint-Saens, Camille. -- Symphonies, no. 3, op. 78, C minor
"Organ" -- Performed by Pierre Cochereau ; Herbert von Karajan ;
Vienna Philharmonic. -- Deutsche Grammophon, p1982. -- 1 compact
disc. -- 400 063-2.

Sibelius, Jean. -- Symphonies, no. 2, op. 43, D. Finlandia. --
Performed by Yoel Levi ; Cleveland Orchestra. -- Telarc, p1984.
-- 1 compact disc. -- CD 80095 Telarc.

SYMPHONIES, SELECTIONS

Beethoven, Ludwig van. -- Symphonies, no. 9, op. 125, D. 4th
movement. Selections, Finale allegro assai vivace. -- Pure
classics. -- Realistic, 198? -- 1 compact disc. -- 51-5001.

Rimsky-Korsakov, Nikolai. -- Scheherazade, 2nd movement. --
Pure classics. -- Realistic, 198? -- 1 band of 1 compact disc. --
51-5001.

TONE POEMS

Debussy, Claude Achille. -- Iberia. -- Performed by Eugene Ormandy
; Philadelphia Orchestra. -- CBS Records, 19? -- 1 side of 1
cassette. -- BT 14168.

Debussy, Claude Achille. -- La Mer. -- Performed by Dimitri
Mitropoulos ; Philharmonic Symphony of New York. -- CBS Records,
19? -- 1 side of 1 cassette. -- BT 14168.

VIDEOCASSETTES

Cataloging videocassettes, as seen in the example above, is no
more a problem than cataloging other forms of nonbook nonprint material, except for one necessity: an annotation must be provided the
user. Much like videocassettes on the one hand and games on the
other are canned programs for the computer, four of which are shown
as examples. All of these three types of nonbook material are
entered under title.

Catalogers have always searched for a personal name under which
an item might be entered, even treating corporate bodies as people
until the early 1970's. However, a computer can find searchable
fields either by being programmed to key on the marks of punctuation which are required for International Bibliographic Description
or by searching for individual terms within the entry as shown in
two of the computer-program examples. However, information is lost
when art prints and sound recordings are entered other than under
the individual artist or individual composer . Showing, for
instance, Leonard Bernstein as the entry followed by a composer's
name -- Brahms -- gives the patron of a library just what is
sought, sound recordings of Bernstein conducting an orchestra that
is playing Brahms. However, even here, as shown elsewhere, a unit
entry is a successful method of cataloging. The patron would just
have to read further in the entry.

However, motion pictures and portfolios are best entered under
the title even when an individual's name may be firmly attached to
the item. A film by John Huston may be a handy way of identifying
a work, but it scarcely conveys the facts. Granted John Huston is

the director, the film exists because of the cooperation of many
people.

Exactly like motion pictures are videocassettes, but they are
especially useful for a few viewers, unlike motion pictures which
may be seen by thousands at one time. Videocassettes have,
therefore, changed from simply being motion pictures converted to
another form of storage to individual methods of instruction.

FORMAT

Enter under title and include other names as found. Usually
this is not on cassette itself, the site of information along with
the tape itself. The tape must be reviewed and any facts that are
needed gained from the credits, that portion of the motion picture
which tells who is responsible for it. These are almost always at
the beginning of a motion picture, although occasionally, they are
at the end. The cardboard container cannot be trusted, although
plastic containers may provide many details as was shown with the
videocassette of Verdi's opera, Aida.

For videocasettes, the size must be specified. There are only
two, VHS and Beta. Beta was developed by Sony which was very
reluctant to license other manufacturers, hence the greater
popularity of VHS. They are the same in quality. Physical
description then gives (1) the type of cassette, (2) after a colon,
the time in minutes, and (3) after a semicolon, the facts about the
film or the tape if the work was directly recorded by a video-
camera. This deviates from AACR practice which uses parenthesis to
record the time, thereby limiting the searching abilities of a
computer if the cataloging is made in machine readable form.

FORMAT

Title / writer and director. -- Producer or production company,
date. -- Physical description: type of cassette : minutes
the cassette runs ; sound or silent, black and white or colored. -- Series. -- Notes.
-- Summary of about 100 words.
Tracing

1. The General was Buster Keaton's favorite film of the many he
made. It set new standards for the motion picture at the time of
its release because the flow of action and the comic situations
complement each other. On the cassette is a firmly glued label
with registered trademark Video Images, a warning in a logo, and
the words, A VIDEO YESTERDAY RECORDING. This is repeated on
the label along the back. Below it are these words in this order:
527. THE GENERAL. (1926) The BUSTER KEATON classic of the Civil
War. Silent film with music score. 105 minutes. From the opening
frames of the videocassette the further information is obtained:
Joseph M. Schenck presents Buster Keaton in The General; United
Artists Production; and on the next frame written and directed by
Buster Keaton and Clyde Buckman. This is enough for the cataloging
shown. The videocassette is treated as a reprint of the original
film, and even the name of Rosa Rio who added sound with her
performance on the Hammond organ is recorded.

1.   Videocassette
The General / written and directed by Buster Keaton and Clyde
    Buckman. -- United Artists, 1926. -- 1 Beta videocassette
    105 min. : silent with music, b&w . -- (Video Yesteryear,
    no. 527). -- Organ music by Rosa Rio, c1984.
-- Keaton plays a Confederate engineer on a railroad
determined to retrieve his locomotive, The General, from the
Union forces which have stolen it. Based on an actual
incident of the Civil war, the comedy results from one of the

longest chase scenes on film, led by Keaton, with photography
reminiscent of the works of Matthew Brady.
1. Silent film comedies. I. Keaton, Buster, 1895-1966.

2. The next example is a French film with English subtitles. The
labels on the videocasette give only the following information:

Murray Hill

VIDEO

RULES OF THE GAME
(1939)
Dalio, Nora Gregor,
Mila Parely
107 mins.
B&W

This is repeated on the label along the side that is not pushed
into the videocassette recorder, along with the number of this
cassette as furnished by the Murray Hill Video company. The
equivalent of a title page is found in the opening frames, which
gives the facts in French and English. Except for parallel titles,
which are required in such instances, there is little difference in
the cataloging of this and the previous example.

2.   Videocassette
The Rules of the game = La Regle du jeu : a film fantasy / by
   Jean Renoir ; subtitles by Daniel Behrman. -- Claude
   Renoir   Productions, 1939. -- 1 Beta videocassette :
   107 min. ; sd., b&w . -- (Murray Hill Video, 88397 X)
   -- Dialog in French with English subtitles.
   -- The problems of modern love and life in pre-World War II
France as seen by several characters each of whom has changed
but expects everyone else to remain the same. The viewer is
warned that the film is entertainment, not social criticism,

before the story begins, but its use of irony and its wit
makes both viewpoints valid.

     1. Film comedies. I. La Regle du jeu. II. Renoir, Jean.

3. This same pattern is followed in the next videocassette, except
that the facts of the film from which the tape was made differ.
What makes this an interesting film is the novel on which it was
based. The opening frame gives this information: RKO Radio
Pictures / presents / LESLIE HOWARD / in / OF HUMAN BONDAGE /
with Bette Davis / Francis Dee. Kay Johnson / Reginald Denny. At
the bottom of the screen is Copyright MCMXXXIV by RKO Radio
Pictures. The next frame gives on the name of the director, John
Cromwell, and the frame after that shows the author of the screen
play, Lester Cohen and continues with the words "from the novel by
W. Somerset Maugham." Four more of the actors are given in the
next frame. At the bottom of a list of players is Alan Hale /
Reginald Sheffield / Reginald Owen / Desmond Roberts. Only the
last actor named is no longer remembered. Each of the others had
long and distinguished film careers. The question for the
cataloger is how much of this should appear on the entry for the
picture, as much a problem when cataloging the original film as for
the videotape. What is shown below is a reasonable compromise,
suitable for any library that does not specialize in film history.

    3.
                                                  Videocassette

Of human bondage / by Lester Cohen, based on the novel by W.
    Somerset Maugham ; directed by John Cromwell ; with Leslie
    Howard and Bette Davis. -- RKO Radio Pictures, 1934. -- 1
    Beta videocassette : 84 min. ; sd., b&w. -- (Murray Hill
    Video no. 83619)
    -- Following Maugham's novel with considerable license, this
    film recounts the struggles of a young lame Englishman to
    become a doctor despite his love for Mildred, a waitress, who
    becomes his mistress and nemesis. After she destroys his
    possessions and he finds himself without funds, he meets a

sensible girl whose love reclaims him.
1. Film drama. I.Cohen Lester. II.Cromwell, John. III.
Howard, Leslie. IV.Davis, Bette. V. Maugham, W. Somerset.

4. Anthologies are not common in videocassettes, but the next
example is one of those which are rather more plentiful, collections of short comedies by a famous comedian. Sometimes a short
motion picture will be eked out with a short comedy, but usually
the motion picture alone is reproduced. The next three examples
show all these variations.

4.   Videocassette
   An evening with W. C. Fields : three comedies : The dentist
   / produced by Mack Sennett ; directed by Leslie Pearce :
   The pharmacist / produced by Mack Sennett ; directed by
   Arthur Ripley ; story by W. C. Fields : The golf special-
   ist   / produced by Louis Brock ; directed by Monte Brice.
   -- Paramount ; Radio Pictures distributed by RKO, c1930.
   1 Beta cassette : approx. 90 min. ; sd., b&w. --
   (Great moments in television no. 3002)
   -- A trilogy of early Fields comedies. As the dentist Fields
   plays fraudulent golf, then tries to prevent his daughter's
   elopement while working on the teeth of a female contor-
   tionist and a man with a long black beard. As the pharmacist,
   Fields runs a drugstore and a family upstairs, and as the golf
   specialist, he adds new twists to his cheating golfer routine.
   1. Film comedies. II. Fields, W. C. III. Sennett, Mack. IV.
   Title: The dentist. V. Title: The parmacist. VI. Title: The
   golf specialist.

                                           Videocassette
   The Great dictator / written, directed, and scored by Charles
   Chaplin ; with Jack Oakie and Paulette Goddard. -- RBC
   Films, c1940; renewed 1968 by Roy Export Establishment. --

1 Beta cassette : 126 min. ; sd., b&w. -- (Playhouse video
no. 3008)
-- Charles Chaplin plays a Jewish barber who loses his memory
for twenty years. He returns to his ghetto shop in the
capital of Tomania, ruled by Adenoid Hynkel, a dictator played
by Chaplin. The flier Chaplin rescued reappears and saves the
barber and his girl friend, Paulette Goddard, from
persecution, temporarily. Hynkel meets with Napaloni,
dictator of Bacteria, played by Jack Oakie, who is ready to
invade a neighboring country before Hynkel can get his troops
to its border. Sentenced to a concentration camp, the barber
and the flier escape, as the invasion begins, mistaken for the
great dictator and his aide.
     1. Film comedies. I. Chaplin, Charles. II. Oakie, Jack.
III. Goddard, Paulette.

                                        Videocassette
The court jester / written, produced, and directed by Norman
     Panama and Melvin Frank : with Danny Kaye, Glynis Johns,
     Basil Rathbone [et al.]   -- Dena Enterprises, c1955;
renewed 1983 by Paramount Pictures. -- 1 Beta cassette : 101
min. ; sd., color. -- (Paramount Home   Video, 5512)
-- Kaye plays the guardian of a boy whose backside is marked
with the purple pimpernel which proves that he is the true
heir to the throne. He wishes to play a bigger part in the
plans of the outlaws trying to overthrow the usurper of the
throne. Posing as a court jester, he is hypnotized by a witch
and rapidly dubbed a knight so he can joust with other
knights. With the help of midgets, he defeats a swordsman,
unseats the usurper, and reinstates the rightful, though
immature, monarch whose backside makes everyone kneel.
     1. Film comedies. I. Panama, Norman. II. Frank, Melvin. III.
Kaye, Danny. IV. Johns, Glynis. V. Rathbone, Basil.

Videocassette

Donald's bee pictures. -- Walt Disney Productions, c1935. --1
Beta cassette : 49 min. ; sd., color. -- (Walt Disney Home
Video, 255 B) -- Contents: Inferior decorator. - Honey
harvester. - Slide, Donald, slide. - Window cleaners. - Bee
at the beach. - Bee on guard. - Let's stick together.
-- These Donald Duck cartoons, produced in the 1930's,
preserve the ill-tempered duck's fruitless confrontations with
a bee, part of the reality that doesn't respect him. The
history of the cartoons and Director Jack Hannah's part in
them are explained before the seven short pieces of unapol-
ogetic slapstick.
   1. Animated cartoons. II. Hannah, Jack. III. Disney, Walt.

5. Videocasettes are especially useful as media of instruction.
The following example shows one of those available. Various kinds
of workout tapes and exercise instruction are avalable along with
everything from how to play bridge to how to paint with
watercolors.

5.   Videocassette

French : all the words and phrases you need for easy travel.
   -- Crown Publishers, pc1984. -- 1 Beta cassette : 60 min. ;
   sd., color. -- (Crown Video Living language) -- ISBN #0-517-
   555611.
-- An elementary course in five sections giving the words, and
phrases used at the airport, the hotel, on the street, at the
restaurant, and at the department store. The student is
helped with subtitles when needed and encouraged to practice
what he has learned.
   1. French language -- Video instruction.

6. Finally, as with the videocassette of Aida the cataloging of
which is shown in the section above, the recording of visual

information along with sound may preserve performances for all
time. Vast numbers of videotapes are made to feed the insatiable
monster of television programming. Many individuals with
videocassette recorders take whole performances off the line and
preserve them for later viewing, very likely this performance. The
following ballet has been broadcast several times along with other
works of the American Ballet Theatre. A library that does
recording of this sort is liable to a lawsuit for the infringement
of copyright. The home owner has the privilege under the rule of
fair use. It is best for a library to buy videocassettes if they
are to be lent to the public, a valid use of public library funds.

6.   Videocassette
Don Quixote : Kitri's wedding / choreography by Mikhail
    Baryshnikov ; after Marius Petipa and Alexander Gorsky ;
    with music by Ludwig Minkus ; arranged with additional music
    by Patrick Flyn. -- American Theatre Ballet, 1983. -- 1 Beta
    cassette ; 86 min. : sd., color. -- (Thorn EMI Video, TXE 28
    00). -- Danced by Baryshnikov with Cynthia Harvey as his
    partner.
    -- Baryshnikov has recreated the choreography of the Russian
    Ballet from the time of the czars to the present in this full-
    length production of a ballet known only from the pas de deux
    which is often performed as a showpiece for the best dancers.
    This production captures all the good humor and great fun of
    the original story as told by Cervantes.

GAMES

The period of the late 70's and early 80's will be remembered
as the time when home computers became the appliance of choice of
many millions of Americans. A new market sprang up, not only of
the machines themselves but of software for the machines, the
hardware everyone either wanted or hated. Using a computer is
quite easy, no harder than using a typewriter and in many ways
much easier. Public libraries will, sooner or later, have to lend
programs to be tried out by borrowers who own a computer of some
sort. Eventually, all libraries that serve a community interested
in computers will have to do the same.

The Anglo-American Cataloging Rules second edition contains
rules for the cataloging of "machine-readable data" suitable only
for large university libraries with mainframe computers. The 64K
home computer has never even been thought of. The cataloging
proposed and exemplified here is for the sort of canned programs
sold in department stores as well as computer stores. The program
is stored on magnetic tape in a cassette or on a special diskette,
the ultimate development of the old computer disks as large as a
serving tray.

What the user must know, along with the title and producer of
the program, is what computer can utilize it, how much memory is
required, and how the program is stored. Whether the program is
stored on a diskette or in a cassette that is exactly the size of
audio cassettes (and utilizes sound to activate the computer) is
less important if both access devices are used, but vital if either
one is the sole means of putting a program into the computer.

the kind written. Everyone will use it for his own purposes, and the library only welcomes trouble if the summary is judgmental. Some will agree and be silent; others will disagree noisily. This cataloging has been shown without summaries but with the critical information displayed in the proper areas of the cataloging entry.

At the head of the entry is the general material designation. The AACR rules specify "Machine-Readable Data." But this cataloging is not for the data but the container of the data. Since either cassettes or diskettes are used, the phrase chosen is "Computer cassette" or "Computer diskette," which will inform the patron what kind of container is available. It is best that he read another card if what he finds is not what he wants. The phrase, "Computer data," could be used when the library has both cassette and diskette storage for the data.

In the physical description area, nothing more than cassette is needed. However, there are at present three sizes of diskette, a large one, a small one, and a smaller one. In place of a summary, the notes have been placed where a summary would be, which is just where the International Bibliographic Description would place them. This information is vital and may govern the use of the program.

All of these programs except one have books accompanying or as a vital part of the information. This variation is shown as well: accompanying text when the diskette is separate and accompanying text when the diskette is contained in it.

Computer games are commonplace. One example is given along with examples of the three kinds of games that follow: those with pieces; those that not only have pieces but also equipment; and those that are nonverbal. The cataloging of games is covered in Chapter 10 of the AACR Rules. These examples follow the rules.

1.   Computer diskette
DOS : [disk operating system] / IBM. -- Version 1.10 -- The
   company, c1982. -- 1 diskette (5 in.) + Looseleaf notebook
   in container, 24 x 21 cm.
-- For IBM Personal Computers, 128 KB minimum.

2.   Computer diskette
Visiword / VisiCorp. -- The company, c1983. -- 1 diskette (5
   in.) + Looseleaf notebook. -- Includes Quickstart course.
-- For IBM Personal Computers, 192 KB minimum.

3.   Computer diskette
Executive filer : the complete information organizer / Paperback Software. -- The company, c1985. -- 1 diskette (5 in.)
   in pouch of paperback book, 198 p., 23 cm.
-- For IBM Personal Computer, DOS version 2.0, 192 KB minimum.

4.   Computer diskette
Gambler : Black jack, solitaire, keno / Keypunch Software. --
   The company, c1985. -- 1 diskette (5 in.)
-- For IBM / XT / AT personal computers, 384 KB minimum.

5.   Game
Third dimension one / Mag-nif. -- The company, c1972. -- 1
   puzzle : 18 pieces of clear plastic in container 12 x 11 x
   9 cm.

6.   Game
Cube twister / Nordevco. -- The company, 198? -- 1 jigsaw
   puzzle ; 100 pieces in box 5 x 11 x 11 cm. -- (Hav.a.cube
   puzzles, 8199-1)

7.   Game
Scrabble : crossword game / Selchow & Righter. -- Deluxe
   edition. -- The company, c1948. -- 1 puzzle : 4 plastic
   tile holders, 120 tiles, one board on swivel base in
   container 6 x 43 x 43 cm.

Subject Headings

The short-cut procedure of using only subject headings for the description of material must be utilized when there is nothing to cite except the material itself, usually pictures and locally produced realia. The subject headings given below are exemplary rather than complete. A library should use those below if listed or add subject headings as needed. There is no need to include see-also references, because the classified list relates one heading to another, no matter how remotely. What would be a see reference from an unused heading to the preferred term are treated as headings in the alphabetic list and included with the preferred heading in the classified list. Headings may be added as needed, even those in a different language or even in a writing system other than the Roman alphabet. For convenience, headings in other languages should be alphabetized in separate lists, a necessity for headings in other writing systems and desirable for headings in languages other than English, which may have different rules of filing its alphabet. All the headings are related, thus avoiding the problem of unrelated headings which have to be known in advance to be found.

The classification used is decimal, like the Dewey Decimal Classification found in the eighth edition of Sears Subject Heading List, but with three features of the Universal Decimal Classification. One decimal point may be added to another. The colon is used to relate two concepts with the understanding that each term will appear as the entry word. Zeroes are not used at the end of any numbers.

The alphabetic list precedes the classified list. Both are essential in this method: the latter to show all the headings in

one general area of associations, the former to show all the
headings in the list to make the areas of associations findable. A
borrower should go to the one that answers the question best: What
should I look up to find pictures of cruise ships or is the term
"Cruise ship" a subject heading? The same answer will be found in
both lists and may be approached either by the area of associations
that includes cruise ships or under that heading in the alphabetic
list.

The rules for the choice of headings are found below. Following these rules, the librarian should be able to develop a service-
able list that fits the library being organized.

Semantic Rules

1. Use the actual name of persons, places, and things where possible. These are not shown in the list except as examples, for
instance "PANAMA CANAL   386.4."
2. Use the class names of groups of persons, types of places, and
kinds of things, for instance "CANALS   386.4."
3. Use class names of classes when essential, but avoid abstract
and meaningless terms like situations, conditions, democracy,
happiness, and so on, for instance "THE ARTS 7."

Grammatical Rules

1. Use one word for topical headings where available. If there is
no class name, a series of terms may be used, each listed
separately in the alphabetic list. Rivers, streams, and creeks are
all forms of natural waterways, but the heading is "333.785 Rivers
; Streams ; Creeks ". Each is listed: "RIVERS   333.785," STREAMS
333.785," and "CREEKS   333.785." The abbreviation "etc." is not

employed after a series a words and not after a single term as in
the Library of Congress List of Subject Headings.

2. Use the plural of count nouns and the singular of mass nouns.
Avoid articles unless an abstract use of a noun is preferred. For
instance "FANS   391.42," "RICE   633.18" and "THE HEART   574.12."
The latter term represents the biological approach to the heart in
living organisms not the anatomical approach of medicine.

3. Use the nominal form of verbs when necessary, but avoid terms
that are non pictorial in nature, for instance "Children playing,"
but not   *Children dreaming.

4. Avoid prepositional phrases and conjunctions where possible
unless a part of a familiar term. For instance, "BOWS AND ARROWS
625.393" but not *Areas of the Brain. This is listed as "BRAIN
AREAS   612.812."

Use of the List

A heading may have two or more classifications and will be
listed once under each classification number. Semantic areas can be
enlarged by using a colon to relate one heading to another. The
subject heading for costumes is enlarged by listing it as "390.2
COSTUMES : NOBILITY" and is also listed under each of these terms
in the alphabetic list, "NOBILITY : COSTUMES   309.2" as well as
"COSTUMES : NOBILITY   309.2." This avoids prepositions and also
lists the heading in both the ways under which it would be sought.

Any heading may be expanded to include all the names of individuals, particular places, and special named things. If a classification number is desired, some variation of the Cutter system can
be used. The first letter of the entry is followed by two or three
numbers representing the rest of the entry. A good system can be
found on the telephone dial. For instance, if "386.4 CANALS" is
to include headings for all the different canals in the world, the

headings included can be listed as "386.4P252 PANAMA CANAL " and "386.4S839 SUEZ CANAL" to follow "386.4K435 KIEL CANAL."

The suggested classification numbers in the list are based on the Universal Decimal Classification. When it is desired to show a locality with a heading, the number of the locality from either the Dewey system tables or the Universal Classification can be used. Localities are shown after a period. In the example above "386.4 CANALS" can be expanded to listf the places where there are waterways for ships and barges, for instance "386.4.43 CANALS : GERMANY". This heading would be listed both under CANALS and under GERMANY as "CANALS : GERMANY 386.4.43" and "GERMANY : CANALS 386.4.43" and possible under the names of each of the canals, for instance "386.4.43K435 KIEL CANAL".

Programs are available for alphabetizing lists by system. The classified list must be keyboarded. A program should provide that a semi-colon indicates that the classification number is used after each heading preceding sign or another semi-colon. The program should also specify that the classification number is placed after the last heading listed and that all the headings are alphabetized. The rules for alphabetization are word by word and letter by letter within words with a space regarded as coming before A. Hyphens and apostrophes are disregarded.

The picture is entirely visual and cannot define or describe abstract concepts such as *Communication or *Mathmatics. Verbal material very often deals with some abstract concept which cannot be pictured. Where the heading is abstract, it is suitable for a pamphlet file but not for a picture collection. The headings below are meant for a collection of pictures of any kind and for realia. They are an expansion and refinement of the classified list in the Encyclopedia of Library and Information Science, vol. 5., pp.66 - 134.

Alphabetic List of Subject Headings

ABBEYS 727.7

ABDOMINAL MUSCLES 611.77

ABERDEEN CATTLE 636.22

ABORTION CLINICS 363.46

ABSTRACTIONIST ART 762.8

ABSTRACTIONIST
PAINTINGS 758.9

ABSTRACTIONIST
SCULPTURES 736.9

ABUTMENTS 721.4

ACADEMIC APPAREL 378.25

ACADEMIC LIBRARIES 027.7

ACADEMIC PARADES 378.1

ACANTHUS 583.81

ACCESSORIES 391.1

ACCIDENTS 155.936

ACCORDIONS 785.6

ACCOUNTING BOOKS 657.5

ACCOUNTING MACHINES 657

ACROBATICS 797.9

ACRYLICS 751.2

ADDING MACHINES 657

ADMIRALS 359.331

ADOLESCENTS 649.4

ADULT BOOKSTORES 363.47

ADULT EDUCATION CLASSES 374

ADULT THEATRES 363.47

ADULTS 304.24

ADVERTISING ART
DEPARTMENTS 659.3

ADVERTISING METHODS 659

ADVERTISING
PHOTOGRAPHY 659.4

AEGEAN ARCHITECTURE 723.6

AERIAL PHOTOGRAPHS 778

AEROBIC EXERCISES 799.95

AFRICAN FIGURES 733.8

AFRICAN SCULPTURES 733.8

AFRICAN VIOLETS 583.83

AGATES 559.6

AGRICULTURAL
STRUCTURES 631.2

AILANTHUS 583.23

AIR BATTLES 358.41

AIR CONDITIONERS 697

AIR TERMINALS 726.36

AIRBRUSH DRAWINGS 741.9

AIRBRUSH PAINTING 751.9

AIRCRAFT 387.1

AIRCRAFT CARRIERS 625.96

AIRCRAFT
CREWS 155.965, 387.11

AIRCRAFT FIELD
SPRAYING 632.9

AIR-CUSHION VEHICLES 625.88

AIRLINE TICKET COUNTERS 387

AIRPLANE INTERIORS 387.3

AIRPLANE
PERSONNEL 155.965, 387.11

AIRPLANES 625.83

APPLES 634.1

APPLIQUE 746.8

APRICOTS 634.32

AQUARIUMS 639.7

AQUATIC SPORTS 798.9

AQUATINTS 766.7

ARABIAN HORSES 636.11

ARCH BRIDGES 626.28

ARCHERY 799.82

ARCHES 721.7, 726.95

ARCHITECTURAL DETAILS 757.9

ARCHITECTURAL DRAWINGS 72

ARCHITECTURAL
 PAINTINGS 757.9

ARCHITECTURAL
 RENDERINGS 72

ARCTIC ENVIRONMENTS 575.3

ARISTOCRATS 305.52

ARITHMETIC PROBLEMS 513

ARK OF THE COVENANT 241.52

ARM EXERCISING 799.91

ARM MUSCLES 611.76

ARMOR 739.9

ARMORED VEHICLES 358.18

ARMS 739.9

ARMY CAMPS 355.41

ARMY LIBRARIES 355.346

ARMY OFFICERS 355.331

ARROWROOT 633.65

ARROWROOT PLANTS 584.22

ART DECO STYLE 761

ART GALLERIES 726.91

ART METALWORK 739

ART NOUVEAU 761.4

ART STYLES 76

ARTESIAN WELLS 551.497

ARTICHOKES 635.29

ARTIFICIAL
 ENVIRONMENTS 613.5

ARTIFICIAL FLOWERS 744.6

ARTIFICIAL POOLS 715.2

ARTISTS 927

THE ARTS 7

ASPARAGUS 635.21

ASSES 599.63

ASTEROIDS 523.44

ASTERS 583.54

ASTRODOMES 726.84

ATOLLS 551.424

ATOMIC-POWER PLANTS 622.6

ATOMS 539.1

ATTICS 648.9, 747.49

AUDIENCES 302.33

AUDIOVISUAL DEVICES 371.35

AUDITORIUMS 726.83

AURORA BOREALIS 538.77

AURORAS 538.77

AUTISTIC STUDENTS 371.94

AUTOMOBILE MECHANICS 654.1

AUTOMOBILE PARTS 654.2

AUTOMOBILE RACING 798.6

AUTOMOBILE TIRE
 MANUFACTURING 678

AVALANCHES 551.3

AVIAN EGGS 598.24

AVOCADOS 634.66

AZTEC ARCHITECTURE 723.96

BABIES 155.42

BABOONS 599.96

BABY CARE 649.1

BACTERIA 589.8

BACKYARDS 713.6

BADGERS 599.892

BADLANDS 333.73

BADMINTON 796.7

BAKERIES 665

BALALAIKA 782.7

BALANCES 542.3

BALCONIES 722.2

BALCONY CONSTRUCTION 694.5

BALERS 631.36

BALL GAMES 796

BALL GOWNS 391.34

BALLET PERFORMANCES 792.5

BALLROOM DANCING 793.5

BALLROOMS 747.7

BALLS 395.8

BALUSTRADES 722.9

BAMBOO 584.9, 633.59

BANANA PLANTS 584.23

BANANAS 634.77

BANDICOOTS 599.24

BANK BUILDINGS 332

BANKS 332.1

BANQUET HALLS 747.7

BANQUETS 642.4

BAPTISMAL SERVICE 265.1

BAR MITZVAH 392.3

BARBECUES 641.5

BARBERSHOP QUARTETS 788.2

BARGELLO 746.6

BARGES 386.42

BARLEY 584.96, 633.16

BARNS 631.22

BAROMETERS 551.64

BARRACKS 355.12

BARRAGE BALLOONS 625.81

BAROQUE
  ARCHITECTURE 725.2

BAROQUE ART 707

BAROQUE SCULPTURE 735.5

BARREL ORGANS 789.1

BARS 726.73

BASALT 552.3

BASEBALL 797.5

BASILICAS 727.2

BASKET BRIDGES 626.22

BASKETBALL 796.3

BASKETBALL GAMES 796.3

BASKETRY 746.4

BASS DRUMS 786.3

BASSES 597.7

BASSOONS 783.7

BATHHOUSES 726.74

BATHING 613.4

BATHROOM FIXTURES 644.4

BATHROOMS 644.4, 747.46

BATHS 615.6

BATIK 746.9

BATS 599.4

BATTALIONS 355.31

BATTLESHIPS 625.94

BAY WINDOWS 722.5

BEACHES 551.46

BEAKERS 542.2

BEANS 635.37

BEARS 599.88

BEAVERS 599.33

BEDDING 644.6

BEDROOMS 644.5, 747.44

BEDS 749.1

BEDSTEADS 644.5

BEE DANCES 63.3

BEE HIVES 638.1

BEE LARVAE 638.4

BEECH TREES 583.98

BEECHES 634.93

BEEF CATTLE 636.25

BEER 641.23

BEES 596.9

BEETLES 595.8

BEETS 633.41

BEGONIA PLANTS 583.47

BELL TOWERS 726.97

BELLFLOWER PLANTS 583.58

BELLHOPS 647.2

BELLS 786.6

BELT BUCKLES 739.4

BELTS 391.45

BENEFICIAL ANIMALS 591.6

BENEFICIAL PLANTS 581.6

BENT GRASSES 633.23

BERRIES 634.7

BETROTHAL CEREMONIES 392.4

BETTING 799.2

BEVERAGES 613.3, 641.2, 641.75

BEVERLY HILLS

   ESTATES 384.875

BIBLES 22

BICYCLE PATHS 712.2

BICYCLE RACES 798.4

BICYCLES 388.5, 712.2

BIG BEN 529.71

BILLBOARDS 627.9

BILLIARDS 794.5

BIRCH TREES 583.98

BIRCHES 634.94

BIRD SKELETONS 598.27

BIRDS 598.2

BIRDS' CLAWS 598.25

BIRDS' EGGS 598.24

BIRDS' NESTS 598.23

BIRDS OF PARADISE 598.64

BIRDS OF PREY 598.8

BIRTHING CENTERS 392.13

BIRTHS 304.63

BISCUITS 641.85

BISHOPS 755.8

BISON 599.75

BITUMINOUS COAL 553.26

BLACK HOLES 523.28

BLACK RACES 572.6

BLACKBERRIES 634.71

BLACKBIRDS 598.66

BLACKJACK TABLES 794.7

BLACK-VEILED HATS 391.83

BLANKETS 644.6

BLIND MAN'S BLUFF 793.9

BLIND PEOPLE 362.41

BLIND STUDENTS 371.911

BLIZZARDS 551.56

BLOCK BOOKS 092

BLOCKADES 625.2

CATALPA TREES 583.53

CATAPULTS 625.398

CATASTROPHES 155.935

CATBIRDS 598.56

CATHEDRALS 727.2

CATHOLIC CHURCHES 727.12

CATS 599.83, 636.8

CATTLE 599.76, 636.2

CAUCASOIDS 572.2

CAULIFLOWER 635.24

CAVE EXPLORATION 798.3

CAVE PEOPLES 155.964

CAVES 551.447

CEDAR TREES 585.5

CEDARS 634.97

CELEBRITY FOOTPRINTS 384.873

CELERY 635.27

CELESTE 758.8

CELLOS 782.3

CEMETERIES 393.12, 718.1

CENTAURS 398.28

CENTERPIECES 642.9

CERAMIC FIGURES 738.8

CERAMIC FIGURINES 738.8

CERAMIC MANUFACTURING 669

CERAMICS 738

CEREAL GRAIN
   CULTIVATION 633.1

CEREAL GRASSES 633.25

CEREALS 641.31

CHAIN STORES 381.2

CHAIRS 645.6, 749.7

CHAISES LONGUES 749.8

CHALK DRAWINGS 741.2

CHAMBER ORCHESTRAS 787.7

CHAMPAGNES 641.759

CHANDELIERS 748.6

CHAPERONS 392.7

CHAPLAINS 248.89

CHARCOAL DRAWINGS 741.1

CHASMS 551.447

CHATEAUX 729.6

CHECKERS 794.2

CHEESE PRODUCTION 637.5

CHEESES 641.37

CHEMICAL ENGINEERING
   EQUIPMENT 66

CHEMICAL GLASSWARE 542.2

CHEMICAL WARFARE
   TROOPS 358.3

CHEMISTRY SCALES 542.3

CHEMISTRY LABORATORIES 542.1

CHEMISTS 540.9

CHERIMOYA 634.48

CHERRIES 634.36

CHESSBOARDS 794.1

CHESSMEN 794.1

CHESTNUTS 634.53

CHESTS 749.2

CHICKADEES 598.53

CHICKEN POX 614.65

CHICKENS 598.44, 636.51

CHICKS 598.44

CHICORY 633.78, 635.25

CHIHUAHUA 636.79

CHILD DEVELOPMENT
   CHARTS 612.68

CHILD LABORERS 331

CLAY 731.2

CLAY MODELING CLASSES 372.53

CLEANING STAFF 652.7

CLEARING 631.61

CLERKS 652.2

CLIFF STONE CARVINGS 718.4

CLIPPERS 625.92

CLITORIS 612.64

CLOCK TOWERS 726.98

CLOCKCASES 749.4

CLOCKWORKS 681

CLOISONNE 738.4

CLOSED-CIRCUIT TELEVISION
  DISPLAYS 653.8

CLOSETS 648.9

CLOTHES MENDING 646.6

CLOUD CHAMBERS 539.6

CLOUDS 551.62

CLOVER 633.32

CLOVES 633.85

CLYDESDALE HORSES 636.14

COAL 553.2

COBBLERS 688

COBRAS 598.13

COCKATOOS 636.596

COCKROACHES 595.3

COCKTAIL PARTIES 395.6

COCKTAILS 641.26, 641.757

COCOA 641.755

COCOA TREES 633.74

COCONUT FIBER 633.58

COCONUTS 634.61

COFFEE 633.73

COFFEE BREWING 641.753

COFFEE-MAKING
  MACHINES 641.753

COINS 332.42, 658

COIR 633.58

COLA 633.76

COLA DRINKS 645.752

COLD FRAMES 631.26

COLD STORAGE 641.44

COLLAGES 751.8

COLLEGE ATHLETES 378.3

COLLEGE BUILDINGS 378, 728.5

COLLEGE CHAPELS 728.6

COLLEGE LIBRARIES 728.7

COLLEGE STADIUMS 728.9

COLLEGE STUDENTS 378.2

COLLIES 636.74

COLON 574.8

COLONIAL ARCHITECTURE 725.4

COLOR CHARTS 535.6, 752

COLUMNS 721.6

COMBAT SOLDIERS 355.45

COMBAT UNITS 355.35

COMBINES 631.35

COMETS 523.6

COMMANDOS 356.167

COMMENCEMENT 378.24

COMMERCIAL BUILDINGS 726.2

COMMITTEES 302.34

COMMODITY MARKETS 332.64

COMMON PEOPLE :
  COSTUMES 390.4

COMMONS 713

COMMUNITY CENTERS 711.5

COMPACT DISCS 789.9

COSTUMED FIGURES 756.7

COSTUMED SINGERS 788.9

COSTUMES 391

COSTUMES :

  COMMON PEOPLE 390.4

COSTUMES : NOBILITY 390.2

COSTUMES : SLAVES 390.2

COTILLIONS 793.7

COTTAGE INDUSTRIES 338.634

COTTAGES 729.5

COTTON 633.51

COTTONTAILS 599.32

COUNSELORS 158.3

COUNTER DISPLAYS 659.8

COUNTRY CLUBS 713.8

COURTHOUSES 726.15 2

COURTSHIP 392.4

COVER CROPS 631.42

COWORKERS 158.261

COWPEAS 633.33

COWS 636.2, 599.76

COYOTES 599.85

CRABS 594.6

CRANBERRIES 634.76

CRANES 598.31, 628.6

CRAYFISH 594.5

CRAYON DRAWINGS 741.3

CREAM 637.3

CREAM PUFFS 641.86

CREEKS 333.785, 551.481

CREMATORIA 393.2

CREVICES 551.4

CREWEL WORK 746.7

CREWMEN 359.338

CRIBLE ENGRAVINGS 767.3

CRICKET 797.5

CRICKETS 595.5

CRIMINAL TYPES 364.3

CRIMINALS 364.3

CRIPPLED STUDENTS 371.916

CROCHET HOOKS 646.4

CROCHETING 746.5

CROCODILES 598.15

CROQUET 797.3

CROSS BARS 795.9

CROSS STITCH 746.6

CROSS-COUNTRY SKIING 798.83

CROWBARS 731.9

CROWDS 302.33

CROWS 598.66

CRUCIFIXION 232.4

CRUISE SHIPS 386.24

CRUISERS 625.95

THE CRUSADES 940.1

CRUSHED-ICE DRINKS 641.28

CRUSHING MACHINES 661

CRYPTOGAMS 586

CRYSTAL DRINKING

  GLASSES 748.8

CRYSTAL GAZERS 133.3

CRYSTAL GROWTH 548.82

CRYSTAL STRUCTURES 548.8

CRYSTALS 548

CUBES 516.6

CUBIST ART 762.4

CUCKOOS 598.49

CUCUMBERS 635.33

CULTIVATION 631.5

CUMULUS CLOUDS 551.626

CUPOLAS 721.8

CURLING 798.89

CURRANTS 634.73

CURRENCY 332.4

CUSTARD APPLES 583.13, 634.48

CUSTOMS HOUSES 726.16

CUSTOMS INSPECTORS 336.26

CUSTOMS STAMPS 768.6

CUT GLASS 748.7

CUT GLASS BOWLS 748.7

CUTLASSES 739.96

CUTTLEFISH 593.8

CUTTING TOOLS 623.2

CYCLING 798.4

CYCLING PATHS 388.52

CYCLONES 551.54

CYMBALS 786.4

CYPRESS 634.97, 583.61

CYPRESS TREES 585.2

DADAIST ART 763

DAGGERS 625.397, 739.92

DAGUERROTYPES 775

DAIRIES 637

DAIRY BARNS 637.1

DAM SITES 628.1

DAMS 622.1, 628.1, 631.27

DANCE BANDS 787.2

DANCE CONTESTS 792.6

DANCE HALLS 726.87

DANCE ORCHESTRAS 787.5

DANCES 395.8

DANDELIONS 635.25

DARNING 646.6

DART BOARDS 794.3

DART GAMES 794.3

DARTS 794.3

DATA PROCESSING
   EQUIPMENT 653

DATES 634.62

DEAF PEOPLE 362.42

DEAF STUDENTS 371.912

DEAF-MUTE LANGUAGE 419

DEATH CEREMONIES 393

DEBUTANTES 392.32

DEBUTS 392.32

DECANTERS 748.8

DECISION CHARTS 519.8

DECKS 722.3

DECORATIVE LETTERING 745.1

DEEP FREEZING 641.44

DEER 599.71, 636.28

DEER FLIES 596.3

DEER HUNTERS 639.1

DEER HUNTING 639.1

DEFORMED FEET 618.5

DEFORMED HANDS 618.5

DEFORMED LIMBS 618.4

DEFORMITIES 618

DEHYDRATING FOODS 641.33

DEIMOS 523.41

DELETERIOUS PLANTS 581.9

DELINQUENT STUDENTS 371.93

DELTAS 551.45

DEMONS 235.4

DENS 644.8, 747.41

DEPARTMENT STORES 381.1

DESK CLERKS 647.2

DESKS 651.1

DESTROYERS 625.98

DETAIL DRAWINGS 692.3

DETAIL FINISHING 698

DETERGENTS 648.1

DEVASTATED AREAS 355.43

DEVELOPING PHOTOGRAPHS 772

DEVILS 235.4

DEWBERRIES 634.73

DIAMONDS 557.2

DICTATION MACHINES 653.6

DICTIONARIES 403

DIGESTIVE ORGANS 611.3

DIGESTIVE TRACT
  DIAGRAMS 612.3

DIKES 551.86

DINING AREAS 644.3

DINING CARS 385.5

DINING ROOMS 642.5, 747.43

DINNER PARTIES 395.4

DINOSAURS 568

DIPLOMATS 327

DIRIGIBLE BALLOONS 625.82

DISCIPLES 225, 755.5

DISCOUNT STORES 381.2

DISEASE CARRIERS 614.4

DISEASE MANIFESTATIONS 614.7

DISEASED ANIMALS 591.2

DISHWASHING 648.7

DITCHES 532.3

DIVING 798.97

DNA STRUCTURES 571

DOBERMAN PINSCHERS 636.72

DOCKS 625.6, 712.7, 726.37

DOG RACING 799.5

DOGFIGHTS 358.41

DOGS 599.85, 636.7

DOLL FURNITURE 744.15

DOLLHOUSES 744.13

DOLPHINS 599.54

DOMES 721.8

DOMESTIC ARCHITECTURE 729.1

DONKEYS 599.63, 636.16

DOOR HANGING 698.5

DOORS 722.4

DOOR-TO-DOOR SELLERS 381.4

DOUBLE BASS 782.4

DOVES 636.55

DOWNHILL SKIING 798.81

DRAFT HORSES 636.14

DRAFTING EQUIPMENT 604.2

DRAGONFLIES 595.6

DRAGONS 398.74

DRAINAGE
  DITCHES 628.4, 631.62

DRAPED FIGURES 743.6, 756.5

DRAPERIES 645.4, 743.6, 747.2

DRAUGHTS 794.2

DRAWING CLASSES 372.52

DRAWING ROOMS 747.42

DRAWINGS 741

DREAMS 135

DRESSMAKING MACHINES 687

DRIED EGGS 637.9

DRIED GRASSES 745.26

DRIED MILK 637.6

DRIFTWOOD 745.25

DRILLING PLATFORMS 629.2

DRILLS 355.5

DRINKING ACTIVITIES 394.12

DRIP-METHOD
  IRRIGATION 631.68

DRIVE-INS 726.72

DROMEDARIES 599.78

DRONES 638.2

DROUGHT DAMAGE 632.4

DRUG ADDICTION
  CHARTS 613.8

DRUG ADDICTS 157.6, 362.293

DRUG PUSHERS 363.45

DRUG TRAFFIC 363.45

DRUPACEOUS FRUITS 634.3

DRYING FOODSTUFFS 641.43

DUCK HUNTING 639.2, 799.85

DUCKS 598.34, 636.56

DUDE RANCHES 798.2

DUELS 394.82

DUGONG 599.57

DUPLEXES 729.2

DUST STORMS 551.57

DUTCH PAINTINGS 758.4

DWARFS 573.4, 618.1

DYES 547.9

EAGLES 598.85

EARLY CHRISTIAN
  ARCHITECTURE 724.2

EARLY GREEK
  SCULPTURES 734.1

THE EARTH 525

EARTHENWARE 738.3

EARTHQUAKE DAMAGE 363.345

EARTHQUAKES 155.935, 363.345

EARTHWORM CULTURE 638.7

EARTHWORMS 594.1

EASTER CHURCH
  SERVICES 263.93

EASTER EGGS 744.8

EASTER PARADES 394.28

EASTERN ORTHODOX
  CHURCHES 727.14

EATING ACTIVITIES 394.1

EBONY PLANTS 583.68

ECHIDNAS 599.15

ECLAIRS 641.86

ECLIPSES 523.78

ECOLOGICAL CHARTS 575

ECONOMISTS 923

EDIBLE PLANTS 581.65

EGG DECORATIONS 744.7

EGG PRODUCTION 637.8

EGGPLANTS 635.36

EGGS 637.9

EGRETS 598.32

EGYPTIAN ARCHITECTURE 723.5

EGYPTIAN STATUARY 733.2

EJACULATORY
  FUNCTIONS 612.62

ELECTRIC GAUGES 622.8

ELECTRIC SUPPLY METERS 622.8

ELECTRIC-POWER
  GENERATORS 622.3

ELECTRIC-POWER LINES 622.5

ELECTRIC-POWER
  STATIONS 622.7
ELECTRON MICROSCOPES 577.1
ELECTRON PATTERNS 539.15
ELECTRONIC ORGANS 785.7
ELEMENTARY
  SCHOOLS 372.1, 728.2
ELEPHANT SEALS 599.898
ELEPHANTIASIS 618.6
ELEPHANTS 599.6
ELEVATED RAILWAYS 627.6
ELIZABETHAN
  ARCHITECTURE 725.1
ELK 599.72, 636.28
EMBALMING 393.4, 614.82
EMBROIDERY 746.7
EMERALDS 557.8
EMERY WHEELS 623.5
EMPTY LOTS 717.8
EMU 598.42
ENAMELS 738.4
ENCHANTED FORESTS 398.48
ENCYCLOPEDIAS 403
ENGINEERS 620.9
ENGLISH HORNS 783.6
ENGLISH PAINTINGS 758.5
ENGLISH SPARROWS 598.65
ENGRAVINGS 766.3
ENLARGED ORCHESTRAL
  GROUPS 787.9
ENLISTED MEN 355.333
ENSLAVING CAPTIVES 399.8
ENTRANCES 722.4
ENVIRONMENTAL HAZARDS 613.1

EPIDEMICS 614
EPIDEMICS CHARTS 614
EPISCOPAL PALACES 727.9
EQUESTRIAN FIGURES 756.8
EQUESTRIAN SPORTS 799.1
EQUESTRIAN STATUES 719.9
EQUINES 636.1
EQUIPMENT REPAIR 654
EQUIPMENT SHEDS 631.25
ERECT PENISES 612.6
EROTICA 756.9
ERUPTIVE DISEASES 614.6
ESCALATORS 722.81
ESOPHAGUS 574.2
ESPARTO GRASS 633.58
ESTATE GARDENS 717.6
ESTUARIES 575.65
ETCHINGS 766.8
ETHNIC GROUPS 155.84
ETRUSCAN
  ARCHITECTURE 723.6
ETRUSCAN FIGURES 734.5
EUPHONIUM 784.8
EUROPA 523.4
EUROPEAN PAINTINGS 758
EVERGREEN FORESTS 634.95
EVOLUTION CHARTS 573
EXCAVATION 627.2
EXECUTIVE MANSIONS 726.13
EXECUTIVES 652.1
EXERCISE 649.8
EXERCISE DIAGRAMS 613.7
EXERCISING 799.9
EXHIBITION BUILDINGS 726.91

FILBERTS 634.54

FILE FOLDERS 651.7

FILING BOXES 651.7

FILING CABINETS 651.5

FILLING STATIONS 726.39

FILM 776

FILM CASSETTES 776

FILTERS 542.6

FINCHES 598.69, 636.592

FINGER PAINTING 751.7

FINGER RINGS 739.5

FIRE ALARMS 643.4

FIRE EXTINCTION 363.374

FIRE HAZARDS 363.372

FIRE STATIONS 726.19

FIREMEN 352.3

FIREPLACES 697.5, 749.3

FIRES 363.37

FIREWORKS 662

FIRS 634.98

FIRST COMMUNION 265.2

FISH CULTURE 639.7

FISHES 597

FISHING NETS 639.4

FISHING POLES 639.6

FISHING VESSELS 639.3

FISHING WEIRS 639.4

FLAG SIGNALS 625.73

FLAMES 541.4

FLASKS 542.2

FLATCARS 385.74

FLAX 583.21, 633.52

FLEAS 596.1, 614.45

FLICKERS 598.48

FLIES 596, 614.42

FLOOD DAMAGE 363.343, 632.4

FLOODS 155.935, 363.343, 551.489

FLOORING 694.3

FLOORS 722.9, 747.3

FLOW CHARTS 519.7

FLOWER ARRANGEMENTS 745.2, 757.7

FLOWER GARDENS 635.6, 717.2

FLOWERING PLANTS 583

FLOWERS 757.7

FLUORESCENCE 535.3

FLUIDS 532

FLUTES 783.1

FLYCASTING 639.6

FLYING FISH 597.5

FLYING FOXES 599.42

FLYSWATTERS 648.8

FOAMS 541.3

FOLDING PAPER 732.7

FOLK DANCES 793.3

FOOD CHAINS 575.1

FOOD PREPARATION 641.41

FOODS 641.3

FOOT SOLDIERS 356.1

FOOTBALL GAMES 796.4

FOOTBALL PLAYERS 796.4

FOOTWEAR MANUFACTURING 688

FORAGE CROPS 633.2

FORAMINIFERA 592.2

FOREST AREAS 718.8

FOREST ENVIRONMENTS 575.7

FORESTS 333.75, 634.9

GAMBLING 363.42

GAME 641.32, 641.39

GAMES 394.3, 649.7

GANYMEDE 523.451

GARAGE SALES 381.9

GARDEN GREENS 635.2

GARDENS 635

GARMENT CUTTING 687

GASES 533.8

GATES 719.6

GAY BARS 363.49

GAY MEN 363.49

GAY RIGHTS

PARADES 306.76, 363.492

GAZELLES 599.74

GEESE 598.34, 636.57

GEIGER COUNTERS 539.5

GEM CUTTING 737.2

GEMS 557

GENERALS 355.32

GENERATORS 537.2

GENETIC CHARTS 571

GENITAL HERPES 614.75

GENRE PAINTINGS 754

GENTIAN 583.73

GEOGRAPHY CLASSES 372.89

GEOLOGIC ERAS 551.75

GEOLOGIC STRUCTURES 551.8

GEOLOGISTS 550.9

GEOMETRIC DESIGNS 762.2

GEOMAGNETISM 538.7

GEORGIAN ARCHITECTURE 725.4

GERBILS 599.36

GERMAN MEASLES 614.64

GERMAN MYTHIC FIGURES 293

GERMAN PAINTINGS 758.3

GERMANIC GODS 293

GEYSERS 551.498

GHOSTS 133.1, 398.8

GIANTS 398.24, 573.8, 618.3

GIBBONS 599.97

GIFTED STUDENTS 371.95

GIN 641.25

GINGER PLANTS 584.21

GINGKO TREES 585.6

GIRAFFES 599.73

GIRL SCOUTS 369.43

GIRLS 155.433, 649.4

GLACIERS 551.3

GLANDULAR ORGANS 611.5

GLASS 691.6, 748

GLASS BLOWING 677.5, 748.1

GLASS LAMPS 748.6

GLASS MANUFACTURE 677

GLASS MOSAICS 748.5

GLASS PAINTING 748.3

GLASS TUBING 542.5

GLOBES 912

GLOCKENSPIEL 785.8

GLOVES 391.12

GLOXINIA 583.82

GLUE POTS 731.7

GLUING MATERIALS 732.9

GLUING PAPER PIECES 732.9

GOATS 599.77, 636.3

GOD 211, 755.1

GODDESSES 292

GOLD 546.2

GROUND COVER 717

GROUP ACTIVITIES 791

GROUSE 598.43

GRYPHONS 398.76

GUARD TOWERS 365.61

GUARDS 652.9

GUAVAS 634.49

GUERNSEY CATTLE 636.23

GUERRILLAS 355.425

GUIDED MISSILES 358.17

GUILDS 338.632

GULLIES 628.7

GULLS 598.34

GUINEA FOWL 636.52

GUITARS 782.5

GUNS 355.8

GUNSHOT WOUNDS 617.3

GYMNASIUMS 726.86

GYMNASTICS 797.6

GYMNOSPERMS 585

GYPSUM 552.62

GYPSUM MINES 556

HAIL 551.35

HAILSTONE DAMAGE 632.1

HAILSTONES 551.3

HAILSTORMS 551.35

HAIR 611.79

HAIR STYLES 391.5

HAIRPIECES 391.54

HALLOWEEN 394.25

HAMMERS 623.6, 731.9

HAMMOCK BRIDGES 626.22

HAMSTERS 599.36

HAND GRENADES 625.42

HANDBALL 796.1

HANDICAPPED STUDENTS 371.91

HANDICRAFT SALES 338.642

HANDICRAFTS CLASSES 372.55

HANDSET TELEPHONES 625.71

HANGARS 726.36

HANGING 617.5

HARA KIRI 394

HARBOR PATROLS 363.286

HARBORS 625.6

HARES 599.31

HARNESS RACES 799.3

HARPSICHORDS 785.1

HARROWS 631.32

HARVESTING 631.5

HATS 391.15

HAUNTED HOUSES 398.84

HAWKS 598.87, 636.599

HAY 633.2

HAZARDOUS MATERIAL
   HANDLING 604.7

HAZELNUTS 634.54

HEADSTONES 718.3

HEALTH CLUBS 727.76

HEARING DIAGRAMS 612.84

THE HEART 574.12

HEART-LUNG MACHINES 615.8

HEATH PLANTS

HEATING 697

HELIPORTS 712.9

HELMETS 739.98

HEMLOCK 634.98

HEMP 633.56

HOSPITAL BUILDINGS 726.52

HOSPITALS 362.1

HOT CHOCOLATE 641.755

HOTBEDS 631.26

HOTEL LOBBIES 647.3, 747.6

HOTEL REGISTRATION
  AREAS 647.4

HOTELS 729.7

HOUNDS 636.75

HOURGLASSES 529.725

HOUSE BUILDING 694

HOUSE CONSTRUCTION 643.1

HOUSE DRESSES 391.32

HOUSE FLIES 596

HOUSE PAINTS 698.1

HOUSE PLANS 692

HOUSE RENTALS 643.2

HOUSE SALE 643.2

HOUSE WRENS 598.54

HOUSEBOATS 729.94

HOUSEHOLD BURGLAR
  ALARMS 643.3

HOUSEHOLD EQUIPMENT 644

HOUSEHOLD FURNISHINGS 644

HOUSEHOLD SECURITY 643.3

HOUSEKEEPING ACTIVITIES 648

HOUSEPLANTS 635.8

HOUSES 643

HOUSE-TO-HOUSE
  FIGHTING 355.426

HOVERCRAFT 625.88

HOWITZERS 625.33

HUCKLEBERRIES 634.72

HUCKLEBERRY PLANTS 583.62

HUMAN ANATOMY 611

HUMAN BRAIN 612.81

HUMAN CORPSES 614.8

HUMAN EARS 612.84

HUMAN EYES 612.83

HUMAN FETUSES 612.66

HUMAN FIGURES 756

HUMAN RACES 572

HUMAN STARVATION 618.7

HUMAN SKELETON 611.7

HUMAN SKULLS 611.73

HUMAN VISCERA 611.9

HUMMINGBIRDS 598.71

HUMPBACK WHALES 599.53

HUNTING 639, 799.8

HUNTING DEER 799.86

HUNTING DOGS 799.84

HUNTING ELK 799.86

HUNTING HORNS 784.9

HUNTING LODGES 729.93

HUNTING SCENES 757.5

HURRICANES 551.52

HUSKING 631.57

HYDROPONIC GARDENING 635.9

HYDROTHERAPY
  EQUIPMENT 615.6

HYENAS 599.82

HYGIENE CHARTS 613

ICE CARVINGS 737.8

ICE CREAM 637.7, 641.81

ICE CREAM SUNDAES 641.81

ICE CRYSTALS 536.5

ICE CUBES 536.5

JACKALS 599.85

JACKRABBITS 599.31

JACOBEAN
  ARCHITECTURE 725.2

JADE 559.2

JAIN TEMPLES 294.4

JANITORS 652.7

JAPANESE
  ARCHITECTURE 723.2

JAPANESE FLOWER
  ARRANGEMENTS 745.22

JAPANESE INK
  PAINTINGS 751.14

JAPANESE PAINTINGS 759.2

JAPANESE SCULPTURES 733.7

JAR CUTTING 748.2

JAYS 598.63

JEEPS 355.27

JELLYFISH 592.6

JERUSALEM ARTICHOKES 633.48

JESUS 225, 755.2

JET PLANES 625.85

JEWELED EASTER EGGS 744.8

JEWELRY 391.7

JEWELRY REPAIR 739.3

JIU JITSU 798.7

JOGGING 799.96

JOUSTS 394.84

JUBILEES 394.43

JUDEAN ARCHITECTURE 723.42

JUDGES 347.1

JUMPING JACKS 799.93

JUNGLE GYMS 795.9

JUNIOR HIGH SCHOOLS 728.3

JUNK 731.3

JUPITER 523.45

JUPITERIAN MOONS 523.451

JUTE 633.55

JUVENILE DELINQUENTS 364.36

KAFIR CORN 633.17

KANGAROOS 599.22

KARATE 798.7

KETTLEDRUMS 786.2

KEYBOARD INSTRUMENTS 785

KICK BOXING 798.7

KIDNEY FUNCTIONS 612.5

KILLER WHALES 599.52

KILNS 738.1

KINDERGARTEN CLASSES 372.21

KINGFISHERS 598.75

KINGS 398.34

KITCHEN EQUIPMENT 644.1

KITCHEN LINEN 644.2

KITCHENS 644.1, 747.48

KITE FLYING 795.2

KITES 598.84, 795.2

KITSCH 761.2

KIWI 598.42

KNEADING DOUGH 641.88

KNEE BENDS 799.97

KNICKNACK STANDS 749.4

KNITTING 746.5

KNITTING NEEDLES 646.6

KNIVES 731.5

KNOTS 514

KOALAS 599.23

MELONS 635.31

MEMORIAL PARKS 718.1

MEMORIAL PLAQUES 719.7

MEMORIAL STATUARY 719.9

MEMORIAL WALLS 726.96

MEN 155.632

MEN'S CHOIRS 788.2

MEN'S HAIRCUTS 391.52

MEN'S NIGHTWEAR 391.26

MEN'S SUITS 391.2

MEN'S UNDERWEAR 391.25

MENSERVANTS 647.1

MENTALLY RETARDED
  PEOPLE 025.7, 097, 362.3

MENTALLY-RETARDED'S
  FACILITIES 726.56

MERCHANT SEAMEN 331.79

MERCHANT SHIPS 625.92

MERCURY 523.41

MERMAIDS 398.27

MERMEN 398.27

MERRY-GO-ROUNDS 795.6

MESAS 551.434

MESOPOTAMIAN
  ARCHITECTURE 723.46

METABOLISM DIAGRAMS 612.4

METAL 731.2

METAL CASTING 732.3

METAL ENGRAVINGS 767

METAL FIGURES 739.8

METALS 546

METAMORPHIC ROCKS 552.5

METEOR SHOWERS 523.5

METEORS 523.5

METER MAIDS 389.32

MEZZOTINTS 766.6

MICE 599.38

MICROBES 576.1

MICRO-ORGANISMS 576, 592.1

MICROSCOPES 577

MICROTOMES 577.2

MICROWAVE OVENS 641.49

MIDDLE SCHOOLS 728.3

MIDGETS 573.6, 618.1

MIGRANT WORKER
  STUDENTS 371.965

MILDEW 632.5

MILKWEED PLANTS 583

MILKY WAY 523.25

MILLET 584.91

MILITARY
  AIRCRAFT 358.4, 625.8

MILITARY BANNERS 355.15

MILITARY
  BRIDGES 358.22, 625.55

MILITARY CEREMONIES 355.17

MILITARY
  COMMUNICATIONS 625.7

MILITARY DEMOLITION 358.23

MILITARY FORTIFICATION 625

MILITARY HIGHWAYS 625.5

MILITARY HOSPITALS 355.345

MILITARY OFFICERS 355.331

MILITARY PARADES 355.16

MILITARY PRISONS 365.4

MILITARY ROADS 358.22, 625.5

MILITARY SCHOOLS 373.24

MILITARY TENTS 355.129

THE MOON 523.3

MOORISH ARCHITECTURE 724.4

MOPPING FLOORS 648.3

MOPS 648.3

MORACEOUS FRUITS 634.46

MORAYS 597.4

MORTARS 625.33

MORNING-GLORY PLANTS 583.78

MOSAIC PAINTING 751.6

MOSAIC MURALS 748.5

MOSAICS 738.5

MOSQUES 297.3, 727.4

MOSQUITOES 596.4, 614.43

MOSSES 588

MOTEL GAME ROOMS 747.6

MOTEL OFFICES 647.4

MOTELS 729.7

MOTHERS 155.646

MOTHS 596.2, 596.7

MOTION PICTURE
  CELEBRITIES 384.87

MOTION PICTURE
  COSTUMES 384.88

MOTION PICTURE CREWS 384.85

MOTION PICTURE
  DIRECTORS 384.83

MOTION PICTURE FILM 777

MOTION PICTURE
  PERFORMERS 384.86

MOTION PICTURE
  PREMIERS 384.871

MOTION PICTURE SETS 384.891

MOTION PICTURE
  STUDIOS 384.81

MOTION PICTURES 384.8

MOTORBOATS 798.92

MOTOR-COACH HOMES 729.97

MOTORCYCLE RACES 798.5

MOUNTAIN CLIMBING 798.1

MOUNTAINS 551.43

MOUNTING GEMS 739.3

MOURNING ACTIVITIES 393.6

MOURNING GARB 391.83

MOUSETRAPS 648.8

MOVABLE BRIDGES 626.27

MOVING WALKWAYS 388.62

MOWERS 631.35

MUEZZINS 297.6

MULBERRIES 634.47

MULBERRY TREES 583.96

MULCH TILLAGE 631.41

MULES 636.17

MULLAHS 297.6

MULTIPLE ARTS 765

MULTIPLE DWELLINGS 729.1

MUMMIFICATION 614.82

MUSEUM EXHIBITS 069.5

MUSEUMS 069

MUSHROOM CAVES 635.5

MUSHROOM CULTIVATION 635.5

MUSCLES 611.74, 743.3

MUSCULAR SYSTEMS 743.3

MUSEUMS 711.5, 726.91

MUSIC BOXES 786.9

MUSIC CLASSES 372.87

MUSIC RECORDING 789

MUSICAL CHAIRS 793.9 2

MUSICAL DEVICES 789

PARKING AREAS 712.3

PARKING LOTS 389.2

PARKING METER

READERS 389.32

PARKING METERS 389.3

PARKS 333.78, 711.2

PARKWAYS 714

PARLORS 747.42

PARQUET FLOORING 747.3

PARROTS 598.47, 636.594

PARSEE DEATH TOWERS 393.5

PARSNIPS 633.45

PARSONAGES 727.9

PARTITION FRAMES 694.4

PARTRIDGES 598.45

PARTY GAMES 793.9

PASSEMENTERIE 746.3

PASSENGER AIRPLANES 387.1

PASSENGER TRAINS 385.2

PASSENGER WAITING

ROOMS 385.4

PASSERIFORMES 598.5

PASSIONFLOWER PLANTS 583.44

PASTA DISHES 641.74

PASTEL DRAWINGS 741.4

PASTURES 333.74

PATENT-OFFICE DRAWINGS 608

PATIOS 644.9, 722.3

PATHOLOGY CHARTS 616

PATROL BOATS 625.98

PATTERNS 646.9

PAUL BUNYAN 398.242

PEA PLANTS 583.32

PEACE PIPES 399.2

PEACHES 634.38

PEACHICKS 636.54

PEACOCKS 598.45, 636.54

PEAHENS 636.54

PEANUTS 633.37

PEARS 634.2

PEAS 635.38

PEASANTS 305.56

PEARL CULTURE 558

PEARL DIVERS 558.2

PEARLS 558

PEAT 553.24

PECAN TREES 583.97

PECANS 634.52

PECCARIES 599.68

PEDESTALS 721.5

PEDESTRIAN CROSSINGS 712.3

PELICANS 598.37

PEN AND INK DRAWINGS 741.6

PENCIL DRAWINGS 741.5

PENCILS 651.8

PENGUINS 598.38

THE PENIS 574.93

PENITENTIAL SERVICES 265.6

PENS 651.8

PENTHOUSE GARDENS 717.4

PEPPER 641.33

PEPPER VINES 633.89

PEPPERS 635.35

PERCHERON HORSES 634.14

PERCHES 597.7

PERCHING BIRDS 598.5

PERCUSSION INSTRUMENTS 786

PERFORATING TOOLS 623.4

PRISONERS 155.962

PRISONERS OF WAR 331.51

PRISONS 365, 726.6

PRIVATE ELEMENTARY
  SCHOOLS 372.12

PRIVATE LIBRARIES 027.1

PROCESSIONS 394.5

PROFESSORS 378.1

PROJECTILES 531.5

PROPELLER-DRIVEN
  AIRPLANES 625.84

PROSTITUTES 306.74

PROTESTANT CHURCHES 727.18

PROTOZOA 592

PRUNING 631.55

PSYCHATRIC DEVICES 615.4

PSYCHIATRIC HOSPITAL
  BUILDINGS 726.54

PSYCHIATRIC HOSPITALS 362.21

PSYCHIATRIC WARDS 362.22

PSYCHOLOGICAL
  LABORATORIES 150.7

PSYCHOLOGISTS 921.5

PSYCHONEUROTIC
  PATIENTS 157.3

PSYCHOTIC PATIENTS 157.2

PUBLIC ELEMENTARY
  SCHOOLS 372.11

PUBLIC GARAGES 726.38

PUBLIC HIGH SCHOOLS 373.21

PUBLIC HOUSEHOLD
  EMPLOYEES 647.2

PUBLIC HOUSING 363.5

PUBLIC LIBRARIES 027.4

PUBLIC LIBRARY
  BUILDINGS 726.92

PUBLIC PERFORMANCES 79

PUBLIC STRUCTURES 726

PUFFINS 598.33

PUMPKINS 635.32

PUMPS 622.4

PUNCHES 623.4

PUNK ROCK STARS 788.9

PURITANS 285.9

PURSES 391.1

PUSHCART PEDDLERS 381.5

PUSH-UPS 799.94

PYGMIES 573.5

PYRAMIDS 516.7

QUAIL 598.43

QUARRIES 554.2

QUEEN BEES 638.2

QUOITS 795.5

RABBIT DAMAGE 632.7

RABBITS 599.32

RACCOONS 599.87

RACEHORSES 636.12

RACETRACKS 726.89

RADAR 625.74

RADAR PLATFORMS 629.1

RADIATION BELTS 538.75

RADIO BROADCASTING 384.54

RADIO WAVES 537.52

RADIOACTIVE ELEMENTS 546.8

RADIOLARIA 592.3

RENAISSANCE
  RELIGIOUS ART 246.4
RENAISSANCE
  SCULPTURES 735.4
REPAIR PITS 654.7
REPTILES 598.1
RESERVOIRS 333.786
RESIDENTIAL BUILDINGS 729
RESIDENTIAL INTERIOR
  DECORATION 747.4
RESIN-PRODUCING
  INSECTS 638.6
RESPIRATORY CHARTS 612.2
RESPIRATORY ORGANS 611.2
RESTAURANT BUILDINGS 726.71
RESTAURANTS 642.5
RESURRECTION 232.5
RETARDED STUDENTS 371.92
REVEGETATION 631.63
REVOLVERS 625.37
RHEAS 598.41
RHESUS MONKEYS 599.94
RHINOCEROSES 599.66
RHUBARB 635.28
RIB CAGE 611.72
RICE 633.18
RICE FIELDS 633.19
RICE PADDIES 633.19
RICE PLANTING 633.18
RICE PLANTS 584.98
RICKETSIAE 576.6
RIDING CLUBS 726.89
RIDING EXHIBITIONS 799.4
RIFLES 625.36, 799.81
RIFTS 551.84

RIOT DAMAGE 363.347
RIOTERS 303.6
RITUAL SUICIDES 394.9
RIVER BOATS 386.32
RIVER ICE 551.38
RIVER PASSENGER SHIPS 386.33
RIVERFRONT PARKS 718.7
RIVERS 333.785, 551.481
RIVETING EQUIPMENT 623.8
ROAD CONSTRUCTION 627.1
ROAD GRADING 627.3
ROADBED PREPARATION 627.2
ROADRUNNERS 598.48
ROADS 388, 631.27
ROADSIDE
  BEAUTIFICATION 627.8
ROADSIDE CAFES 388.42
ROADSIDE LITTER 627.9
ROASTING 641.48
ROBINS 598.58
ROCK ART 702
ROCK FORMATIONS 553.1
ROCK GARDENS 635.6
ROCK HYRAXES 599.61
ROCK STARS 788.8
ROCKET LAUNCHERS 625.411
ROCKET PLANES 625.86
ROCKETS 625.41
ROCKS 552
ROCKY MOUNTAIN SPOTTED
  FEVER 614.66
ROCOCO ARCHITECTURE
  725.3
RODENTS 599.3
RODEO DRIVE SHOPS 384.876

SALMON 597.6

SALOONS 394.12

SALT 641.33

SALT-WATER
  ENVIRONMENTS 575.6

SALVATION ARMY 267.1

SAND 555.2

SAND DOLLARS 592.8

SAND PAINTING 751.7

SANDALWOOD TREES 583.95

SANDWICHES 641.79

SANDPIPERS 598.33

SANDSTONE 552.6

SAPODILLA PLANTS 583.69

SAPPHIRES 557.6

SASSAFRAS 633.84

SATAN 133.42

SATANIC RITUALS 133.42

SATELLITES 625.89

SATURN 523.46

SAUNAS 726.76

SAUTEEING 641.47

SAWMILLS 676

SAWS 623.2

SAXIFRAGE 583.35

SAXOPHONES 783.4

SCALDS 617.1

SCALPING CAPTIVES 399.4

SCARLET FEVER 614.62

SCARVES 391.17

SCHOLASTIC PRANKS 378.34

SCHOOL BANDS 372.873

SCHOOL BOYS 371.9

SCHOOL
  BUILDINGS 371.61, 728

SCHOOL BUSES 371.872

SCHOOL CAFETERIAS 371.71

SCHOOL CHILDREN 649.3

SCHOOL
  DEMONSTRATIONS 371.81

SCHOOL
  DORMITORIES 371.871

SCHOOL GIRLS 371.9

SCHOOL GROUNDS 371.62

SCHOOL NEWSPAPER
  WORK 371.89

SCHOOL
  PHOTOGRAPHY 371.89

SCHOOL
  PLAYGROUNDS 371.62

SCHOOL ROOMS 747.9

SCHOOL
  SUPERINTENDENTS 371.2

SCHOOL VANDALISM 371.58

SCHOOL VIOLENCE 371.58

SCHOOLS 371

SCIENTISTS 925

SCISSORS 646.5

SCORPIONS 595.2

SCOTTISH DANCING 793.3

SCRAPERS 624.8, 631.33

SCRATCHBOARD
  DRAWINGS 741.8

SCREENS 749.5

SCUBA DIVING 798.99

SCULPTURES 73

SEA EAGLES 598.86

SEA HORSES 597.5

SEA LIONS 599.896

SEA ONIONS 594.4

SEA SPIDERS 594.9

SEA URCHINS 592.9

SEAFOOD 641.38

SEAMS 646.8

SEAPORTS 712.7

SEAS 333.914

SEASCAPES 757.2

SEASHORES 551.46

SEASONAL PARTIES 793.2

SEAWALLS 628.3

SECONDARY SCHOOLS 728.3

SECONDHAND STORES 381.3

SECRET POLICE 363.283

SECRETARIES 652.5

SECRETARY BIRDS 598.83

SECURITY ALARMS 384.7

SECURITY PERSONNEL 652.9

SEDGES 584.8

SEED-BEARING PLANTS 582

SEEDLESS PLANTS 586

SEEDERS 631.34

SEEDS 631.51

SEESAWS 795.7

SEDIMENTARY ROCKS 552.6

SELTZER WATER 641.751

SEMAPHORES 384.92, 625.73

SEMI-PRECIOUS STONES 559

SENIOR-CITIZENS'
  HOMES 726.57

SENNA PLANTS 583.33

SEQUOIA 634.99

SERFS 326

SERGEANTS 355.333

SERIGRAPHS 766.5

SERMON ON THE
  MOUNT 241.53

SERVICE CLUB
  MEETINGS 369.5

SEVEN DEADLY SINS 241.3

SEWAGE DISPOSAL
  OPERATIONS 629.3

SEWAGE DISPOSAL
  PLANTS 629.2

SEWAGE TREATMENT
  PLANTS 363.7

SEWER LINES 629.45

SEWING CLASSES 372.54

SEWING EQUIPMENT 646

SEWING MACHINES 646.1

SEX DIFFERENCES 155.33

SEX EDUCATION
  CLASSES 372.37

SEX HYGIENE
  DIAGRAMS 613.9

SEX ORGANS 574.9

SEXUAL INTERCOURSE 612.61

SHACKS 729.95

SHADE TREES 716.4

SHAFT SINKING 624.4

SHAMPOOING 613.4

SHARECROPPERS 305.56

SHARKS 597.1

SHEARS 646.5

SHEEP 599.77, 636.3

SHEEPDOGS 636.74

SOYBEANS 633.34

SPACE BATTLES 398.56

SPACE MEN 398.52

SPACE PHOTOGRAPHY 779

SPACE SHIPS 398.5

SPACECRAFT 625.89

SPACECRAFT CREWS 155.966

SPAGHETTI 641.74

SPANIELS 636.77

SPARKLING

  WINE 641.22, 641.759

SPEAKER SYSTEMS 789.4

SPEAR FISHING 799.7

SPEARS 625.394

SPECTROSCOPES 543

SPECTROSCOPIC

  PICTURES 543.1

SPELUNKING 798.3

SPERM DIAGRAMS 612.63

SPERM WHALES 599.56

SPHERES 516.8

SPHYGMOMANOMETERS 612.16

SPICE CROPS 633.8

SPICES 641.33

SPIDERS 595.2, 614.46

SPILLWAYS 532.2

SPINACH 635.22

SPINAL COLUMN 611.71

SPINAL CORD 612.82

SPINNING 746.1

SPIRITUALIST MEDIUMS 133.9

SPIROCHETES 589.9

THE SPLEEN 574.64

SPONGES 592.4

SPORT CLOTHES 391.24

SPORT FISHING 639.5, 799.6

SPORTING DOGS 636.75

SPORTS 649.8, 795, 797.7

SPRINGS 551.49

SPRINKLERS 333.913, 628.5

SPRUCE 634.96

SQUARE DANCES 793.4

SQUARES 516.2

SQUASH 796.9

SQUASHES 635.32

SQUID 593.9

SQUIRRELS 599.34

STAB WOUNDS 617.2

STADIUMS 726.84

STAGE PLAYS 792.1

STAIN DIAGRAMS 577.3

STAINED GLASS 748.3

STAIRCASES 722.7

STAIRWAY

  CONSTRUCTION 694.6

STAIRWAYS 719.2

STALLIONS 636.1

STARFISH 592.7

STARLESS AREAS 523.28

STARLINGS 598.62

STARS 523.8

STATE VISITS 394.44

STATUARY 73

STATUES 719.9

STEAM ENGINES 621.1

STEAM PIPES 621.3

STEEL BEAMS 691.7

STEEL MILLS 672, 726.46

SUCKERS 631.53

SUEZ CANAL 386.4

SUGAR 641.32

SUGAR BEETS 633.63

SUGAR CANE 584.92, 633.61

SUGAR MAPLES 633.64

SUGAR PLANTS 633.6

SUGAR REFINERIES 666

SUMAC 583.28

SUMMER COTTAGES 729.92

THE SUN 523.7

SUNDAY CHURCH
  SERVICES 363.4

SUNDAYS 263.3

SUNDIALS 529.72

SUNFLOWERS 583.56

SUNSPOTS 523.74

SUPREME COURT
  JUSTICES 347.1

SURF 551.47

SURF RIDING 798.93

SURFACE MINE
  RECLAMATION 631.63

SURFACE-TO-AIR
  MISSILES 625.45

SURFERS 798.93

SURGERIES 615.7

SURGICAL NURSES 610.7

SURREALIST ART 763

SURVIVAL TECHNIQUES 613.6

SUSPENSION BRIDGES 626.21

SUTTEES 393.67

SWALLOWS 598.52

SWAMPS 333.918

SWANS 598.35, 636.58

SWEEPING FLOORS 648.2

SWEET CORN 635.39

SWEET POTATOES 633.47

SWEET SORGHUM 633.62

SWIFTS 598.77

SWIM MEETS 798.96

SWIMMING 798.95

SWIMMING POOL
  BUILDINGS 726.78

SWIMMING POOLS 726.78

SWINE 636.4

SWING BRIDGES 626.27

SWINGS 795.6

SWITCHBOARD
  OPERATORS 652.6

SWORD DANCES 793.6

SWORDS 625.396, 739.94

SYMBOLIC LOGIC
  PROBLEMS 511.3

SYMPHONIC BANDS 787.4

SYMPHONIC CHOIRS 788.4

SYMPHONY ORCHESTRAS 787.8

SYNAGOGUES 296.6

SYNAPSE 612.8

SYNTHESIZERS 785.7

SYPHILIS 614.74

SYRUP 641.32

TABLE DECORATIONS 642.9

TABLE FURNISHINGS 642.8

TABLE PIECES 735.2

TABLE SERVICE 642

TABLE SETTINGS 642.6

UNDERWATER MINING 624.6
UNDERWATER SALVAGE 628.9
UNDERWATER TREASURE
  HUNTING 628.9
UNICORNS 398.78
UNIFORMED PEOPLE 390.5
UNITED NATIONS 341.23
UNIVERSITY
  BUILDINGS 378, 728.5
UNIVERSITY CHAPELS 728.6
UNIVERSITY LIBRARIES 728.7
UNIVERSITY RESEARCH
  FACILITIES 728.8
UNIVERSITY STADIUMS 728.9
UNSOPHISTICATED
  INSTRUMENTS 786.8
UPHOLSTERY 645, 747.2
URANIUM MINES 553.9
URANUS 523.47
URBAN COMMUNITIES 155.942
URBAN LITTER 717.8
URBAN RENEWAL AREAS 711.9
URBAN RESIDENTIAL
  AREAS 711.6
URBAN SCENES 757.3
URBAN STRUCTURAL
  FEATURES 719
UROGENITAL ORGANS 611.6
THE UTERUS 574.97

VACANT LOTS 333.77
VACATION
  HOUSES 643.7, 729.92
VACCINATION 614.5

VACUUM CLEANERS 648.5
VAGINA 574.96
VAGINAL CANAL 612.64
VALERIAN PLANTS 583
VALLEYS 551.44
VAMPIRE BATS 599.44
VAMPIRES 398.25
VAN ALLEN BELT 538.75
VANILLA 633.82
VAULTS 721.7
VEGETABLE GARDENS 635.1
VEINS 551.86
VEINS : PLANTS 581.2
VENETIAN BLINDS 645.4
VENISON 641.39
VENTILATION 697
VENUS 523.42
VERANDAS 644.9, 722.1
VERMIN 591.8
VERTEBRAE 611.71
VETERINARY
  HOSPITALS 726.59
VERTICAL-LIFT
  BRIDGES 626.27
VERTICAL-LIFT
  PLANES 625.87
VERVAIN PLANTS 583.86
VETCHES 633.35
VETERANS 331.52
VICE PRESIDENTS 353.1
VICTORIAN ART 708
VICUNAS 599.79, 636.29
VILLAS 729.6
VINES 582.6, 716.8

WITCHES 133.43, 398.38

WITCH-HAZEL PLANTS 583.36

WIZARDS 398.36

WOLVES 599.86

THE WOMB 574.97

WOMBATS 599.26

WOMEN 155.633

WOMEN'S CHORAL
  GROUPS 788.3

WOMEN'S DRESSES 391.3

WOMEN'S HAIR STYLES 391.55

WOOD 731.1

WOOD CARVINGS 737.4

WOOD ENGRAVINGS 766.1

WOOD LICE 594.3

WOOD-BURNING STOVES 697.7

WOODLANDS 575.7

WOODPECKERS 598.48

WORD PROCESSORS 651.3

WORK CLOTHES 391.23

WORKING DOGS 636.72

WORLD WAR I,
  1914-1918 940.3

WORLD WAR II,
  1939-1945 940.5

WORMS 594.1

WORSHIPPERS 248.3

WOUNDS 617

WREATHS 745.28

WRENS 598.54

WRESTLING 798.7

WRIST WATCHES 529.76

WRITERS 928

XYLOPHONES 785.9

X-RAYS 539.4

Y. M. C. A. 267.3

Y. W. C. A. 267.5

YACHT CLUB
  BUILDINGS 726.88

YACHTS 625.91

YAMS 584.27

YARD SALES 381.9

YARN 646.3

YEW TREES 585.4

YOGA EXERCISES 799.99

YOUTH CAMPS 647.8

YOUNG ANIMALS 591.3

YOUNG MEN 155.532

YOUNG PEOPLE 305.23

YOUNG WOMEN 155.533

YUPPIES 305.55

ZEBRAS 599.64, 636.18

THE ZODIAC 133.5

ZOOLOGICAL GARDENS 713.4

ZOOS 713.4

Classified List of Subject Headings

002   BOOKS

02   LIBRARIES

022.3   LIBRARY BUILDINGS

022.4   LIBRARY BOOKSTACKS

022.9   CARD CATALOGS

023   LIBRARIANS

025.7   BOOKPLATES ; NUMBERED BOOKS

027.1   PRIVATE LIBRARIES

027.4   PUBLIC LIBRARIES

027.7   ACADEMIC LIBRARIES

06   CONFERENCES

069   MUSEUMS

069.5   MUSEUM EXHIBITS

07   NEWSPAPERS

091   MANUSCRIPTS ; PALM-LEAF BOOKS

092   BLOCK BOOKS

093   INCUNABULA

095   BOOKBINDING

097   BOOKPLATES

099   MINIATURE BOOKS ; OVERSIZE BOOKS

133.1   GHOSTS

133.3   FORTUNE-TELLERS ; CRYSTAL GAZERS

133.324 TAROT CARDS

133.42 SATAN ; SATANIC RITUALS

133.43 WITCHES

133.5   THE ZODIAC

133.6   PALM-READING CHARTS

133.9   SPIRITUALIST MEDIUMS

133.93 OUIJA BOARDS

135   DREAMS

138   PHYSIOGNOMY CHARTS

139   PHRENOLOGY CHARTS

150.7   PSYCHOLOGICAL LABORATORIES

152.148 OPTICAL ILLUSIONS

152.322 CONDITIONED REFLEX TESTING

152.42   FACIAL EXPRESSION

155.284 RORSCHACH TESTS

155.33   SEX DIFFERENCES

155.42   BABIES

155,432 BOYS

155.433 GIRLS

155.532 YOUNG MEN

155.533 YOUNG WOMEN

155.632 MEN

155.633 WOMEN

155.646 PARENTS ; FATHERS ; MOTHERS

155.84   ETHNIC GROUPS

155.935 CATASTROPHES ; EARTHQUAKES ; FLOODS

155.936 ACCIDENTS

155.942 URBAN COMMUNITIES

155.943 SUBURBAN COMMUNITIES

155.944 RURAL COMMUNITIES

155.945 SLUM HOUSING

155.962 PRISONERS

155.963 SUBMARINE CREWS

155.964 CAVE PEOPLES

155.965 AIRCRAFT CREWS

155.966 SPACECRAFT CREWS

157.2   PSYCHOTIC PATIENTS

157.3   PSYCHONEUROTIC PATIENTS

157.6   DRUG ADDICTS ; ALCOHOLICS

157.7   TRANSVESTITES

157.8   MENTALLY RETARDED INDIVUALS

158.2   COOPERATIVE GROUPS

158.24 FAMILIES

158.25 NEIGHBORS

158.26 COWORKERS

158.3   COUNSELORS

158.4   LEADERS

211   GOD

22   BIBLES

222   OLD TESTAMENT PROPHETS

225   JESUS ; DISCIPLES ; LAST SUPPER

226   THE NATIVITY ; WISE MEN ; SHEPHERDS

232.1   CHRIST

232.4   CRUCIFIXION

232.5   RESURRECTION

232.9   THE ANNUNCIATION

235.2   SAINTS

235.3   ANGELS

235.4   DEVILS ; DEMONS

241.3   CARDINAL SINS ; SEVEN DEADLY SINS

241.52 TEN COMMANDMENTS ; ARK OF THE COVENANT

241.53 SERMON ON THE MOUNT

246.1   BYZANTINE ICONS

246.2   GOTHIC RELIGIOUS ART ; GOTHIC CATHEDRALS

246.4   RENAISSANCE RELIGIOUS ART ; RENAISSANCE CHURCHES

246.9   CHURCH BUILDINGS

247.1   CHURCH FURNITURE ; PEWS ; CHOIR STALLS

248.3   WORSHIPPERS

248.89 MINISTERS ; PRIESTS ; CHAPLAINS

248.942 MONKS

248.943 NUNS

263.1   SABBATH

263.3   SUNDAYS

363.4   SUNDAY CHURCH SERVICES

263.91 CHRISTMAS CHURCH SERVICES

263.92   HOLY WEEK CHURCH SERVICES

263.93   EASTER CHURCH SERVICES

265.1   BAPTISMAL SERVICE

265.2   CONFIRMATION ; FIRST COMMUNION

265.4   ORDINATION

265.5   CHURCH WEDDINGS ; MATRIMONIAL SERVICES

265.6   PENITENTIAL SERVICES ; CONFESSION BOXES

265.7   EXTREME UNCTION SERVICES ; ANOINTING THE SICK

265.8   FAITH HEALERS

265.82   VISITING THE SICK

265.85   FUNERALS ; GRAVESIDE SERVICES

265.92   CHURCH CONSECRATIONS

265.94   EXORCISTS ; EXORCISM RITES

266   MISSIONARIES

267.1   SALVATION ARMY

267.3   Y.M.C.A.

267.5   Y.W.C.A.

271.1   MEDIEVAL ABBEYS

271.7   MEDIEVAL MONKS

271.72   MONASTERIES

271.9   MEDIEVAL NUNS

271.92   CONVENTS

285.9   PURITANS

291   MYTHOLOGICAL BEASTS

292   GREEK GODS ; ROMAN GODS ; GODDESSES

293   GERMANIC GODS ; GERMAN MYTHIC FIGURES

294.3   BUDDHIST TEMPLES ; PAGODAS

294.36   BUDDHIST MONKS ; BUDDHIST ABBOTS

294.4   JAIN TEMPLES

294.5   HINDU TEMPLES

294.56   HINDU HOLY MEN

294.6   SIKHS

296.6   SYNAGOGUES

297   ISLAMIC RITUALS ; ISLAMIC HOLY PLACES

297.12 THE KORAN
297.3 MOSQUES
297.6 MULLAHS ; MUEZZINS ; IMAMS
302.33 AUDIENCES ; CROWDS ; BUS PASSENGERS
302.34 COMMITTEES
303.6 RIOTERS ; MOBS
303.62 TERRORISTS
303.64 BOMBED BUILDINGS ; WAR DAMAGE
304.28 POLLUTED STREAMS ; LITTERED STREETS
304.63 BIRTHS
304.64 CORPSES
305.23 YOUNG PEOPLE
304.24 ADULTS
304.26 OLD PEOPLE
305.52 ARISTOCRATS ; WEALTHY PEOPLE
305.55 WHITE-COLLAR WORKERS ; YUPPIES
305.56 LABORERS ; PEASANTS ; SHARECROPPERS
306.74 PROSTITUTES
306.76 HOMOSEXUAL GROUPS ; GAY RIGHTS PARADES
311 GRAPHS
321 GOVERNMENT OFFICES ; BUREAUCRATS
323.4 CIVIL RIGHTS DEMONSRATIONS
324.5 POLITICIANS ; POLITICAL MEETINGS
324.6 POLLING PLACES ; VOTING MACHINES
325.1 IMMIGRANTS
325.73 AMERICANIZATION CLASSES
326 SLAVES ; SERFS
327 DIPLOMATS
328 LEGISLATURES ; CONGRESS
329 POLITICAL PARTY ACTIVITIES
331.31 CHILD LABORERS
331.51 PRISONERS OF WAR ; CONVICTS
331.52 VETERANS
331.55 APPRENTICES

331.79 MERCHANT SEAMEN

331.87 LABOR UNION MEETINGS

331.89 STRIKERS ; PICKET LINES

332.1   BANKS ; BANK BUILDINGS

332.4   CURRENCY ; LEGAL TENDER INSTRUMENTS

332.42 COINS ; GOLD COINS ; SILVER COINS

332.45 PAPER MONEY

332.63 STOCK MARKETS

332.64 COMMODITY MARKETS

333.53 TENANTS

333.54 LANDLORDS

333.73 WASTELANDS ; BADLANDS

333.74 PASTURES ; MEADOWS

333.75 FORESTS

333.76 FARM LANDS

333.77 VACANT LOTS

333.772 STREETS ; HIGHWAYS

333.78 PARKS

333.782 WILDERNESS AREAS

333.784 LAKES

333.785 RIVERS ; STREAMS ; CREEKS

333.786 RESERVOIRS

333.9   WATER SUPPLY

333.91 WATER TREATMENT PLANTS

333.913 IRRIGATION DITCHES ; SPRINKLERS

333.914 OCEANS ; SEAS

333.917 SHORELANDS

333.918 SWAMPS

336.26 CUSTOMS INSPECTORS ; TARIFF COLLECTORS

336.27 TAX STAMPS

338.632 GUILDS

338.634 COTTAGE INDUSTRIES

338.64 SHOPS ; BOUTIQUES

338.642 HANDICRAFT SALES

338.65 FACTORIES

341.22 LEAGUE OF NATIONS

341.23 UNITED NATIONS

347   LAW COURTS

347.1   JUDGES ; SUPREME COURT JUSTICES

352.2   POLICEMEN

352.3   FIREMEN

353.1   PRESIDENTS ; VICE PRESIDENTS

353.12 PRESIDENTIAL CABINETS

355.12 BARRACKS

355.129 MILITARY TENTS ; TWO-MAN SHELTERS

355.13 MEDALS

355.14 MILITARY UNIFORMS

355.15 MILITARY BANNERS ; REGIMENTAL FLAGS

355.16 MILITARY PARADES

355.17 MILITARY CEREMONIES

355.27 MILITARY VEHICLES ; JEEPS

355.31 MILITARY UNITS ; BATTALIONS ; REGIMENTS

355.32 GENERALS

355.331 MILITARY OFFICERS ; ARMY OFFICERS

355.333 ENLISTED MEN ; SERGEANTS ; CORPORALS

355.345 MILITARY HOSPITALS

355.346 ARMY LIBRARIES

355.35 COMBAT SOLDIERS ; COMBAT UNITS

355.4   CAMOUFLAGE

355.41 ARMY CAMPS

355.425 GUERRILLAS

355.426 HOUSE-TO-HOUSE FIGHTING

355.43 DEVASTATED AREAS ; BOMBED CITIES

355.5   TACTICAL EXERCISES ; DRILLS

355.71 PRISONER-OF-WAR CAMPS

355.73 TARGET RANGES

355.8   GUNS

356.1   FOOT SOLDIERS ; INFANTRY TROOPS

356.164 SKI TROOPS

356.166 PARATROOPERS

356.167 COMMANDOS ; RANGERS

357.1   HORSE CAVALRY

357.5   MECHANIZED CAVALRY

358.13   ANTIAIRCRAFT GUNS

358.17   GUIDED MISSILES

358.18   TANKS ; ARMORED VEHICLES

358.2   BOMB DISPOSAL UNITS

358.22   MILITARY ROADS ; MILITARY BRIDGES

358.23   MILITARY DEMOLITION

358.3   CHEMICAL WARFARE TROOPS

358.4   MILITARY AIRCRAFT

358.41   DOGFIGHTS ; AIR BATTLES

358.42   BOMBERS

358.43   FIGHTER PLANES

358.44   RECONNAISSANCE PLANES

358.45   RECONNAISSANCE SATELLITES

359.1   WARSHIPS

359.331 ADMIRALS

359.332 NAVAL OFFICERS

359.338 SAILORS ; CREWMEN

359.96   MARINE CORPSMEN

359.97   COAST GUARD

361.77   RED CROSS WORKERS

362.1   HOSPITALS

362.19   CHILDREN'S WARDS

362.21   PSYCHIATRIC HOSPITALS

362.22   PSYCHIATRIC WARDS

362.292 ALCOHOLICS

362.293 DRUG ADDICTS

362.3   MENTALLY RETARDED PEOPLE

362.41   BLIND PEOPLE

362.42   DEAF PEOPLE

362.5   TRAMPS

362.6   OLD PEOPLE

362.7   CHILDREN

362.73 ORPHANS ; ORPHANAGES

362.78 RURAL YOUTH

362.79 CITY YOUTH

363.12 TRAFFIC ACCIDENTS

363.2   POLICEMEN

363.24 POLICE RADIO

363.25 POLICE INTERROGATION

363.254 POLYGRAPH TESTS ; LIE DETECTORS

363.282 SHERIFFS ; MARSHALS

363.283 SECRET POLICE

363.284 NARCOTICS AGENTS

363.285 BORDER PATROLS

363.286 HARBOR PATROLS

363.342 TORNADO DAMAGE ; TORNADOES

363.343 FLOOD DAMAGE ; FLOODS

363.345 EARTHQUAKE DAMAGE ; EARTHQUAKES

363.347 RIOT DAMAGE

363.37 FIRES

363.372 FIRE HAZARDS

363.374 FIRE EXTINCTION

363.42 GAMBLING ; GAMBLERS

363.45 DRUG TRAFFIC ; DRUG PUSHERS

363.46 ABORTION CLINICS

363.463 ANTI-ABORTION DEMONSTRATIONS

363.47 ADULT THEATRES ; ADULT BOOKSTORES

363.49 GAY BARS ; GAY MEN ; LESBIANS

363.492 GAY RIGHTS PARADES

363.5   PUBLIC HOUSING

363.6   HISTORIC LANDMARKS

363.7   SEWAGE TREATMENT PLANTS

363.732 POLLUTANTS

363.738 OIL SLICKS ; OIL SPILLS
363.739 SMOKESTACKS ; SMOKE CLOUDS ; SMOG SCENES
363.78   RATS
363.8   FAMINE
364.3   CRIMINALS ; CRIMINAL TYPES
364.36   JUVENILE DELINQUENTS
365   PRISONS
365.4   MILITARY PRISONS ; PRISON CAMPS
365.5   PRISON GROUNDS
365.52   PRISON GATES
365.54   PRISON WALLS
365.6   PRISON GUARDS
365.61   GUARD TOWERS
365.64   PRISON RIOTS
365.65   PRISON LABORERS
366.1   FREEMASONS
369.43   BOY SCOUTS
369.43   GIRL SCOUTS
369.47   CAMP FIRE GIRLS
369.5   SERVICE CLUB MEETINGS ; ROTARY CLUBS
371   SCHOOLS
371.1   TEACHERS
371.2   SCHOOL SUPERINTENDENTS ; PRINCIPALS
371.25   CLASSES
371.32   TEXTBOOKS
371.35   AUDIOVISUAL DEVICES
371.54   CORPORAL PUNISHMENT
371.58   SCHOOL VANDALISM ; SCHOOL VIOLENCE
371.61   SCHOOL BUILDINGS
371.62   SCHOOL GROUNDS ; SCHOOL PLAYGROUNDS
371.71   SCHOOL CAFETERIAS
371.81   SCHOOL DEMONSTRATIONS ; STUDENT PROTESTS
371.871 SCHOOL DORMITORIES
371.872 SCHOOL BUSES

371.89 SCHOOL NEWSPAPER WORK ; SCHOOL PHOTOGRAPHY

371.9   STUDENTS ; SCHOOL BOYS ; SCHOOL GIRLS

371.91 HANDICAPPED STUDENTS

371.911 BLIND STUDENTS

371.912 DEAF STUDENTS

371.916 CRIPPLED STUDENTS ; PHYSICALLY DISADVANTAGED
        STUDENTS

371.92 RETARDED STUDENTS

371.93 DELINQUENT STUDENTS

371.94 AUTISTIC STUDENTS

371.95 GIFTED STUDENTS

371.96 SLUM STUDENTS

371.965 MIGRANT WORKER STUDENTS

372.1   ELEMENTARY SCHOOLS

372.11 PUBLIC ELEMENTARY SCHOOLS

372.12 PRIVATE ELEMENTARY SCHOOLS

372.13 EXPERIMENTAL SCHOOLS

372.21 KINDERGARTEN CLASSES

372.35 NATURE STUDY CLASSES

372.37 SEX EDUCATION CLASSES

372.4   READING CLASSES

372.52 DRAWING CLASSES

372.53 CLAY MODELING CLASSES

372.54 SEWING CLASSES

372.55 HANDICRAFTS CLASSES

372.82 HOME ECONOMICS CLASSES

372.86 PHYSICAL EDUCATION CLASSES

372.87 MUSIC CLASSES

372.873 SCHOOL BANDS

372.89 GEOGRAPHY CLASSES

373.21 PUBLIC HIGH SCHOOLS

373.22 BOARDING SCHOOLS

373.24 MILITARY SCHOOLS

373.25 VOCATIONAL SCHOOLS

373.27 APPRENTICESHIP ACTIVITIES

374   ADULT EDUCATION CLASSES

374.4   CORRESPONDENCE SCHOOLS

377.1   CONVENT SCHOOLS ; RELIGIOUS SCHOOLS

377.3   MONASTIC SCHOOLS

377.6   MISSION SCHOOLS

378   COLLEGE BUILDINGS ; UNIVERSITY BUILDINGS

378.1   PROFESSORS ; ACADEMIC PARADES

378.2   COLLEGE STUDENTS

378.24 COMMENCEMENT ; GRADUATION CEREMONIES

378.25 ACADEMIC APPAREL

378.3   COLLEGE ATHLETES

378.31 FRATERNITIES

378.32 SORORITIES

378.33 FRATERNITY PARTIES ; SORORITY PARTIES

378.34 SCHOLASTIC PRANKS

381.1   SHOPS ; STORES ; DEPARTMENT STORES

381.2   CHAIN STORES ; DISCOUNT STORES

381.3   SECONDHAND STORES

381.4   DOOR-TO-DOOR SELLERS

381.5   PUSHCART PEDDLERS

381.8   OUTDOOR MARKETS

381.9   GARAGE SALES ; YARD SALES

383.1   POST OFFICES

383.2   POSTAL DELIVERIES ; POSTAL VEHICLES ; POSTAL
        CLERKS

383.3   PONY EXPRESS

384.3   TELEGRAPH POLES ; TELEPHONE POLES

384.4   SUBMARINE CABLE SHIPS

384.52 PORTABLE TELEPHONES

384.53 RADIOS

384.54 RADIO BROADCASTING

384.55 TELEVISION BROADCASTING

384.552 TELEVISION SETS

384.553 TELEVISION GAME SHOWS

384.554 TELEVISION CAMERA OPERATORS

384.555 TELEVISION ANNOUNCERS

384.556 TELEVISION PERFORMERS

384.557 TELEVISION SERIES

384.6 TELEPHONES

384.61 TELEPHONE SWITCHBOARDS

384.62 TELEPHONE OPERATORS

384.63 TELEPHONE LINEMEN

384.7 SECURITY ALARMS

384.8 MOTION PICTURES

384.81 MOTION PICTURE STUDIOS

384.82 SOUND STAGES

384.83 MOTION PICTURE DIRECTORS

384.84 CAMERAMEN

384.85 MOTION PICTURE CREWS

384.86 MOTION PICTURE PERFORMERS

384.87 MOTION PICTURE CELEBRITIES

384.871 MOTION PICTURE PREMIERS

384.872 HOLLYWOOD WALK OF FAME

384.873 CELEBRITY FOOTPRINTS ; GRAUMAN'S CHINESE
           THEATRE

384.874 HOLLYWOOD PARTIES

384.875 BEVERLY HILLS ESTATES

384.876 RODEO DRIVE SHOPS

384.88 MOTION PICTURE COSTUMES ; COSTUME DESIGNERS

384.891 MOTION PICTURE SETS

384.892 WESTERN-MOVIE SETS

384.893 OUTDOOR SETS

384.894 INDOOR SETS

384.895 ON-LOCALE ACTIVITIES

384.9 VISUAL SIGNALS

384.91 SMOKE SIGNALS

384.92 SEMAPHORES

385   RAILROADS

385.2   PASSENGER TRAINS

385.3   RAILROAD DEPOTS

385.4   PASSENGER WAITING ROOMS

385.5   DINING CARS

385.6   SLEEPING CARS

385.7   RAILROAD SWITCHBOARDS

385.72 FREIGHT TRAINS

385.73 FREIGHT CARS

385.74 FLATCARS

385.76 FREIGHT YARDS

385.8   FUNICULAR RAILROADS ; INCLINED RAILWAYS

386.2   SHIPS

386.24 CRUISE SHIPS

386.26 TANKERS

386.28 CONTAINER PORTS ; CONTAINER VESSELS

386.31 FERRIES

386.32 RIVER BOATS

386.33 RIVER PASSENGER SHIPS ; PADDLEWHEEL STEAMERS

386.4   CANALS ; SUEZ CANAL ; PANAMA CANAL

386.42 CANAL BOATS ; BARGES

387   AIRPORTS ; AIRLINE TICKET COUNTERS ; AIRPORT WAITING
        ROOMS

387.1   AIRCRAFT ; PASSENGER AIRPLANES

387.11 AIRCRAFT CREWS ; AIRPLANE PERSONNEL

387.2   LANDING FIELDS ; RUNWAYS

387.3   AIRPLANE INTERIORS

387.4   FREIGHT AIRCRAFT

388   ROADS ; HIGHWAYS

388.1   EXPRESSWAYS

388.2   OFF RAMPS

388.3   BUSES

388.32 BUS STATIONS

388.4   TRUCKS ; TRAILER TRUCKS

388.42 TRUCK STOPS ; ROADSIDE CAFES

388.5   BICYCLES

388.52 CYCLING PATHS

388.6   SIDEWALKS

388.62 MOVING WALKWAYS

388.7   TRAMS

388.74 TRAMWAYS

388.8   SUBWAYS

388.82 SUBWAY TRAINS

388.83 SUBWAY PASSENGERS

388.84 SUBWAY STATIONS

388.85 SUBWAY TRACKS

389.1   TRAFFIC SIGNS

389.2   PARKING LOTS

389.3   PARKING METERS

389.32 PARKING METER READERS ; METER MAIDS

390.1   ROYAL COSTUMES

390.2   NOBILITY : COSTUMES

390.3   SLAVES : COSTUMES

390.4   COMMONALTY : COSTUMES

390.5   UNIFORMED PEOPLE

391   COSTUMES

391.1   ACCESSORIES ; PURSES

391.12 GLOVES ; MITTENS

391.13 SHOES

391.14 HOSIERY

391.15 HATS

391.16 SHIRTS ; BLOUSES

391.17 NECKWEAR ; TIES ; SCARVES

391.18 TROUSERS ; PANTS ; SLACKS

391.2   MEN'S SUITS

391.23 WORK CLOTHES

391.24 SPORT CLOTHES

391.25 MEN'S UNDERWEAR

391.26 MEN'S NIGHTWEAR

391.3 WOMEN'S DRESSES

391.32 HOUSE DRESSES

391.34 BALL GOWNS

391.42 FANS ; PARASOLS ; UMBRELLAS

391.43 EYEGLASSES ; MONOCLES ; LORGNETTES

391.44 BUTTONS

391.45 BUCKLES ; BELTS

391.5 HAIR STYLES

391.52 MEN'S HAIRCUTS

391.54 TOUPEES ; HAIRPIECES

391.55 WOMEN'S HAIR STYLES

391.56 WIGS

391.63 COSMETICS

391.64 TATTOOS

391.7 JEWELRY

391.82 WEDDING DRESSES

391.83 MOURNING GARB ; BLACK-VEILED HATS

391.9 NUDES

391.92 MALE NUDES

391.93 FEMALE NUDES

391.94 NUDIST CAMPS

391.95 NUDIST ACTIVITIES

391.96 NUDE SUNBATHING

392.1 CHILDBIRTH

392.12 MATERNITY WARDS

392.13 BIRTHING CENTERS

392.2 CHILDREN PLAYING

392.21 PARK PLAYGROUNDS

392.3 INITIATION RITES ; BAR MITZVAH

392.32 DEBUTS ; DEBUTANTES

392.4 COURTSHIP : BETROTHAL CEREMONIES

392.5 WEDDINGS

392.6 DWELLING PLACES

392.62 SUBURBAN HOUSES

392.63 FAMILY LIFE

392.7 CHAPERONS

392.8 OLD PEOPLE'S HOMES

392.9 NURSING HOMES

393 DEATH CEREMONIES

393.1 BURIAL

393.12 CEMETERIES

393.2 CREMATORIA

393.3 FUNERALS

393.32 FUNERAL HOMES

393.4 EMBALMING

393.5 EXPOSURE : CORPSES ; PARSEE DEATH TOWERS

393.6 MOURNING ACTIVITIES

393.65 WAKES

393.67 SUTTEES

394.1 EATING ACTIVITIES

394.12 DRINKING ACTIVITIES : SALOONS

394.13 SMOKING ; PIPES ; CIGARS ; CIGARETTES

394.21 FASTING ACTIVITIES

394.22 CARNIVALS ; MARDI GRAS

394.24 HOLIDAY FESTIVIES

394.25 HALLOWEEN ; TRICK-OR-TREAT COSTUMES

394.26 THANKSGIVING DINNERS

394.27 CHRISTMAS ACTIVITIES

394.28 EASTER PARADES

394.3 GAMES ; TOYS

394.4 OFFICIAL CEREMONIES

394.41 CORONATIONS

394.42 INAUGURATIONS

394.43 JUBILEES

394.44 STATE VISITS

394.45 TRIUMPHAL PARADES

394.5 PARADES ; PROCESSIONS

394.6 PAGEANTS

394.7 FAIRS

394.8 CHIVALRIC ACTIVITIES

394.82 DUELS

394.84 JOUSTS

394.9 RITUAL SUICIDES ; HARA KIRI

394.95 CANNIBALS

395 SOCIAL OCCASIONS

395.2 TEA PARTIES

395.4 DINNER PARTIES

395.6 COCKTAIL PARTIES

395.8 DANCES ; BALLS

395.9 RECEPTIONS

398 STORYTELLERS

398.2 LEGENDARY PEOPLE

398.21 OGRES

398.22 FAIRIES

398.23 LEPRECHAUNS

398.24 GIANTS

398.242 PAUL BUNYAN

398.25 VAMPIRES

398.26 WEREWOLVES

398.27 MERMAIDS ; MERMEN

398.28 CENTAURS

398.32 HEROES

398.34 KINGS

398.36 SORCERERS ; WIZARDS

398.38 WITCHES

398.4 MAGIC CASTLES

398.42 MAGIC RINGS

398.44 MAGIC WANDS

398.46 MAGIC CARPETS

398.48 ENCHANTED FORESTS

398.5 SPACE SHIPS

398.54 EXTRATERRESTRIAL CREATURES

398.56 SPACE BATTLES

398.6 LEGENDARY PLACES

398.62 IMAGINARY CITIES

398.64 IMAGINARY PLANETS

398.7 LEGENDARY ANIMALS

398.72 PHOENIXES

398.74 DRAGONS

398.76 GRIFFINS ; GRYPHONS

398.78 UNICORNS

398.8 GHOSTS

398.84 HAUNTED HOUSES

399 WAR DANCES

399.2 PEACE PIPES

399.3 FEATHERED HEADDRESSES

399.4 SCALPING CAPTIVES

399.6 TORTURING CAPTIVES

399.8 ENSLAVING CAPTIVES

403 DICTIONARIES ; ENCYCLOPEDIAS

419 SIGN LANGUAGE ; DEAF-MUTE LANGUAGE ; MANUAL ALPHABET

509.2 MATHEMATICIANS

511.3 SYMBOLIC LOGIC PROBLEMS

512 ALGEBRA PROBLEMS

513 ARITHMETIC PROBLEMS

514 KNOTS ; LINKS ; BRAIDS

515 CALCULUS PROBLEMS

516.1 PLANE GEOMETRICAL FIGURES

516.2 SQUARES

516.3 TRIANGLES

516.4 CIRCLES

516.5 SOLID GEOMETRICAL FIGURES

516.6 CUBES

516.7 PYRAMIDS

516.8   SPHERES

516.9   CONES

517   TRIGONOMETRIC PROBLEMS

519.7   COMPUTER PROGRAMMING CHARTS ; FLOW CHARTS

519.8   DECISION CHARTS

521   TELESCOPES

523   NIGHT SKIES

523.1   CONSTELLATIONS

523.2   GALAXIES

523.25   MILKY WAY

523.27   NEBULAS

523.28   BLACK HOLES ; STARLESS AREAS

523.3   THE MOON

523.4   SOLAR SYSTEM

523.41   MERCURY

523.42   VENUS

523.43   MARS

523.431 DEIMOS ; PHOBOS ; MARTIAN MOONS

523.44   ASTEROIDS ; PLANETOIDS

523.45   JUPITER

523.451 CALLISTO ; EUROPA ; GANYMEDE ; IO ; JUPITERIAN
         MOONS

523.46   SATURN

523.47   URANUS

523.48   NEPTUNE

523.49   PLUTO

523.5   METEORS ; METEOR SHOWERS

523.6   COMETS

523.7   THE SUN

523.74   SUNSPOTS

523.75   SOLAR FLARES ; SOLAR CORONA

523.78   ECLIPSES

523.8   STARS

525   THE EARTH

529.3   CALENDARS

529.35   MAYAN CALENDARS

529.7   TIMEPIECES

529.71   OUTDOOR CLOCKS ; BIG BEN

529.72   SUNDIALS

529.725 HOURGLASSES

529.727 WATER CLOCKS

529.73   GRANDFATHER CLOCKS

529.74   MANTEL CLOCKS

529.75   ALARM CLOCKS

529.76   WATCHES ; WRIST WATCHES

531.1   WAVES

531.3   SHOCK WAVES

531.5   PROJECTILES ; TRAJECTORIES

532   FLUIDS

532.1   NOZZLES

532.2   WEIRS ; SPILLWAYS

532.3   PIPES ; DITCHES

532.4   TURBULENT FLUIDS

533.5   SUBMERGED BODIES

533.6   BUBBLES

533.7   OSMOSIS EXPERIMENTS

533.8   GASES

534   SOUND WAVES

535   LIGHT

535.1   PRISMS

535.2   MIRRORS

535.3   PHOSPHORESCENCE ; FLUORESCENCE ; LUMINESCENCE

535.4   HOLOGRAMS

535.5   LIGHT BEAMS

535.6   COLOR CHARTS

535.8   OPTICAL FIBERS

536.2   CONDUCTION CURRENTS

536.3   CONVECTION CURRENTS

536.4   BOILING WATER

536.5   ICE CUBES ; ICE CRYSTALS

537.2   GENERATORS

537.3   TURBINES

537.5   RADIOS

537.52 RADIO WAVES

535.6   TELEVISION SETS

538   MAGNETS

538.1   MAGNET EXPERIMENTS

538.4   MAGNETIC SUBSTANCES ; IRON FILINGS

538.7   GEOMAGNETISM

538.75 RADIATION BELTS ; VAN ALLEN BELT

538.77 AURORAS ; AURORA BOREALIS

539.1   ATOMS

539.15 ELECTRON PATTERNS

539.2   MOLECULES

539.3   NUCLEAR PARTICLES

539.4   X-RAYS

539.5   GEIGER COUNTERS

539.6   CLOUD CHAMBERS

540.1   ALCHEMISTS

540.9   CHEMISTS

541.2   MOLECULAR DIAGRAMS

541.3   FOAMS ; LATHERS ; FROTHS

541.4   FLAMES

542.1   CHEMISTRY LABORATORIES

542.2   CHEMICAL GLASSWARE ; TEST TUBES ; BEAKERS ;
        FLASKS

542.3   CHEMISTRY SCALES ; BALANCES

542.4   BUNSEN BURNERS

542.5   BLOWPIPES ; GLASS TUBING

542.6   FUNNELS ; FILTERS

542.7   TITRATION EQUIPMENT

542.8   COMPUTERS

551.36 LAKE ICE

551.38 RIVER ICE

551.41 CONTINENTS

551.42 ISLANDS

551.424 REEFS ; ATOLLS

551.43 MOUNTAINS ; HILLS

551.434 PLATEAUS ; MESAS

551.44 VALLEYS ; RAVINES ; CANYONS

551.447 CAVES ; CREVICES ; CHASMS

551.45 DELTAS

551.46 SEASHORES ; BEACHES

551.47 WAVES ; SURF

551.48 LAKES ; PONDS

551.481 RIVERS ; STREAMS ; CREEKS

551.484 WATERFALLS

551.489 FLOODS

551.49 WELLS ; SPRINGS

551.497 ARTESIAN WELLS

551.498 GEYSERS

551.5 WIND ; BREEZES

551.52 HURRICANES

551.54 TORNADOES ; CYCLONES

551.55 THUNDERSTORMS

551.56 SNOWSTORMS ; BLIZZARDS

551.57 DUST STORMS

551.61 RAINFALL ; RAIN

551.62 CLOUDS

551.622 CIRRUS CLOUDS

551.624 STRATUS CLOUDS

551.626 CUMULUS CLOUDS

551.628 NIMBUS CLOUDS

551.63 WEATHER VANES

551.64 BAROMETERS

551.65 THERMOMETERS

551.66	WEATHER SATELLITES
551.67	WEATHER BALLOONS
551.7	STRATIGRAPHIC CHARTS
551.75	GEOLOGIC ERAS
551.8	GEOLOGIC STRUCTURES
551.82	FAULTS
551.84	RIFTS
551.86	VEINS ; DIKES
552	ROCKS
552.1	IGNEOUS ROCKS ; LAVA
552.2	OBSIDIAN
552.3	BASALT
552.4	PLUTONIC ROCKS ; GRANITE
552.5	METAMORPHIC ROCKS ; SLATE
552.52	LIMESTONE
552.54	MARBLE
552.6	SEDIMENTARY ROCKS ; SANDSTONE
552.62	GYPSUM
553	MINES
553.1	ROCK FORMATIONS
553.2	COAL
553.24	PEAT
553.25	LIGNITE ; BROWN COAL
553.26	BITUMINOUS COAL
553.28	ANTHRACITE COAL
553.3	OIL WELLS
553.4	IRON MINES
553.5	COPPER MINES
553.6	GOLD MINES ; GOLD ORE
553.62	PLACER MINES
553.64	GOLD DUST
553.66	GOLD NUGGETS
553.7	TIN MINES
553.9	URANIUM MINES

554.2   QUARRIES

554.4   MARBLE QUARRIES

555.2   SAND

555.4   GRAVEL

556   GYPSUM MINES

557   GEMS ; PRECIOUS STONES

557.2   DIAMONDS

557.4   RUBIES

557.6   SAPPHIRES

557.8   EMERALDS

558   PEARL CULTURE ; PEARLS

558.2   PEARL DIVERS

559   SEMI-PRECIOUS STONES

559.2   JADE

559.4   TURQUOISE

559.6   AGATES

56   FOSSILS

561   FOSSIL PLANTS

562   PETRIFIED WOOD

563   FOSSIL PROTOZOA

564   FOSSIL MOLLUSKS

565   FOSSIL WORMS

566   FOSSIL INSECTS

567   FOSSIL FISH

568   DINOSAURS

569.1   FOSSIL BIRDS

569.5   FOSSIL ANIMALS

571   GENETIC CHARTS ; DNA STRUCTURES

572   HUMAN RACES

572.2   WHITE RACES ; CAUCASOIDS

572.4   BROWN RACES ; MONOGOLOIDS

572.6   BLACK RACES ; NEGROIDS

573   EVOLUTION CHARTS

573.3   PREHISTORIC MAN

573.4	DWARFS
573.5	PYGMIES
573.6	MIDGETS
573.8	GIANTS
573.9	PHYSICAL ANOMALIES ; FREAKS
574.1	CIRCULATORY SYSTEM
574.12	THE HEART
574.2	THE LUNGS
574.3	TEETH
574.4	ESOPHAGUS ; THE STOMACH
574.5	THE LIVER
574.6	INTERNAL ORGANS
574.62	THE PANCREAS
574.64	THE SPLEEN
574.7	SMALL INTESTINES
574.8	LARGE INTESTINES ; COLON ; ANUS
574.9	SEX ORGANS
574.92	MALE SEX ORGANS
574.93	THE PENIS
574.94	TESTICLES
574.95	FEMALE SEX ORGANS
574.96	VAGINA
574.97	THE UTERUS ; THE WOMB
574.98	OVARIES
574.99	HERMAPHRODITIC SEX ORGANS
575	ECOLOGICAL CHARTS
575.1	FOOD CHAINS
575.2	ANIMAL MIGRATIONS
575.3	ARTIC ENVIRONMENTS
575.4	TROPICAL ENVIRONMENTS
575.5	FRESH-WATER ENVIRONMENTS
575.6	SALT-WATER ENVIRONMENTS
575.65	ESTUARIES
575.7	FOREST ENVIRONMENTS ; WOODLANDS

575.8	GRASSLANDS ; MEADOWS ; PRAIRIES
575.9	TIMBERLINE ENVIRONMENTS ; TUNDRA
576	MICRO-ORGANISMS
576.1	MICROBES
576.6	RICKETSIAE
576.7	VIRUSES
576.8	FUNGUS
577	MICROSCOPES
577.1	ELECTRON MICROSCOPES
577.2	MICROTOMES
577.3	STAIN DIAGRAMS
577.4	PLANT TISSUE SLIDES
577.8	ANIMAL TISSUE SLIDES
578	STUFFED ANIMALS ; TAXIDERMY DISPLAYS
579	SKELETONS
58	THE PLANT KINGDOM
581.2	PLANT CIRCULATION SYSTEMS ; VEINS : PLANTS
581.3	STEMS ; LEAVES; FRONDS
581.4	ROOTS
581.5	POLLEN
581.6	BENEFICIAL PLANTS ; MEDICINAL PLANTS
581.65	EDIBLE PLANTS
581.7	POISONOUS PLANTS
581.8	ALLERGENIC PLANTS
581.9	WEEDS ; DELETERIOUS PLANTS ; PLANT PESTS
582	SEED-BEARING PLANTS
582.1	HERBACEOUS PLANTS
582.2	HERBACEOUS FLOWERING PLANTS ; SUCCULENTS
582.3	HERBACEOUS SHRUBS
582.4	TREES
582.5	SHRUBS
582.6	VINES
583	FLOWERING PLANTS
583.11	WATER-LILIES

583.12 MAGNOLIAS
583.13 CUSTARD APPLES
583.14 VIOLETS
583.15 PINKS
583.16 TEA PLANTS ; CAMELLIAS
583.17 MALLOWS
583.18 LINDEN TREES
583.19 SILK-COTTON TREES
583.21 FLAX
583.22 LIGNUM VITAE
583.23 AILANTHUS
583.24 MAHOGANY TREES
583.25 HOLLY
583.26 GRAPE VINES
583.27 CASHEW TREES
583.28 SUMAC
583.31 MIMOSA
583.32 PEA PLANTS
583.33 SENNA PLANTS
583.34 ROSES
583.35 SAXIFRAGE
583.36 WITCH-HAZEL PLANTS
583.41 MYRTLE TREES
583.42 BRAZIL-NUT TREES
583.43 POMEGRANATES
583.44 PASSIONFLOWER PLANTS
583.45 GOURD VINES
583.46 PAPAYA PLANTS
583.47 BEGONIA PLANTS
583.48 CACTUS PLANTS
583.49 CARROT PLANTS
583.51 HONEYSUCKLE PLANTS
583.52 VALERIAN PLANTS
583.53 CATALPA TREES

583.54 ASTERS
583.55 CRYSANTHEMUMS
583.56 SUNFLOWERS
583.57 BLUEBELLS
583.58 BELLFLOWER PLANTS
583.59 LOBELIA PLANTS
583.61 HEATH PLANTS
583.62 HUCKLEBERRY PLANTS
583.63 WINTERGREEN PLANTS
583.67 PRIMROSES
583.68 EBONY PLANTS
583.69 SAPODILLA PLANTS
583.71 MILKWEED PLANTS
583.72 OLIVE TREES
583.73 GENTIAN
583.74 PHLOX
583.75 BORAGE
583.76 FORGET-ME-NOT PLANTS
583.77 NIGHTSHADE PLANTS
583.78 MORNING-GLORY PLANTS
583.81 ACANTHUS
583.82 GLOXINIA
583.83 AFRICAN VIOLETS
583.84 SNAPDRAGON PLANTS
583.85 MINT PLANTS
583.86 VERVAIN PLANTS
583.87 PLANTAIN PLANTS
583.91 POKEWEED
583.92 BUCKWHEAT PLANTS
583.93 LAURELS
583.94 FOUR-O'CLOCK PLANTS
583.95 SANDALWOOD TREES
583.96 MULBERRY TREES
583.97 WALNUT TREES ; HICKORY TREES ; PECAN TREES

583.98 BEECH TREES ; OAK TREES ; BIRCH TREES

583.99 WILLOWS

584.1 ORCHIDS

584.21 GINGER PLANTS

584.22 ARROWROOT PLANTS

584.23 BANANA PLANTS

584.24 PINEAPPLE PLANTS ; BROMELIADS

584.25 IRIS PLANTS

584.26 AMARYLLIS PLANTS

584.27 YAMS

584.3 LILIES

584.4 TRILLIUMS

584.5 PALM TREES

584.6 PANDANA TREES

584.7 WATER PLANTS

584.8 SEDGES

584.9 GRASSES ; BAMBOO

584.91 MILLET

584.92 SUGAR CANE

584.93 MAIZE ; CORN ; INDIAN CORN

584.94 OATS

584.95 WHEAT

584.96 BARLEY

584.97 RYE GRASSES

584.98 RICE PLANTS

585 NAKED-SEED PLANTS ; GYMNOSPERMS

585.1 CONIFERS

585.2 CYPRESS TREES

585.3 PINE TREES

585.4 YEW TREES

585.5 CEDAR TREES

585.6 GINGKO TREES

586 SEEDLESS PLANTS ; CRYPTOGAMS

587 FERNS

588	MOSSES
589	FUNGI
589.3	ALGAE
589.8	BACTERIA
589.9	SPIROCHETES
59	ANIMALS
591.1	ANIMAL SKELETONS ; ANIMAL SKULLS
591.2	DISEASED ANIMALS
591.3	YOUNG ANIMALS ; ANIMAL BABIES
591.4	COMPARATIVE ANATOMY CHARTS
591.5	ANIMAL MIGRATIONS
591.6	BENEFICIAL ANIMALS
591.7	TAME ANIMALS
591.8	VERMIN ; ANIMAL PESTS
591.9	POISONOUS ANIMALS
592	PROTOZOA
592.1	MICRO-ORGANISMS
592.2	FORAMINIFERA
592.3	RADIOLARIA
592.4	SPONGES
592.5	CORALS
592.6	JELLYFISH
592.7	STARFISH
592.8	SAND DOLLARS
592.9	SEA URCHINS
593.1	SHELL FISH ; MOLLUSKS
593.2	OYSTERS
593.3	CLAMS
593.4	MUSSELS
593.5	SNAILS
593.6	WHELKS
593.7	OCTOPUSES
593.8	CUTTLEFISH
593.9	SQUID

594	BUGS
594.1	WORMS ; EARTHWORMS
594.2	SHRIMPS ; PRAWNS
594.3	WOOD LICE
594.4	SEA ONIONS
594.5	LOBSTERS ; CRAYFISH
594.6	CRABS
594.7	HERMIT CRABS
594.8	HORSESHOE CRABS
594.9	SEA SPIDERS
595	INSECTS
595.1	MITES ; TICKS
595.2	SCORPIONS ; SPIDERS
595.3	COCKROACHES
595.4	MANTISES ; PRAYING MANTIS
595.5	CRICKETS ; GRASSHOPPERS ; LOCUSTS
595.6	DRAGONFLIES
595.7	LICE
595.8	BEETLES
595.9	WEEVILS
596	FLIES ; HOUSE FLIES
596.1	FLEAS
596.2	MOTHS
596.3	HORSE FLIES ; DEER FLIES
596.4	MOSQUITOES
596.5	WASPS ; HORNETS
596.6	BUTTERFLIES
596.7	MOTHS
596.8	ANTS
596.9	BEES
597	FISHES
597.1	SHARKS
597.2	RAYS ; SKATES
597.3	STURGEONS

597.4   MORAYS

597.5   SEA HORSES ; FLYING FISH ; STICKLEBACKS

597.6   SALMON ; TROUT

597.7   BASSES ; PERCHES

597.8   SALAMANDERS ; NEWTS

597.9   FROGS ; TOADS

598.1   REPTILES

598.12 SNAKES

598.13 POISONOUS SNAKES ; RATTLESNAKES ; COBRAS

598.14 TURTLES

598.15 CROCODILES ; ALLIGATORS

598.16 LIZARDS

598.2   BIRDS

598.23 BIRDS' NESTS

598.24 BIRDS' EGGS ; AVIAN EGGS

598.25 BIRDS' CLAWS

598.26 FEATHERS

598.27 BIRD SKELETONS

598.3   WATER BIRDS ; WATERFOWL

598.31 CRANES

598.32 EGRETS ; HERON ; STORKS

598.33 PUFFINS ; SANDPIPERS ; PLOVERS

598.34 GULLS ; TERNS

598.35 DUCKS ; GEESE ; SWANS

598.36 ALBATROSSES ; PETRELS

598.37 PELICANS ; BOOBIES ; CORMORANTS

598.38 PENGUINS

598.39 LOONS ; GREBES

598.4   LAND BIRDS

598.41 OSTRICHES ; RHEAS

598.42 EMU ; KIWI ; CASSOWARIES

598.43 PRAIRIE CHICKENS ; GROUSE ; QUAIL

598.44 CHICKENS ; ROOSTERS ; HENS ; CHICKS

598.45 PEACOCKS ; PARTRIDGES ; PHEASANTS

598.46 TURKEYS
598.47 PARROTS ; PARAKEETS ; MACAWS
598.48 WOODPECKERS ; FLICKERS
598.49 ROADRUNNERS ; CUCKOOS
598.5   PERCHING BIRDS ; PASSERIFORMES
598.51 LARKS
598.52 SWALLOWS ; MARTINS
598.53 CHICKADEES ; TITMICE
598.54 WRENS ; HOUSE WRENS
598.56 CATBIRDS ; MOCKINGBIRDS
598.57 THRUSHES
598.58 ROBINS
598.59 WARBLERS
598.61 SHRIKES
598.62 STARLINGS
598.63 MAGPIES ; JAYS
598.64 BIRDS OF PARADISE
598.65 ENGLISH SPARROWS
598.66 BLACKBIRDS ; CROWS ; RAVENS
598.67 ORIOLES
598.68 TANAGERS
598.69 CARDINALS ; FINCHES
598.71 HUMMINGBIRDS
598.73 HORNBILLS
598.75 TOUCAN
598.75 KINGFISHERS
598.77 SWIFTS
598.8   BIRDS OF PREY
598.81 VULTURES
598.82 CONDORS
598.83 SECRETARY BIRDS
598.84 BUZZARDS ; KITES
598.85 EAGLES
598.86 OSPREYS ; SEA EAGLES

598.87 HAWKS
598.88 FALCONS
598.89 OWLS
599   MAMMALS
599.1   MONOTREMES
599.11 PLATYPUSES
599.15 ECHIDNAS
599.2   MARSUPIALS
599.22 KANGAROOS
599.23 KOALAS
599.24 BANDICOOTS
599.25 WALLABIES
599.26 WOMBATS
599.27 OPOSSUMS
599.3   RODENTS
599.31 HARES ; JACKRABBITS
599.32 RABBITS ; COTTONTAILS
599.33 BEAVERS
599.34 SQUIRRELS ; CHIPMUNKS
599.35 PRAIRIES DOGS ; GOPHERS
599.36 HAMSTERS ; GERBILS
599.37 MUSKRATS
599.38 RATS ; MICE
599.39 SHREWS ; VOLES ; MOLES
599.4   BATS
599.42 FLYING FOXES ; FRUIT BATS
599.44 VAMPIRE BATS
599.5   WHALES
599.52 KILLER WHALES ; ORCA ; GRAMPUS
599.53 HUMPBACK WHALES
599.54 DOLPHINS
599.55 PORPOISES
599.56 SPERM WHALES
599.57 SEA COWS ; DUGONG ; MANATEE

599.6   ELEPHANTS

599.61 ROCK HYRAXES ; CONIES

599.62 HORSES

599.63 DONKEYS ; ASSES

599.64 ZEBRAS

599.65 TAPIRS

599.66 RHINOCEROSES

599.67 HIPPOPOTAMUS

599.68 WILD BOARS ; WART HOGS ; PECCARIES

599.69 PIGS

599.7   RUMINANT ANIMALS

599.71 CARIBOU ; DEER

599.72 ELK ; REINDEER

599.73 GIRAFFES

599.74 GAZELLES ; ANTELOPE

599.75 BUFFALOES ; BISON

599.76 CATTLE ; COWS ; BULLS

599.77 SHEEP ; GOATS

599.78 CAMELS ; DROMEDARIES

599.79 LLAMAS ; ALPACAS ; VICUNAS

599.8   CARNIVORES

599.81 CIVETS ; MONGOOSES

599.82 HYENAS

599.83 CATS ; WILDCATS

599.84 LIONS ; TIGERS

599.85 DOGS ; JACKALS ; COYOTES

599.86 WOLVES

599.87 PANDAS ; RACCOONS

599.88 BEARS

599.89 SKUNKS

599.891 WEASELS

599.892 BADGERS

599.893 FERRETS

599.894 MINKS

599.895 OTTERS

599.896 FUR SEALS ; SEA LIONS

599.897 WALRUSES

599.898 ELEPHANT SEALS

599.9   PRIMATES

599.91   LEMURS ; TARSIERS

599.92   MARMOSETS

599.93   MONKEYS ; OLD WORLD MONKEYS

599.94   MACAQUES ; RHESUS MONKEYS

599.95   NEW WORLD MONKEYS

599.96   BABOONS ; MANDRILLS

599.97   GIBBONS

599.98   CHIMPANZEES

599.99   GORILLAS

604.2   DRAFTING EQUIPMENT

604.24   LETTERING CHARTS

604.25   BLUEPRINTS ; PHOTOSTATS

604.6   RECYCLING WASTE MATERIAL

604.7   HAZARDOUS MATERIAL HANDLING

607   INDUSTRIAL EXHIBITS

608   PATENT-OFFICE DRAWINGS

610.2   PHYSICIANS

610.4   NURSES

610.5   RED-CROSS NURSES

610.6   VISITING NURSES

610.7   SURGICAL NURSES

611   HUMAN ANATOMY ; GROSS ANATOMY

611.1   CARDIOVASCULAR SYSTEM

611.2   RESPIRATORY ORGANS

611.3   DIGESTIVE ORGANS

611.4   LYMPH GLANDS

611.5   GLANDULAR ORGANS

611.6   UROGENITAL ORGANS

611.62   MALE GENITAL ORGANS

611.64 FEMALE GENITAL ORGANS

611.7   HUMAN SKELETON

611.71 SPINAL COLUMN ; VERTEBRAE

611.72 RIB CAGE

611.73 HUMAN SKULLS

611.74 MUSCLES

611.75 FACE MUSCLES

611.76 ARM MUSCLES ; SHOULDER MUSCLES

611.77 ABDOMINAL MUSCLES

611.78 LEG MUSCLES ; HIP MUSCLES ; BUTTOCKS

611.79 HAIR ; NAILS

611.8   NERVOUS SYSTEM

611.9   HUMAN VISCERA ; VISCERAL CHARTS

612   PHYSIOLOGICAL CHARTS ; PHYSIOLOGICAL DIAGRAMS

612.1   BLOOD

612.11 RED CORPUSCLES

612.12 WHITE CORPUSCLES

612.15 BLOOD CLOTS

612.16 BLOOD PRESSURE INSTRUMENTS ; SPHYGMOMANOMETERS

612.2   LUNGS ; RESPIRATORY CHARTS

612.3   DIGESTIVE TRACT DIAGRAMS

612.4   METABOLISM DIAGRAMS

612.5   KIDNEY FUNCTIONS

612.6   ERECT PENISES

612.61 SEXUAL INTERCOURSE

612.62 EJACULATORY FUNCTIONS

612.63 SPERM DIAGRAMS

612.64 VAGINAL CANAL ; CLITORIS

612.65 PREGNANCY

612.66 HUMAN FETUSES ; FETAL GROWTH

612.67 CHILDBIRTH

612.68 CHILD DEVELOPMENT CHARTS

612.7   SKIN CARE ; PORES ; PERSPIRATION

612.8   NERVE FIBERS ; SYNAPSE

612.81 HUMAN BRAIN

612.812 BRAIN AREAS

612.82 SPINAL CORD

612.83 HUMAN EYES ; EYE FUNCTIONS

612.84 HUMAN EARS ; HEARING DIAGRAMS

612.85 OLFACTORY FUNCTIONS

613   HYGIENE CHARTS

613.1   ENVIRONMENTAL HAZARDS

613.2   WEIGHT-LOSING CHARTS

613.3   BEVERAGES

613.4   BATHING ; SHAMPOOING ; FACIAL MASSAGES

613.5   ARTIFICIAL ENVIRONMENTS ; SKINNER BOXES

613.6   SURVIVAL TECHNIQUES

613.7   PHYSICAL FITNESS ; EXERCISE DIAGRAMS

613.8   DRUG ADDICTION CHARTS

613.9   FAMILY PLANNING CHARTS ; SEX HYGIENE DIAGRAMS

613.95 CONTRACEPTIVES

614   EPIDEMICS ; EPIDEMICS CHARTS

614.4   DISEASE CARRIERS

614.42 FLIES

614.43 MOSQUITOES

614.44 LICE

614.45 FLEAS

614.46 SPIDERS

614.47 RATS

614.5   VACCINATION ; INOCULATION

614.6   ERUPTIVE DISEASES ; RASHES

614.61 SMALLPOX

614.62 SCARLET FEVER

614.63 MEASLES

614.64 GERMAN MEASLES

614.65 CHICKEN POX

614.66 ROCKY MOUNTAIN SPOTTED FEVER

614.7   DISEASE MANIFESTATIONS

614.72 LEPROSY

614.74 SYPHILIS

614.75 GENITAL HERPES

614.8   HUMAN CORPSES ; CADAVERS

614.82 EMBALMING ; CADAVER PRESERVATION ; MUMMIFICATION

615.1   PHARMACIES

615.2   BLOOD TRANSFUSIONS ; BLOOD BANKS

615.4   PSYCHATRIC DEVICES ; STRAIT JACKETS

615.6   BATHS ; HYDROTHERAPY EQUIPMENT

615.7   SURGERIES ; OPERATING ROOMS ; OPERATIONS

615.8   HEART-LUNG MACHINES

616   PATHOLOGY CHARTS

617   WOUNDS ; INJURIES

617.1   BURNS ; SCALDS

617.2   STAB WOUNDS

617.3   GUNSHOT WOUNDS

617.4   FRACTURES ; COMPOUND FRACTURES

617.5   CHOKING ; STRANGLING ; HANGING

618   DEFORMITIES

618.1   MIDGETS ; DWARFS

618.2   OBESITY

618.3   GIANTS

618.4   DEFORMED LIMBS

618.5   DEFORMED HANDS ; DEFORMED FEET

618.6   ELEPHANTIASIS

618.7   ANOREXIA PATIENTS ; HUMAN STARVATION

619   ANIMAL EXPERIMENTS ; VIVISECTION

620.9   ENGINEERS

621.1   STEAM ENGINES

621.2   BOILERS

621.3   STEAM PIPES

621.4   PRESSURE REGULATORS

622.1   DAMS ; WATER-POWER PROJECTS

622.2   WATERWHEELS

622.3 TURBINES ; ELECTRIC-POWER GENERATORS

622.4 PUMPS

622.5 ELECTRIC-POWER LINES

622.6 ATOMIC-POWER PLANTS

622.7 ELECTRIC-POWER STATIONS

622.8 ELECTRIC SUPPLY METERS ; ELECTRIC GAUGES

623   TOOLS

623.1 PLANING TOOLS ; MILLING TOOLS

623.2 SAWS ; CUTTING TOOLS

623.3 LATHES

623.4 PUNCHES ; PERFORATING TOOLS

623.5 EMERY WHEELS ; GRINDSTONES

623.6 HAMMERS ; POWER HAMMERS

623.7 WELDING EQUIPMENT ; SOLDERING EQUIPMENT

623.8 RIVETING EQUIPMENT

623.9 CLAMPS ; VISES

624.1 OPEN PIT MINES ; STRIP MINING

624.2 UNDERGROUND TUNNELS

624.3 UNDERGROUND BORING ; UNDERGROUND BLASTING

624.4 UNDERGROUND SHAFTS ; SHAFT SINKING

624.5 MINE BEAMS ; TUNNEL SUPPORTS

624.6 UNDERWATER MINING

624.7 MINER'S CAPS ; PORTABLE LAMPS

624.8 CONVEYOR BELTS ; SCRAPERS ; SHUTTLE CARS

624.9 MINE ELEVATORS ; MINE CAGES ; BUCKET SYSTEMS

625   MILITARY FORTIFICATION

625.1 FORTS ; FORTRESSES

625.2 MINE LAYERS ; MINES ; BLOCKADES

625.3 ORDNANCE

625.32 SIEGE GUNS

625.33 FIELD ARTILLERY ; CANNON ; MORTARS ; HOWITZERS

625.34 NAVAL ARTILLERY

625.35 SMALL ARMS

625.36 RIFLES ; MUSKETS ; CARBINES

625.37 REVOLVERS ; PISTOLS ; SIDE ARMS

625.38 AMMUNITION

625.39 PRE-FIREARM WEAPONRY

625.391 MACES

625.392 TOMAHAWKS

625.393 BOWS AND ARROWS

625.394 SPEARS

625.395 LANCES

625.396 SWORDS

625.397 DAGGERS

625.398 CATAPULTS

625.399 SHIELDS

625.4   MODERN WEAPONRY

625.41 ROCKET LAUNCHERS ; ROCKETS

625.42 HAND GRENADES ; TEAR-GAS GRENADES

625.43 INCENDIARY BOMBS ; SMOKE BOMBS

625.44 TORPEDOES

625.45 SURFACE-TO-AIR MISSILES

625.46 AIR-TO-AIR MISSILES

625.47 INTERCONTINENTAL BALLISTIC MISSILES

625.48 MISSILE SITES ; LAUNCHING PITS

625.5   MILITARY ROADS ; MILITARY HIGHWAYS

625.55 MILITARY BRIDGES

625.6   DOCKS ; HARBORS ; NAVAL BASES

625.7   MILITARY COMMUNICATIONS

625.71 HANDSET TELEPHONES

625.72 RADIOS ; TELETYPETWRITERS

625.73 FLAG SIGNALS ; SEMAPHORES

625.74 RADAR

625.8   MILITARY AIRCRAFT

625.81 BARRAGE BALLOONS

625.82 AIRSHIPS ; DIRIGIBLE BALLOONS

625.83 AIRPLANES

625.84 PROPELLER-DRIVEN AIRPLANES

625.85 JET PLANES

625.86 ROCKET PLANES

625.87 VERTICAL-LIFT PLANES

625.88 AIR-CUSHION VEHICLES ; HOVERCRAFT

625.89 RECONNAISSANCE AIRCRAFT ; SATELLITES ; SPACECRAFT

625.9 SHIPS ; NAVAL VESSELS

625.91 WIND-DRIVEN CRAFT ; SAILBOATS ; YACHTS

625.92 MERCHANT SHIPS ; CLIPPERS

625.93 WARSHIPS ; FRIGATES

625.94 FREIGHTERS ; TANKERS

625.95 BATTLESHIPS ; CRUISERS

625.96 AIRCRAFT CARRIERS

625.97 LANDING CRAFT ; TORPEDO BOATS

625.98 DESTROYERS ; PATROL BOATS

625.99 SUBMARINES

626   CONSTRUCTIONS ; CONSTRUCTION SITES

626.1 BUILDING CONSTRUCTIONS ; SKYSCRAPER
       CONSTRUCTIONS

626.2 BRIDGES

626.21 SUSPENSION BRIDGES

626.22 ROPE BRIDGES; HAMMOCK BRIDGES ; BASKET BRIDGES

626.23 WIRE-CABLE BRIDGES

626.24 TRESTLE BRIDGES

626.25 CANTILEVER BRIDGES

626.26 LONG-SPAN GIRDER BRIDGES

626.27 MOVABLE BRIDGES ; SWING BRIDGES ; VERTICAL-LIFT
       BRIDGES

626.28 ARCH BRIDGES

626.29 PONTOON BRIDGES

627.1 ROAD CONSTRUCTION ; TRACK LAYING

627.2 ROADBED PREPARATION ; EXCAVATION

627.3 ROAD GRADING

627.4 RAILROAD SIGNALS ; RAILROAD SWITCHES

627.5 CABLE RAILWAYS ; CABLE CARS

627.6   ELEVATED RAILWAYS

627.7   INCLINED RAILWAYS ; FUNICULAR RAILROADS

627.8   ROADSIDE BEAUTIFICATION

627.9   ROADSIDE LITTER ; BILLBOARDS

628.1   DAMS ; DAM SITES

628.2   EARTHWORK DAMS ; LEVEES

628.3   SEAWALLS

628.4   DRAINAGE DITCHES

628.5   IRRIGATION CANALS ; IRRIGATION DEVICES ;
           SPRINKLERS

628.6   PORT FACILITIES ; CARGO-HANDLING EQUIPMENT ;
           CRANES

628.7   LAND EROSION ; GULLIES

628.8   LAND RECLAMATION PROJECTS

628.9   UNDERWATER SALVAGE ; UNDERWATER TREASURE
           HUNTING

629.1   NAVIGATION AIDS ; LIGHTHOUSES ; BUOYS

629.2   RADAR PLATFORMS ; DRILLING PLATFORMS

629.3   SEWAGE DISPOSAL PLANTS ; SEWAGE DISPOSAL
           OPERATIONS

629.45 SEWER LINES ; STORM SEWERS

629.4   WATER MAINS ; SUBSURFACE WATER PIPES

629.5   WATER-SUPPLY RESERVOIRS

629.6   SALINE WATER CONVERSION PLANTS

629.7   SNOW REMOVAL ; STREET CLEANING

629.8   WATER POLLUTION ; INDUSTRIAL WASTE POLLUTION

629.9   CITY DUMPS ; REFUSE DISPOSAL

631.2   AGRICULTURAL STRUCTURES

631.21 FARMHOUSES

631.22 BARNS

631.23 GRANARIES ; SILOS ; GRAIN ELEVATORS

631.25 MACHINE SHEDS ; EQUIPMENT SHEDS

631.26 GREENHOUSES ; COLD FRAMES ; HOTBEDS

631.27 ROADS ; BRIDGES ; DAMS

631.3 SOIL-WORKING TOOLS

631.31 PLOWS

631.32 HARROWS

631.33 HOES ; SCRAPERS ; WEEDERS ; RAKES

631.34 SEEDERS ; PLANTERS ; FERTILIZER SPREADERS

631.35 MOWERS ; REAPERS ; COMBINES

631.36 THRESHERS ; BALERS

631.37 TRACTORS

631.38 HORSE-DRAWN EQUIPMENT ; ANIMAL-DRAWN PLOWS

631.39 ANIMAL-DRAWN WAGONS ; HORSES AND BUGGIES

631.4 SOILS

631.41 MULCH TILLAGE

631.42 COVER CROPS

631.43 CONTOUR PLOWING

631.44 SOIL EROSION DAMS

631.45 STRIP CROPPING

631.46 LAND USE SURVEYS

631.47 SOIL RENEWAL

631.5 CULTIVATION ; HARVESTING

631.51 SEEDS

631.52 BULBS ; TUBERS

631.53 SUCKERS ; RUNNERS

631.54 PLANT CUTTINGS

631.55 GRAFTING ; PRUNING

631.56 THRESHING

631.57 HUSKING

631.58 WINNOWING

631.61 CLEARING

631.62 DRAINAGE DITCHES

631.63 REVEGETATION ; SURFACE MINE RECLAMATION

631.66 IRRIGATION DITCHES

631.67 WATER CONSERVATION

631.68 DRIP-METHOD IRRIGATION

631.8 FERTILIZERS

631.82 COMPOST HEAPS

631.83 MANURE PILES

632   PLANT DISEASES ; PLANT PESTS

632.1   PLANT INJURIES ; HAILSTONE DAMAGE

632.2   LIGHTNING DAMAGE

632.3   WINDSTORM DAMAGE

632.4   DROUTH DAMAGE ; FLOOD DAMAGE

632.5   RUST ; SMUT ; MILDEW

632.6   WEEDS

632.7   ANIMAL PESTS ; RABBIT DAMAGE

632.8   INSECT PESTS ; PLANT PARASITES

632.9   PEST CONTROL ; AIRCRAFT FIELD SPRAYING

633   FIELD CROPS

633.1   CEREAL GRAIN CULTIVATION

633.11 WHEAT ; WHEAT FIELDS

633.12 BUCKWHEAT

633.13 OATS

633.14 RYE

633.15 CORN ; MAIZE ; CORN FIELDS

633.16 BARLEY

633.17 MILLET ; SORGHUM ; KAFIR CORN

633.18 RICE ; RICE PLANTING

633.19 RICE FIELDS ; RICE PADDIES

633.2   FORAGE CROPS ; HAY

633.21 BLUEGRASSES

633.22 ORCHARD GRASS

633.23 REDTOP ; BENT GRASSES

633.24 TIMOTHY GRASS

633.25 CEREAL GRASSES ; CORNSTALKS

633.26 STRAW

633.3   LEGUME CROPS

633.31 ALFALFA

633.32 CLOVER

633.33 COWPEAS

633.34 SOYBEANS

633.35 VETCHES

633.36 LUPINES

633.37 PEANUTS

633.38 FIELD PEAS

633.4 ROOT CROPS

633.41 BEETS

633.42 TURNIPS ; RUTABAGAS

633.44 CARROTS

633.45 PARSNIPS

633.46 POTATOES

633.47 SWEET POTATOES

633.48 JERUSALEM ARTICHOKES

633.5 FIBER CROPS

633.51 COTTON

633.52 FLAX

633.55 JUTE

633.56 HEMP

633.57 PINEAPPLE FIBERS

633.58 ESPARTO GRASS ; COIR ; COCONUT FIBER

633.59 BAMBOO

633.6 SUGAR PLANTS

633.61 SUGAR CANE

633.62 SWEET SORGHUM ; SORGO

633.63 SUGAR BEETS

633.64 SUGAR MAPLES

633.65 ARROWROOT

633.66 SAGO PALMS

633.67 CASSAVA ; MANIOC ; TROPICAL YAMS

633.7 ALKALOIDAL CROPS

633.71 TOBACCO

633.72 TEA

633.73 COFFEE

633.74 CACAO ; COCOA TREES

633.75 POPPIES

633.76 COLA

633.77 MATE ; PARAGUAY TEA

633.78 CHICORY

633.79 MARIHUANA

633.8 SPICE CROPS

633.81 MINT

633.82 VANILLA

633.83 HOPS

633.84 SASSAFRAS

633.85 CLOVES

633.86 NUTMEG ; MACE

633.87 OILSEED PLANTS

633.88 MUSTARD

633.89 CHILI PEPPERS ; PEPPER VINES

633.9 INDUSTRIAL CROPS

633.91 RUBBER

633.95 OIL PALMS

633.97 INSECTICIDE PLANTS

634 ORCHARDS

634.1 APPLES

634.2 PEARS

634.3 DRUPACEOUS FRUITS

634.32 APRICOTS

634.34 PLUMS

634.36 CHERRIES

634.38 PEACHES ; NECTARINES

634.4 CITRUS FRUITS

634.41 ORANGES

634.42 GRAPEFRUIT

634.43 LEMONS

634.44 LIMES

634.45 KUMQUATS

634.46 MORACEOUS FRUITS ; FIGS

634.47 MULBERRIES ; BREADFRUIT

634.48 CHERIMOYA ; CUSTARD APPLES

634.49 GUAVAS

634.5 NUTS ; NUT FRUITS

634.51 WALNUTS

634.52 PECANS ; HICKORY NUTS

634.53 CHESTNUTS

634.54 FILBERTS ; HAZELNUTS

634.55 ALMONDS

634.56 CASHEWS ; CASHEW NUTS

634.57 PISTACHIOS

634.58 BRAZIL NUTS

634.6 TROPICAL FRUITS

634.61 COCONUTS

634.62 DATES

634.63 OLIVES

634.64 POMEGRANATES

634.65 PAPAYAS

634.66 AVOCADOS ; ALLIGATOR PEARS

634.67 MANGOSTEENS

634.7 BERRIES

634.71 RASPBERRIES ; BLACKBERRIES

634.72 BLUEBERRIES ; HUCKLEBERRIES

634.73 LOGANBERRIES ; BOYSENBERRIES ; DEWBERRIES

634.74 CURRANTS ; GOOSEBERRIES

634.75 STRAWBERRIES

634.76 CRANBERRIES

634.77 BANANAS

634.78 PINEAPPLES

634.8 GRAPES ; VITICULTURE

634.82 GRAPE VINES ; VINEYARDS

634.84 GRAPE DISEASES ; GRAPE PESTS

634.86 GRAPE CULTIVATION

634.88 GRAPE HARVESTING ; GRAPE PICKING

634.9   FORESTS ; SILVICULTURE

634.91 OAKS

634.92 MAPLES

634.93 POPLARS ; BEECHES

634.94 BIRCHES

634.95 EVERGREEN FORESTS

634.96 PINES ; SPRUCE

634.97 CEDARS ; CYPRESS

634.98 FIRS ; HEMLOCK

634.99 SEQUOIA ; REDWOODS

635   GARDENS

635.1   VEGETABLE GARDENS

635.2   SALAD GARDENS ; GARDEN GREENS

635.21 ASPARAGUS

635.22 SPINACH

635.23 CABBAGE ; BRUSSELS SPROUTS

635.24 BROCCOLI ; CAULIFLOWER

635.25 DANDELIONS ; CHICORY

635.26 LETTUCE

635.27 CELERY

635.28 RHUBARB

635.29 ARTICHOKES

635.31 MELONS ; WATERMELONS ; CANTELOUPE ; HONEYDEW

635.32 SQUASHES ; PUMPKINS

635.33 CUCUMBERS

635.34 TOMATOES

635.35 PEPPERS ; GREEN PEPPERS

635.36 EGGPLANTS ; OKRA

635.37 BEANS ; STRING BEANS

635.38 PEAS ; LENTILS

635.39 CORN ; SWEET CORN

635.4   HERB GARDENS

635.5   MUSHROOM CULTIVATION ; MUSHROOM CAVES ; TRUFFLES

635.6   FLOWER GARDENS ; ROCK GARDENS

635.7 WINDOW-BOX GARDENS

635.8 HOUSEPLANTS

635.9 HYDROPONIC GARDENING ; GREENHOUSE GARDENS

636   FARM ANIMALS

636.1 HORSES ; STALLIONS ; MARES ; EQUINES

636.11 ARABIAN HORSES

636.12 RACEHORSES ; TROTTERS

636.13 CARRIAGE HORSES

636.14 DRAFT HORSES ; CLYDESDALE HORSES ; PERCHERON
       HORSES

636.15 PONIES ; SHETLAND PONIES

636.16 DONKEYS

636.17 MULES

636.18 ZEBRAS

636.2 RUMINANTS ; COWS ; BULLS ; CATTLE

636.21 SHORTHORN CATTLE ; HEREFORD CATTLE

636.22 ABERDEEN CATTLE

636.23 GUERNSEY CATTLE

636.24 LONGHORN CATTLE

636.25 BEEF CATTLE

636.26 MILK CATTLE ; MILK COWS

636.27 WATER BUFFALOES

636.28 DEER ; ELK ; CARIBOU ; REINDEER

636.29 ALPACAS ; LLAMAS ; VICUNAS

636.3 SHEEP ; GOATS

636.4 SWINE ; PIGS

636.5 POULTRY

636.51 CHICKENS ; ROOSTERS ; HENS

636.52 GUINEA FOWL

636.53 PHEASANTS ; TURKEYS

636.54 PEACOCKS ; PEAHENS ; PEACHICKS

636.55 PIGEONS ; HOMING PIGEONS ; DOVES

636.56 DUCKS

636.57 GEESE

636.58 SWANS

636.59 CAGED BIRDS

636.591 CANARIES

636.592 FINCHES

636.593 BUDGERIGARS

636.594 PARROTS

636.595 MACAWS

636.596 COCKATOOS

636.597 MYNAHS

636.598 TOUCANS

636.599 HAWKS ; FALCONS

636.7 DOGS

636.71 NONSPORTING DOGS ; POODLES

636.72 WORKING DOGS ; BOXERS ; DOBERMAN PINSCHERS

636.73 SIBERIAN HUSKIES

636.74 COLLIES ; SHEEPDOGS

636.75 SPORTING DOGS ; HOUNDS

636.76 TERRIERS

636.77 SPANIELS

636.78 TOY DOGS ; MINIATURE DOGS ; TOY POODLES

636.79 CHIHUAHUA ; BRUSSELS GRIFFON

636.8 CATS

636.9 WILD-ANIMAL PETS

637 DAIRIES ; MILK PRODUCTION

637.1 DAIRY BARNS

637.2 MILKING MACHINES

637.3 MILK SEPARATORS ; CREAM ; SKIM MILK

637.4 BUTTER CHURNS ; BUTTER PRODUCTION

637.5 CHEESE PRODUCTION

637.6 WHOLE MILK ; DRIED MILK ; CONDENSED MILK

637.7 FROZEN DESSERTS ; ICE CREAM ; SHERBET

637.8 EGG PRODUCTION

637.9 EGGS ; DRIED EGGS

638 INSECT CULTURE

638.1 BEE HIVES ; APICULTURES

638.2 QUEEN BEES ; DRONES

638.3 BEE DANCES ; NECTAR GATHERING

638.4 HONEYCOMBS ; BEE LARVAE

638.5 SILKWORMS

638.6 RESIN-PRODUCING INSECTS ; LAC INSECTS

638.7 EARTHWORM CULTURE

638.8 ANT FARMS

638.9 LADYBUGS ; MANTISES

639   HUNTING

639.1 TRAPPING ; DEER HUNTING ; DEER HUNTERS

639.2 DUCK HUNTING

639.3 FISHING VESSELS ; OYSTER CULTURE

639.4 FISHING NETS ; FISHING WEIRS ; LOBSTER POTS

639.5 SPORT FISHING

639.6 FLYCASTING ; FISHING POLES

639.7 FISH CULTURE ; AQUARIUMS

639.8 WHALING VESSELS ; WHALE HUNTING ; WHALERS

639.9 FROG SPEARING ; SNAKE HUNTING ; SNAKE CULTURE

641.2 BEVERAGES

641.21 RED WINE

641.22 WHITE WINE ; SPARKLING WINE

641.23 BEER ; ALE

641.24 WHISKEY ; BRANDY

641.25 VODKA ; GIN ; TEQUILA

641.26 MIXED DRINKS ; COCKTAILS

641.27 MINT JULEPS

641.28 CRUSHED-ICE DRINKS ; FROZEN COCKTAILS

641.3 FOODS

641.31 CEREALS

641.32 SUGAR ; SYRUP ; GAME

641.33 SPICES ; HERBS ; SALT ; PEPPER

641.34 FRUITS ; FRUIT BOWLS

641.35 NUTS ; NUTMEATS

641.36 MEATS

641.37 CHEESES ; BUTTER ; MILK

641.38 SEAFOOD ; OYSTERS ; CLAMS ; LOBSTERS

641.39 GAME ; PHEASANT ; VENISON

641.4 COOKING

641.41 FOOD PREPARATION ; WASHING VEGETABLES

641.42 CANNING

641.43 DEHYDRATING FOODS ; DRYING FOODSTUFFS

641.44 DEEP FREEZING ; COLD STORAGE

641.45 PICKLING

641.46 SMOKING FOODSTUFFS ; SMOKEHOUSES

641.47 SAUTEEING ; FRYING

641.48 ROASTING ; OVENS ; STOVES

641.49 MICROWAVE OVENS

641.5 OUTDOOR COOKERY ; CAMPFIRES ; BARBECUES

641.6 MEAL INGREDIENTS

641.71 APPETIZERS

641.72 SOUPS

641.73 SOUFFLES

641.74 PASTA DISHES ; SPAGHETTI ; PIZZAS

641.75 BEVERAGES

641.751 TABLE WATER ; MINERAL WATER ; SELTZER WATER

641.752 SOFT DRINKS ; COLA DRINKS

641.753 COFFEE BREWING ; COFFEE-MAKING MACHINES

641.754 TEA BREWING ; TEAPOTS ; STRAINERS ; TEA BAGS

641.755 COCOA ; HOT CHOCOLATE ; CHOCOLATE MILK

641.756 HERB TEAS ; TISANES

641.757 APPERITIF ; SHERRIES ; COCKTAILS

641.758 TABLE WINES

641.759 SPARKLING WINES ; CHAMPAGNES

641.76 MEAT PIES

641.77 STEWS

641.78 SALADS

641.79 SANDWICHES

641.81 ICE CREAM ; ICE CREAM SUNDAES

641.82 SHERBETS ; SORBETS

641.83 PIES ; TARTS

641.84 CAKES

641.85 COOKIES ; BISCUITS

641.86 ECLAIRS ; CREAM PUFFS

641.87 CAKES

641.88 BREAD MAKING ; KNEADING DOUGH

641.89 ROLLS ; BREADS

642   MEALS ; TABLE SERVICE

642.1 FAMILY MEALS

642.2 TV DINNERS

642.3 PICNICS

642.4 BANQUETS

642.5 RESTAURANTS ; DINING ROOMS

642.6 TABLE SETTINGS

642.7 MEAT CARVING

642.8 TABLE FURNISHINGS ; TABLEWARE

642.9 TABLE DECORATIONS ; CENTERPIECES

643   HOUSES

643.1 HOUSE CONSTRUCTION

643.2 HOUSE SALE ; HOUSE RENTALS

643.3 HOUSEHOLD SECURITY ; HOUSEHOLD BURGLAR ALARMS

643.4 FIRE ALARMS ; SMOKE DETECTORS

643.5 MOBILE HOMES

643.6 PREFABRICATED HOUSES

643.7 VACATION HOUSES

643.8 CONDOMINIUMS

643.9 APARTMENTS

644   HOUSEHOLD FURNISHINGS ; HOUSEHOLD EQUIPMENT

644.1 KITCHENS ; KITCHEN EQUIPMENT

644.2 KITCHEN LINEN

644.3 DINING AREAS ; BREAKFAST NOOKS

644.4 BATHROOMS ; BATHROOM FIXTURES

644.5 BEDROOMS ; BEDSTEADS ; MATTRESSES
644.6 BLANKETS ; BEDDING ; PILLOWS
644.7 LIVING ROOMS
644.8 FAMILY ROOMS ; DENS
644.9 PATIOS ; PORCHES ; VERANDAS
645.1 RUGS ; CARPETS
645.2 LINOLEUM ; TILES
645.3 WALLPAPER ; PANELING
645.4 DRAPERIES ; WINDOW BLINDS ; VENETIAN BLINDS
645.5 SLIPCOVERS ; UPHOLSTERY
645.6 CHAIRS ; SOFAS
645.7 LIGHTING FIXTURES ; LAMPS
645.8 OUTDOOR FURNISHINGS
645.9 PORCH SWINGS
646   SEWING EQUIPMENT ; NEEDLES
646.1 SEWING MACHINES
646.2 FABRICS
646.3 THREAD ; YARN
646.4 KNITTING NEEDLES ; CROCHET HOOKS
646.5 SCISSORS ; SHEARS
646.6 DARNING ; CLOTHES MENDING
646.7 BUTTONS ; HOOKS AND EYES
646.8 STITCHES ; SEAMS ; PLEATS
646.9 PATTERNS
647   INSTITUTIONAL HOUSEKEEPING
647.1 MAIDS ; BUTLERS ; MENSERVANTS
647.2 PUBLIC HOUSEHOLD EMPLOYEES ; BELLHOPS ; DESK
       CLERKS
647.3 WAITERS ; WAITRESSES
647.4 HOTEL LOBBIES ; HOTEL REGISTRATION AREAS ; MOTEL
       OFFICES
647.5 BOARDING HOUSES ; BOARDING HOUSE DINING ROOMS
647.6 NURSING HOME FACILITIES
647.7 CAFETERIAS

647.8 YOUTH CAMPS ; HOSTELRIES

647.9 TRAILER CAMPS ; CAMPSITES ; TENT CITIES

648   HOUSEKEEPING ACTIVITIES

648.1 LAUNDERING ; LAUNDRY SOAPS ; DETERGENTS

648.2 SWEEPING FLOORS ; BROOMS

648.3 MOPPING FLOORS ; MOPS

648.4 IRONING CLOTHES

648.5 VACUUM CLEANERS

648.6 PAINTING ; REFINISHING FURNITURE

648.7 DISHWASHING

648.8 FLYSWATTERS ; MOUSETRAPS

648.9 STORAGE AREAS ; CLOSETS ; ATTICS

649   CHILD REARING

649.1 BABY CARE ; INFANT CARE

649.2 PRESCHOOL CHILDREN

649.3 SCHOOL CHILDREN

649.4 ADOLESCENTS ; BOYS ; GIRLS

649.5 FEEDING CHILDREN

649.6 NURSING SICK CHILDREN ; HOME NURSING

649.7 TOYS ; GAMES

649.8 EXERCISE ; SPORTS

649.9 STORYTELLING

651   OFFICES ; BUSINESS OFFICES

651.1 OFFICE FURNITURE ; DESKS

651.2 TYPEWRITERS

651.3 WORD PROCESSORS ; COMPUTERS

651.4 COPYING EQUIPMENT

651.5 FILING CABINETS

651.6 STORAGE CABINETS

651.7 FILE FOLDERS ; FILING BOXES

651.8 PENCILS ; PENS

651.9 INKWELLS ; INK BOTTLES

652   OFFICE PERSONNEL

652.1 EXECUTIVES ; BUSINESS MEN

652.2 CLERKS ; COPYISTS

652.3 COMPUTER OPERATORS

652.4 OFFICE BOYS ; PAGES

652.5 SECRETARIES

652.6 SWITCHBOARD OPERATORS ; RECEPTIONISTS

652.7 JANITORS ; CLEANING STAFF

652.8 WINDOW WASHERS

652.9 GUARDS ; SECURITY PERSONNEL

653 DATA PROCESSING EQUIPMENT

653.1 MAINFRAME COMPUTERS

653.2 MINICOMPUTERS ; COMPUTER DISPLAY EQUIPMENT

653.3 PRINTERS

653.4 COMPUTER ROOMS

653.5 COMPUTER FORMS ; CONTINUOUS PAPER FORMS

653.6 DICTATION MACHINES ; RECORDING DEVICES

653.7 TELETYPE MACHINES

653.8 CLOSED-CIRCUIT TELEVISION DISPLAYS

652.9 TIME CLOCKS

653 SHORTHAND EXAMPLES

654 EQUIPMENT REPAIR

654.1 AUTOMOBILE MECHANICS

654.2 AUTOMOBILE PARTS

654.5 TIRE CHANGING

654.7 REPAIR PITS

657 ACCOUNTING MACHINES ; ADDING MACHINES

657.5 LEDGERS ; ACCOUNTING BOOKS

658 MONEY ; COINS

659 ADVERTISING METHODS

659.1 TELEVISION COMMERCIALS

659.2 NEWSPAPER ADS ; PERIODICAL ADS

659.3 ADVERTISING ART DEPARTMENTS

659.4 ADVERTISING PHOTOGRAPHY

659.5 CAR CARDS

659.6 POSTERS

659.7   WINDOW DRESSING
659.8   COUNTER DISPLAYS
659.9   WALL DISPLAYS
66   CHEMICAL ENGINEERING EQUIPMENT
661   CRUSHING MACHINES ; GRINDING MACHINES
662   FIREWORKS ; EXPLOSIVES
663   WINE VATS
664   BREWERIES
665   BAKERIES
666   SUGAR REFINERIES
667   OIL PRESSES
668   OIL REFINERIES ; OIL TANKS
669   CERAMIC MANUFACTURING ; POTTERS WHEELS
671   FOUNDRIES
672   STEEL MILLS
673   MOLTEN STEEL BUCKETS ; STEEL-MAKING FURNACES
674   TEXTILE MILLS
675   MECHANICAL LOOMS
676   SAWMILLS
677   GLASS MANUFACTURE ; MOLTEN GLASS
677.5   GLASS BLOWING
678   AUTOMOBILE TIRE MANUFACTURING
679   CIGAR MAKING ; CIGARETTE MANUFACTURING
68   PRECISION INSTRUMENTS
681   CLOCKWORK
682   TESTING MACHINES
683   LENS GRINDING
684   PHOTOMETERS
685   POLARIMETERS
686   PRINTING PRESSES ; LINOTYPE MACHINES
687   DRESSMAKING MACHINES ; GARMENT CUTTING
688   FOOTWEAR MANUFACTURING ; COBBLERS ; SHOE REPAIRMEN
689   BOOKBINDERS
691   BUILDING MATERIALS

691.2 TIMBER

691.3 STONE ; STONE CUTTING

691.4 CONCRETE BLOCKS ; CINDER BLOCKS

691.5 BRICKS

691.6 GLASS

691.7 STEEL BEAMS

692   BLUEPRINTS ; HOUSE PLANS ; BUILDING LAYOUT

692.3 DETAIL DRAWINGS

693.2 STONE LAYING

693.4 BRICKLAYING

693.6 PLASTERING

694   HOUSE BUILDING

694.1 FOUNDATIONS

694.2 SIDINGS

694.3 FLOORING

694.4 PARTITION FRAMES

694.5 BALCONY CONSTRUCTION

694.6 STAIRWAY CONSTRUCTION

694.7 SHELF MAKING

694.8 MOLDINGS

694.9 PANELS

695   ROOFING

696   PLUMBING

697   HEATING ; VENTILATION ; FURNACES ; AIR
       CONDITIONERS

697.5 FIREPLACES

697.7 WOOD-BURNING STOVES

698   DETAIL FINISHING

698.1 PAINTING ; HOUSE PAINTS

698.2 BRUSHES ; ROLLERS

698.3 PAINT MIXING

698.4 CALCIMINING ; WHITEWASHING

698.5 DOOR HANGING

698.6 WINDOW INSTALLATION

698.7 RUG LAYING

698.8 LAYING TILES

698.9 PAPERHANGING

7   THE ARTS

701   PRIMITIVE ART ; PREHISTORIC ART

702   PALEOLITHIC ART ; ROCK ART

703   BYZANTINE ART

704   ROMANESQUE ART

705   GOTHIC ART

706   RENAISSANCE ART

707   BAROQUE ART

708   VICTORIAN ART

709   MODERN ART

711   CITY PLANNING

711.1 BUSINESS DISTRICTS ; SHOPPING CENTERS

711.2 INDUSTRIAL PARKS

711.3 RECREATIONAL AREAS ; PARKS ; PLAYGROUNDS

711.4 PERFORMING ARTS CENTERS ; THEATER
       DISTRICTS

711.5 COMMUNITY CENTERS ; LIBRARIES ; MUSEUMS

711.6 URBAN RESIDENTIAL AREAS

711.7 SUBURBAN RESIDENTIAL AREAS

711.8 RURAL RESIDENTIAL AREAS

711.9 URBAN RENEWAL AREAS

712   TRANSPORTATION FACILITIES

712.1 CITY BUSES

712.2 BICYCLE PATHS ; BICYCLES

712.3 PARKING AREAS

712.4 PEDESTRIAN CROSSINGS ; WALKWAYS

712.5 RAILROAD STATIONS

712.6 BUS STATIONS

712.7 SEAPORTS ; DOCKS ; MARINAS

712.8 AIRPORTS ; RUNWAYS

712.9 HELIPORTS

713   COMMONS ; BUSINESS DISTRICT PARKS

713.1   FAIRGROUNDS

713.2   AMUSEMENT PARKS

713.3   BOTANICAL GARDENS

713.4   ZOOLOGICAL GARDENS ; ZOOS

713.5   FRONT YARDS

713.6   BACKYARDS

713.7   HOME GARDENS

713.8   COUNTRY CLUBS

713.9   INDUSTRIAL PLANTS

714   FREEWAYS ; PARKWAYS

715.2   ARTIFICIAL POOLS

715.4   NATURAL POOLS ; LAKES

715.6   FOUNTAINS

715.8   CASCADES

716.2   TOPIARY WORK

716.4   SHADE TREES

716.6   SHRUBBERY

716.8   VINES

717   GROUND COVER

717.2   FLOWER GARDENS

717.4   PENTHOUSE GARDENS ; ROOFTOP GARDENS

717.6   ESTATE GARDENS ; CASTLE GARDENS

717.8   EMPTY LOTS ; URBAN LITTER

718.1   CEMETERIES ; MEMORIAL PARKS ; GRAVEYARDS

718.2   TOMBS ; MAUSOLEUMS

718.3   GRAVESTONES ; HEADSTONES

718.4   NATURAL MONUMENTS ; CLIFF STONE CARVINGS

718.5   WILDLIFE PRESERVES

718.6   WATER-SUPPLY RESERVOIRS

718.7   RIVERFRONT PARKS

718.8   FOREST AREAS

718.9   RECLAIMED LAND

719   URBAN STRUCTURAL FEATURES

719.1 MONUMENTS

719.2 STAIRWAYS

719.3 TERRACES

719.4 FENCES ; STONE WALLS

719.5 RUINS ; PRESERVED ARCHITECTURAL FEATURES

719.6 GATES

719.7 MEMORIAL PLAQUES

719.8 MONOLITHS ; OBELISKS

719.9 MEMORIAL STATUARY ; STATUES ; EQUESTRIAN
       STATUES

72   ARCHITECTURAL DRAWINGS ; ARCHITECTURAL
       RENDERINGS

721   STRUCTURAL ELEMENTS

721.2 FOUNDATIONS

721.3 WALLS

721.4 PIERS ; ABUTMENTS

721.5 COLUMNS ; POSTS ; PEDESTALS

721.6 ROOFS ; GABLES

721.7 ARCHES ; VAULTS

721.8 DOMES ; CUPOLAS

721.9 NICHES

722.1 PORCHES ; VERANDAS

722.2 BALCONIES

722.3 DECKS ; PATIOS

722.4 DOORS ; ENTRANCES

722.5 WINDOWS ; BAY WINDOWS

722.6 FANLIGHTS

722.7 RAMPS ; STAIRCASES

722.8 ESCALATORS ; OUTDOOR ELEVATORS

722.9 FLOORS ; BALUSTRADES

723   ANCIENT ARCHITECTURE ; ORIENTAL
       ARCHITECTURE

723.1 CHINESE ARCHITECTURE

723.2 JAPANESE ARCHITECTURE

723.3   KOREAN ARCHITECTURE

723.42 JUDEAN ARCHITECTURE

723.44 PERSIAN ARCHITECTURE

723.46 MESOPOTAMIAN ARCHITECTURE

723.5   EGYPTIAN ARCHITECTURE

723.6   ETRUSCAN ARCHITECTURE ; AEGEAN
         ARCHITECTURE

723.7   ROMAN ARCHITECTURE

723.8   GREEK ARCHITECTURE

723.92 BUDDHIST ARCHITECTURE

723.94 HINDU ARCHITECTURE

723.96 AZTEC ARCHITECTURE ; MAYAN ARCHITECTURE

724   MEDIEVAL ARCHITECTURE

724.2   EARLY CHRISTIAN ARCHITECTURE

724.3   BYZANTINE ARCHITECTURE

724.4   MOORISH ARCHITECTURE

724.5   ROMANESQUE ARCHITECTURE ; NORMAN
         ARCHITECTURE

724.6   GOTHIC ARCHITECTURE

725   MODERN ARCHITECTURE

725.1   RENAISSANCE ARCHITECTURE ; ELIZABETHAN
         ARCHITECTURE

725.2   JACOBEAN ARCHITECTURE ; BAROQUE
         ARCHITECTURE

725.3   ROCOCO ARCHITECTURE ; CHURRIGUERESQUE
         ARCHITECTURE

725.4   GEORGIAN ARCHITECTURE ; COLONIAL
         ARCHITECTURE

725.5   CLASSIC REVIVAL ARCHITECTURE

725.6   GOTHIC REVIVAL ARCHITECTURE

725.7   ROMANESQUE REVIVAL ARCHITECTURE

725.8   EXPRESSIONIST ARCHITECTURE

725.9   FUNCTIONALIST ARCHITECTURE

726   PUBLIC STRUCTURES

726.1 GOVERNMENT BUILDINGS

726.12 CAPITOLS ; LEGISLATIVE BUILDINGS

726.13 ROYAL PALACES ; EXECUTIVE MANSIONS

726.14 GOVERNMENT OFFICE BUILDINGS

726.15 COURTHOUSES

726.16 CUSTOMS HOUSES

726.17 POST OFFICES

726.18 POLICE STATIONS ; POLICE BARRACKS

726.19 FIRE STATIONS

726.2 COMMERCIAL BUILDINGS ; SHOPPING MALLS

726.32 RAILROAD DEPOTS ; RAILROAD PASSENGER
        STATIONS

726.34 ROUNDHOUSES ; TOOL SHOPS ; SIGNAL
        BUILDINGS

726.35 BUS TERMINALS

726.36 AIRPORTS ; AIR TERMINALS ; HANGARS

726.37 FERRY STATIONS ; DOCKS

726.38 PUBLIC GARAGES

726.39 FILLING STATIONS

726.42 INDUSTRIAL BUILDINGS

726.44 MANUFACTURING PLANTS ; FACTORIES

726.46 STEEL MILLS

726.48 SHIPYARDS

726.52 HOSPITAL BUILDINGS

726.54 PSYCHIATRIC HOSPITAL BUILDINGS

726.56 MENTALLY-RETARDED'S FACILITIES

726.57 SENIOR-CITIZENS' HOMES ; OLD FOLKS' HOMES

726.59 VETERINARY HOSPITALS

726.6 PRISONS ; REFORM SCHOOLS ; BORSTALS

726.71 RESTAURANT BUILDINGS

726.72 FAST-FOOD RESTAURANTS ; DRIVE-INS

726.73 TAPROOMS ; BARS ; TAVERNS ; INNS

726.74 BATHHOUSES

726.76 SAUNAS ; HEALTH CLUBS

726.78 SWIMMING POOL BUILDINGS ; SWIMMING POOLS

726.79 CASINOS ; AMUSEMENT PARK BUILDINGS

726.8   RECREATION BUILDINGS

726.81 CONCERT HALLS

726.82 OPERA HOUSES

726.83 THEATERS ; AUDITORIUMS

726.84 STADIUMS ; ASTRODOMES ; AMPHITHEATERS ;
        GRANDSTANDS

726.85 BOWLING ALLEYS

726.86 GYMNASIUMS

726.87 SKATING RINKS ; DANCE HALLS

726.88 YACHT CLUB BUILDINGS ; CANOE CLUB
        BUILDINGS

726.89 RACETRACKS ; RIDING CLUBS

726.91 EXHIBITION BUILDINGS ; ART GALLERIES ;
        MUSEUMS

726.92 PUBLIC LIBRARY BUILDINGS

726.93 BRANCH LIBRARY BUILDINGS

726.94 TEMPORARY LIBRARY STRUCTURES ; BOOKMOBILES

726.95 ARCHES ; TRIUMPHAL ARCHES

726.96 MEMORIAL WALLS

726.97 TOWERS ; BELL TOWERS ; OBSERVATORY TOWERS

726.98 CLOCK TOWERS

726.99 BRIDGES ; TUNNELS

727   RELIGIOUS STRUCTURES

727.1   CHURCHES

723.12 CATHOLIC CHURCHES ; ROMAN CATHOLIC
        CHURCHES

723.14 EASTERN ORTHODOX CHURCHES ; RUSSIAN
        ORTHODOX CHURCHES

723.16 ANGLICAN CHURCHES

723.18 PROTESTANT CHURCHES

727.2   CATHEDRALS ; BASILICAS

727.3   TEMPLES ; SHRINES

727.4 MOSQUES ; MINARETS

727.5 BUDDHIST TEMPLES ; PAGODAS

727.6 HINDU TEMPLES

727.7 MONASTERIES ; ABBEYS

727.8 CONVENTS ; NUNNERIES

727.9 EPISCOPAL PALACES ; PARSONAGES ; RECTORIES

728   SCHOOL BUILDINGS

728.1 ONE-ROOM SCHOOLHOUSES

728.2 ELEMENTARY SCHOOLS

728.3 SECONDARY SCHOOLS ; JUNIOR HIGH SCHOOLS ;
       MIDDLE SCHOOLS

728.4 HIGH SCHOOLS ; HIGH SCHOOL STADIUMS

728.5 COLLEGE BUILDINGS ; UNIVERSITY BUILDINGS ;
       CLASSROOM BUILDINGS

728.6 COLLEGE CHAPELS ; UNIVERSITY CHAPELS

728.7 COLLEGE LIBRARIES ; UNIVERSITY LIBRARIES

728.8 UNIVERSITY RESEARCH FACILITIES

728.9 COLLEGE STADIUMS ; UNIVERSITY STADIUMS

729   RESIDENTIAL BUILDINGS ; DOMESTIC
       ARCHITECTURE

729.1 MULTIPLE DWELLINGS

729.2 DUPLEXES ; TOWNHOUSES ; ROW HOUSES

729.3 TENEMENTS

729.4 APARTMENT HOUSES ; CONDOMINIUMS

729.5 BUNGALOWS ; COTTAGES

729.6 MANSIONS ; VILLAS ; CASTLES ; CHATEAUX ;
       PALACES

729.7 HOTELS ; MOTELS

729.8 FARMHOUSES ; FARM COTTAGES

729.91 SOLAR HOUSES

729.92 VACATION HOUSES ; SUMMER COTTAGES

729.93 CABINS ; HUNTING LODGES

729.94 HOUSEBOATS

729.95 SHACKS ; LEAN-TO STRUCTURES

729.96 MOBILE HOMES ; TRAILERS ; CARAVANS

729.97 MOTOR-COACH HOMES

729.98 CAMPERS ; TENTS

729.99 OPEN-AIR SETTLEMENTS

73   SCULPTURES ; STATUARY

731.1   STONE ; WOOD

731.2   METAL ; CLAY ; PLASTER

731.3   WIRE ; ROPE ; PAPER ; PAPIER MACHE

731.4   FOUND OBJECTS ; JUNK

731.5   CHISELS ; KNIVES

731.6   TROWELS

731.7   GLUE POTS

731.8   WELDING EQUIPMENT

731.9   PLIERS ; CROWBARS ; HAMMERS

732.1   CHISELING STONE

732.2   CARVING WOOD ; WHITTLING

732.3   POURING MOLTEN METAL ; METAL CASTING

732.4   TWISTING WIRE ; TWISTING ROPE

732.5   MOLDING CLAY

732.6   PLASTERING FORMS

732.7   FOLDING PAPER

732.8   WELDING METAL ; WELDING JUNKYARD PIECES

732.9   GLUING MATERIALS ; GLUING PAPER PIECES

733.1   PREHISTORIC CARVINGS

733.2   EGYPTIAN STATUARY

733.3   SOUTHEAST ASIAN STATUARY

733.4   BUDDHIST IMAGES

733.5   HINDU FIGURES

733.6   CHINESE FIGURES ; CHINESE FIGURINES

733.7   JAPANESE SCULPTURES

733.8   AFRICAN FIGURES ; AFRICAN SCULPTURES

733.9   MAYAN FIGURES

734   CLASSICAL STATUARY

734.1   EARLY GREEK SCULPTURES

734.2 GREEK SCULPTURES

734.3 GREEK BAS-RELIEF SCULPTURES

734.5 ETRUSCAN FIGURES

734.6 ROMAN SCULPTURES

734.7 ROMAN FIGURINES

734.8 ROMAN BAS-RELIEF SCULPTURES

735.1 MODERN SCULPTURES

735.2 SMALL FIGURINES ; TABLE PIECES

735.3 MARBLE SCULPTURES

735.4 RENAISSANCE SCULPTURES

735.5 BAROQUE SCUPLTURE

735.6 CLASSIC REVIVAL SCULPTURES

736.7 ROMANTIC-PERIOD SCULPTURES

736.8 MODERNISTIC SCULPTURES ; NOUVEAU ART
       ORNAMENTATION

736.9 ABSTRACTIONIST SCULPTURES

737.1 CARVINGS

737.2 GEM CUTTING ; LAPIDARY WORK ; POLISHING
       GEMS

737.3 CAMEOS

737.4 WOOD CARVINGS

737.5 INSCRIPTIONS ; STONE CARVINGS

737.6 IVORY CARVINGS

737.7 NETSUKE

737.8 SOAP CARVINGS ; ICE CARVINGS ; SNOW
       SCULPTURES

737.9 WAX MOLDING ; WAX FIGURES

738   CERAMICS

738.1 POTTER'S WHEELS ; KILNS

738.2 POTTERY ; PORCELAIN PIECES ; CHINAWARE

738.3 EARTHENWARE ; STONEWARE

738.4 ENAMELS ; CLOISONNE

738.5 MOSAICS

738.6 PLASTER ORNAMENTS ; PLASTER ORNAMENTATION

738.7 ORNAMENTAL BRICKS ; ORNAMENTAL TILES

738.8 CERAMIC FIGURES ; CERAMIC FIGURINES

739   ART METALWORK

739.1 PRECIOUS METALS

739.14 GOLD JEWELRY ; GOLD CHAINS

739.16 GOLD COINS

739.18 GOLD CUPS ; GOLD VASES

739.2 SILVERWARE

739.3 MOUNTING GEMS ; REPAIR JEWELRY

739.4 BELT BUCKLES ; SHOE BUCKLES

739.5 FINGER RINGS

739.6 IRONWORK

739.7 BRASS ORNAMENTS ; MONUMENTAL BRASSES

739.8 PEWTER FIGURES ; METAL FIGURES

739.9 ARMS ; ARMOR

739.92 DAGGERS

739.93 SHIELDS

739.94 SWORDS

739.95 SABERS

739.96 CUTLASSES

739.97 BREASTPLATES

739.98 HELMETS

741   DRAWINGS

741.1 CHARCOAL DRAWINGS

741.2 CHALK DRAWINGS

741.3 CRAYON DRAWINGS

741.4 PASTEL DRAWINGS

741.5 PENCIL DRAWINGS

741.6 PEN AND INK DRAWINGS

741.7 SILVERPOINT DRAWINGS

741.8 SCRATCHBOARD DRAWINGS

741.9 AIRBRUSH DRAWINGS

742.1 ANIMATED CARTOONS

742.2 CARTOONS

742.3 CARICATURES

742.4 BOOK JACKETS

742.5 NEWSPAPER CARTOONS

742.6 PERIODICAL CARTOONS

742.7 SHEET MUSIC COVERS

742.8 CALENDARS

742.9 POSTCARDS ; GREETING CARDS

743   PERSPECTIVE

743.1 PORTRAITS

743.2 BONES ; SKELETAL SYSTEMS

743.3 MUSCLES ; MUSCULAR SYSTEMS

743.4 ANATOMY FOR ARTISTS

743.5 NUDE FIGURES

743.6 DRAPED FIGURES ; DRAPERIES

743.7 ANIMALS

743.8 PLANT LIFE

743.9 STILL LIFE

744   ANTIQUES

744.1 ANTIQUE DOLLS

744.13 DOLLHOUSES

744.15 DOLL FURNITURE

744.17 STUFFED ANIMALS ; STUFFED TOYS

744.19 TOY SOLDIERS

744.2 LAMPSHADES

744.3 CANDLE STICKS

744.4 SNUFFBOXES

744.5 COSTUME JEWELRY

744.6 ARTIFICIAL FLOWERS

744.7 EGG DECORATIONS

744.8 EASTER EGGS ; JEWELED EASTER EGGS

745.1 DECORATIVE LETTERING ; CALLIGRAPHY

745.2 FLOWER ARRANGEMENTS

745.21 ORIENTAL FLOWER ARRANGEMENTS

745.22 JAPANESE FLOWER ARRANGEMENTS

745.23 CORSAGES

745.24 BOUTONNIERES

745.25 DRIFTWOOD

745.26 DRIED GRASSES

745.27 WEDDING BOUQUETS

745.28 WREATHS ; FUNERAL WREATHS

745.29 HOLIDAY FLOWER ARRANGEMENTS

746 TEXTILES

746.1 SPINNING ; WEAVING

746.2 LACES ; TATTING

746.3 PASSEMENTERIE ; BRAIDS ; CORDS ; FRINGES

746.4 BASKETRY ; MACRAME

746.5 KNITTING ; CROCHETING

746.6 NEEDLEPOINT ; BARGELLO ; CROSS STITCH

746.7 EMBROIDERY ; CREWEL WORK

746.8 APPLIQUE

746.9 SILK-SCREEN PRINTING ; TIE-DYEING ; BATIK

747 INTERIOR DECORATION

747.1 WALL HANGINGS ; WALLPAPER

747.2 DRAPERIES ; UPHOLSTERY ; CARPETS

747.3 FLOORS ; CARPETS ; PARQUET FLOORING

747.4 RESIDENTIAL INTERIOR DECORATION

747.41 HOME LIBRARIES ; STUDIES ; DENS

747.42 LIVING ROOMS ; DRAWING ROOMS ; PARLORS

747.43 DINING ROOMS

747.44 BEDROOMS

747.45 NURSERIES

747.46 BATHROOMS ; POWDER ROOMS

747.47 RECREATION ROOMS ; FAMILY ROOMS

747.48 KITCHENS

747.49 PANTRIES ; STORAGE ROOMS ; ATTICS

747.5 OFFICE DECORATION

747.6 HOTEL LOBBIES ; MOTEL GAME ROOMS

747.7 BANQUET HALLS ; BALLROOMS

747.8 THEATER LOBBIES ; THEATER DECORATION
747.9 SCHOOL ROOMS ; CLASSROOMS
748   GLASS
748.1 GLASS BLOWING
748.2 BOTTLE CUTTING ; JAR CUTTING
748.3 GLASS PAINTING ; STAINED GLASS
748.4 LEADED GLASS CRAFT
748.5 GLASS MOSAICS ; MOSAIC MURALS
748.6 GLASS LAMPS ; CHANDELIERS
748.7 CUT GLASS ; CUT GLASS BOWLS
748.8 CRYSTAL DRINKING GLASSES ; DECANTERS
748.9 PAPERWEIGHTS
749   FURNITURE
749.1 BEDS ; CANOPIES
749.2 CABINETS ; CHESTS
749.3 FIREPLACES ; MANTELS ; INGLENOOKS
749.4 CLOCKCASES ; KNICKNACK STANDS
749.5 SCREENS ; PICTURE FRAMES
749.6 TABLES
749.7 CHAIRS
749.8 SOFAS ; CHAISES LONGUES
749.9 BUILT-IN FURNITURE
75   PAINTINGS
751.1 WATERCOLORS
751.12 INKS ;
751.13 CHINESE INK PAINTINGS
751.14 JAPANESE INK PAINTINGS
751.15 KOREAN INK PAINTINGS
751.16 INK PAINTINGS
751.2 ACRYLICS
751.3 TEMPERA
751.4 FRESCO PAINTING
751.5 OIL PAINTING
751.6 MOSAIC PAINTING

751.7 FINGER PAINTING ; SAND PAINTING

751.8 COLLAGES

751.9 AIRBRUSH PAINTING

752   COLOR CHARTS

753   MYTHICAL FIGURES ; ALLEGORICAL FIGURES

754   GENRE PAINTINGS

755   RELIGIOUS FIGURES

755.1 GOD

755.2 JESUS CHRIST

755.3 VIRGIN MARY

755.4 MADONNA AND CHILD

755.5 DISCIPLES

755.6 APOSTLES

755.7 SAINTS

755.8 CARDINALS ; POPES ; BISHOPS

755.9 PRIESTS

756   HUMAN FIGURES ; NUDES

756.1 NUDE GROUPS

756.2 NUDE MALES

756.3 NUDE FEMALES

756.4 NUDE CHILDREN

756.5 DRAPED FIGURES

756.6 PORTRAITS ; MINIATURES

756.7 COSTUMED FIGURES

756.8 EQUESTRIAN FIGURES

756.9 EROTICA ; PORNOGRAPHY

757.1 LANDSCAPES

757.2 MARINE SCENES ; SEASCAPES

757.3 URBAN SCENES ; CITYSCAPES

757.4 ANIMALS

757.5 HUNTING SCENES

757.6 STILL LIFE

757.7 PLANT LIFE ; FLOWERS ; FLOWER ARRANGEMENTS

757.8 INDUSTRIAL SUBJECTS ; TECHNICAL SUBJECTS

757.9   ARCHITECTURAL PAINTINGS ; ARCHITECTURAL
        DETAILS
758   EUROPEAN PAINTINGS
758.1   ITALIAN PAINTINGS ; RENAISSANCE PAINTINGS
758.2   FRENCH PAINTINGS
758.3   GERMAN PAINTINGS
758.4   DUTCH PAINTINGS
758.5   ENGLISH PAINTINGS
758.6   AMERICAN PAINTINGS
758.7   PRIMITIVE PAINTINGS
758.8   EXPRESSIONIST PAINTINGS
758.9   ABSTRACTIONIST PAINTINGS
759   ORIENTAL PAINTINGS
759.1   CHINESE PAINTINGS
759.2   JAPANESE PAINTINGS
759.3   KOREAN PAINTINGS
759.4   SOUTHEAST ASIAN PAINTINGS
759.5   TIBETAN PAINTINGS ; NEPALESE PAINTINGS
759.6   INDIAN PAINTINGS
759.7   PERSIAN PAINTINGS
76   ART STYLES
761   ART DECO STYLE
761.2   KITSCH
761.4   ART NOUVEAU
762   FUNCTIONALIST STYLES
762.2   GEOMETRIC DESIGNS
762.4   CUBIST ART
762.6   FUTURIST ART
762.8   ABSTRACTIONIST ART
763   SURREALIST ART ; DADAIST ART
764   POP ART
765   PERFORMANCE ART ; MULTIPLE ARTS
766   PRINTS ; PRINT MAKING
766.1   WOOD ENGRAVINGS

766.2 LINOLEUM-BLOCK PRINTS
766.3 ENGRAVINGS
766.4 LITHOGRAPHS
766.5 SERIGRAPHS
766.6 MEZZOTINTS
766.7 AQUATINTS
766.8 ETCHINGS
767 METAL ENGRAVINGS
767.1 STIPPLE ENGRAVINGS
767.2 LINE ENGRAVINGS
767.3 CRIBLE ENGRAVINGS
767.4 BOOK ILLUSTRATIONS
768 POSTAGE STAMPS
768.2 CANCELLED POSTAGE STAMPS ; CANCELLATIONS
768.4 POSTAL STATIONERY
768.6 GOVERNMENTAL STAMPS ; CUSTOMS STAMPS
768.8 TOBACCO STAMPS
77 PHOTOGRAPHY
771 CAMERAS
772 DEVELOPING PHOTOGRAPHS
773 POSING FIGURES
774 PHOTOGRAPHIC STUDIOS
775 DAGUERROTYPES
776 FILM ; FILM CASSETTES
777 MOTION PICTURE FILM
778 AERIAL PHOTOGRAPHS
779 SPACE PHOTOGRAPHY
781 MUSICAL INSTRUMENTS
782 STRING INSTRUMENTS
782.1 VIOLINS
782.2 VIOLAS
782.3 CELLOS ; VIOLONCELLOS
782.4 DOUBLE BASS
782.5 GUITARS

782.6 MANDOLINS

782.7 BALALAIKA

782,8 IRISH HARPS

782.9 ITALIAN HARPS

783   WIND INSTRUMENTS

783.1 FLUTES

783.2 PICCOLOS

783.3 CLARINETS

783.4 SAXOPHONES

783.5 OBOES

783.6 ENGLISH HORNS

783.7 BASSOONS

783.8 PAN PIPES

783.9 RECORDERS

784   BRASS INSTRUMENTS

784.1 BUGLES

784.2 TRUMPETS ; CORNETS

784.3 FRENCH HORNS

784.4 TROMBONES

784.5 TUBAS

784.6 SOUSAPHONES

784.7 LONG TRUMPETS

784.8 EUPHONIUM

784.9 HUNTING HORNS

785   KEYBOARD INSTRUMENTS

785.1 HARPSICHORDS ; CLAVICHORDS

785.2 PIANOS ; PIANOFORTES

785.3 ORGANS

785.4 MELODIONS

785.6 ACCORDIONS

785.7 ELECTRONIC ORGANS ; SYNTHESIZERS

785.8 GLOCKENSPIEL ; CELESTE

785.9 XYLOPHONES

786   PERCUSSION INSTRUMENTS

786.1 SNARE DRUMS
786.2 KETTLEDRUMS
786.3 BASS DRUMS
786.4 CYMBALS
786.5 TRIANGLES
786.6 GONGS ; BELLS ; CHIMES
786.7 MARACAS ; RATTLES ; CASTANETS ;
786.8 UNSOPHISTICATED INSTRUMENTS ; MUSICAL SAWS
786.9 MECHANICAL INSTRUMENTS ; PLAYER PIANOS ;
       MUSIC BOXES
787   MUSICAL GROUPS
787.1 STRING QUARTETS ; STRING QUINTETS
787.2 DANCE BANDS
787.3 MARCHING BANDS
787.4 SYMPHONIC BANDS
787.5 DANCE ORCHESTRAS
787.6 PIT ORCHESTRAS ; THEATER ORCHESTRAS
787.7 CHAMBER ORCHESTRAS
787.8 SYMPHONY ORCHESTRAS
787.9 ENLARGED ORCHESTRAL GROUPS
788   CHOIRS
788.1 BOY'S CHOIRS
788.2 MEN'S CHOIRS ; BARBERSHOP QUARTETS
788.3 WOMEN'S CHORAL GROUPS
788.4 MIXED CHOIRS ; SYMPHONIC CHOIRS
788.5 OPERA CHORUS
788.6 MALE SINGERS
788.7 FEMALE SINGERS
788.8 ROCK STARS ; POP SINGERS
788.9 PUNK ROCK STARS ; COSTUMED SINGERS
789   MUSICAL DEVICES ; MUSIC RECORDING
789.1 BARREL ORGANS ; STREET ORGANS
789.2 PHONOGRAPHS ; GRAMOPHONES ; WIND-UP
       PHONOGRAPHS

789.3 TURNTABLES

789.4 SPEAKER SYSTEMS

789.5 CASSETTE RECORDERS

789.6 RECORDING STUDIOS

789.7 PHONOGRAPH RECORDS ; PHONOGRAPH CYLINDERS

789.8 SOUND CASSETTES

789.9 COMPACT DISCS

79 PERFORMING ARTS ; RECREATIONAL ACTIVITIES

791 GROUP ACTIVITIES

792 PUBLIC PERFORMANCES

792.1 STAGE PLAYS

792.2 MUSICAL PERFORMANCES

792.3 OPERATIC PERFORMANCES

792.4 OUTDOOR PERFORMANCES

792.5 BALLET PERFORMANCES

792.6 DANCE CONTESTS

792.7 TAP DANCERS

792.8 CHORUS LINES

792.9 MODERN DANCERS ; INTERPETIVE DANCERS

793.1 CHILDREN'S PARTIES

793.2 SEASONAL PARTIES

793.3 FOLK DANCES ; SCOTTISH DANCING

793.4 SQUARE DANCES

793.5 BALLROOM DANCING

793.6 SWORD DANCES ; HIGHLAND FLING

793.7 COTILLIONS

793.8 MAGIC SHOWS ; MAGICIANS PERFORMING

793.9 PARTY GAMES ; BLIND MAN'S BLUFF ; MUSICAL
      CHAIRS

794.1 CHESSBOARDS ; CHESSMEN

794.2 CHECKERS ; DRAUGHTS

794.3 DARTS ; DART GAMES ; DART BOARDS

794.4 BOWLING

794.5 BILLIARDS ; POOL GAMES ; SNOOKER

794.6 CARD GAMES

794.7 BLACKJACK TABLES

794.8 POKER GAMES ; POKER PLAYERS

794.9 ROULETTE TABLES

795   SPORTS ; OUTDOOR GAMES

795.1 LEAPFROG ; HIDE AND SEEK

795.2 KITES ; KITE FLYING

795.3 TOP SPINNING

795.4 ROLLER SKATING

795.5 QUOITS ; HORSESHOES

795.6 SWINGS ; MERRY-GO-ROUNDS

795.7 SEESAWS

795.8 SLIDES

795.9 JUNGLE GYMS ; CROSS BARS

796   BALL GAMES

796.1 HANDBALL ; LAWN BOWLING

796.2 NETBALL ; VOLLEYBALL

796.3 BASKETBALL ; BASKETBALL GAMES

796.4 FOOTBALL GAMES ; FOOTBALL PLAYERS

796.5 SOCCER ; RUGBY

796.6 TENNIS ; LAWN TENNIS

796.7 BADMINTON

796.8 TABLE TENNIS ; PING PONG

796.9 SQUASH

797.1 GOLF

797.2 POLO

797.3 CROQUET

797.4 FIELD HOCKEY ; LACROSSE

797.5 BASEBALL ; CRICKET

797.6 GYMNASTICS

797.7 TRACK AND FIELD SPORTS ; RUNNING ; HIGH
       JUMPS ; POLE VAULTING

797.8 TRAPEZE WORK ; ROPE CLIMBING ; WIRE
       WALKING

797.9 ACROBATICS ; TRAMPOLINES ; TUMBLING ;
       CONTORTION
798   OUTDOOR ACTIVITIES
798.1 HIKING ; MOUNTAIN CLIMBING
798.2 CAMPING ; DUDE RANCHES
798.3 SPELUNKING ; CAVE EXPLORATION
798.4 CYCLING ; BICYCLE RACES
798.5 MOTORCYCLE RACES
798.6 AUTOMOBILE RACING
798.7 WRESTLING ; KARATE ; JIU JITSU ; KICK
       BOXING
798.8 WINTER SPORTS
798.81 SKIING ; DOWNHILL SKIING
798.82 TOBAGGANING ; SLEDDING
798.83 CROSS-COUNTRY SKIING ; SNOWSHOEING
798.84 ICE SKATING
798.85 FIGURE SKATING
798.86 ICE DANCING
798.87 ICE-SKATING RACES
798.88 ICE HOCKEY
798.89 CURLING
798.9 AQUATIC SPORTS ; WATER GAMES
798.91 BOATING ; SAILBOATS ; CANOES ; RAFTING
798.92 MOTORBOATS
798.93 SURF RIDING ; SURFERS
798.94 WATER SKIING
798.95 SWIMMING
798.96 SWIM MEETS
798.97 DIVING
798.98 SKIN DIVING ; SCUBA DIVING
798.99 WATER POLO
799.1 HORSEMANSHIP ; EQUESTRIAN SPORTS
799.2 HORSE RACES ; BETTING
799.3 HARNESS RACES

799.4 RIDING EXHIBITIONS
799.5 DOG RACING
799.6 SPORT FISHING ; ANGLING
799.7 SPEAR FISHING
799.8 HUNTING
799.81 RIFLES ; PISTOLS ; SHOTGUNS
799.82 BOWS AND ARROWS ; ARCHERY
799.83 BOOMERANGS ; BLOWPIPES ; LASSOS
799.84 FALCONS ; HUNTING DOGS
799.85 SHOOTING BIRDS ; DUCK HUNTING
799.86 HUNTING DEER ; HUNTING ELK
799.87 TRAPSHOOTING
799.88 TARGET SHOOTING
799.9 EXERCISING ; CALISTHENICS
799.91 ARM EXERCISING
799.92 TORSO EXERCISES
799.93 JUMPING JACKS
799.94 PUSH-UPS
799.95 AEROBIC EXERCISES ; RUNNING IN PLACE
799.96 RUNNING ; JOGGING
799.97 KNEE BENDS
799.98 SIT-UPS
799.99 YOGA EXERCISES
806 LITERARY SOCIETY MEETINGS
910.4 PIRATES
910.6 SHIPWRECKS
910.8 BURIED TREASURE
912 GLOBES
913 RUINS
921 PHILOSOPHERS
921.5 PSYCHOLOGISTS
922.1 RELIGIOUS LEADERS
922.5 SAINTS
923 SOCIAL SCIENTISTS ; ECONOMISTS

924   LINGUISTS
925   SCIENTISTS
926   INDUSTRIALISTS
927   ARTISTS
928   WRITERS
929   HISTORIANS
940.1   THE CRUSADES
940.3   WORLD WAR I, 1914-1918
940.5   WORLD WAR II, 1939-1945

Index